Scandal in the Ink

*The Cassell Lesbian and Gay Studies list
offers a broad-based platform to lesbian, gay
and bisexual writers for the discussion of
contemporary issues and for the promotion
of new ideas and research.*

COMMISSIONING:
Steve Cook
Roz Hopkins

CONSULTANTS:
Liz Gibbs
Keith Howes (Australia)
Christina Ruse
Peter Tatchell

Scandal in the Ink

Male and Female Homosexuality in Twentieth-century French Literature

Christopher Robinson

CASSELL

Cassell
Villiers House
41/47 Strand
London WC2N 5JE

387 Park Avenue South
New York, NY 10016–8810

First published 1995

British Library Cataloguing-in-Publication Data
A catalogue record for this book is available from the British Library.

ISBN 0–304–32705–0 (paperback)

Typeset by Fakenham Photosetting Ltd, Fakenham, Norfolk
Printed and bound in Great Britain by Mackays of Chatham plc

Contents

Please no
were

Acknowledgements

I am grateful to the Governing Body of my college for sabbatical leave and other research assistance; to Professor Malcolm Bowie and Dr Ann Jefferson for their helpful comments on the informal paper (delivered to their Modern French Studies graduate seminar) which grew into Chapter 5; to Ian Watson and Marjorie Mayo for their efforts to keep me sane during the writing process; and above all to Paul Rees, who not only offered me patient criticism and unstinting affectionate support but whose intellectual stimulation was essential to the fertilization of many of my ideas.

Introduction

WHY write a book about homosexuality and contemporary French literature? The case for looking at literature about homosexuality is simple enough. Lesbians and gay men need to become better acquainted with creative writing by and about homosexuals because literature is a mirror of society's perceptions. Studying it helps us to understand how and why homosexuals have represented themselves, or have been represented by heterosexuals, in certain ways and in certain social contexts. The case for looking at literature in general from a specifically gay and lesbian angle is equally simple.[1] There is a need for critical works written from a specifically gay perspective on *any* sort of literature, because traditional criticism is partisan, writing to a hidden agenda which treats certain criteria as 'objective' when they are based on loaded assumptions. This need is particularly pressing where the study of works by gay authors, or overtly about homosexual issues, is concerned.

Whether intentionally or not, the critical establishment uses its authority to promote prejudice. It indulges in censorship: critics play down or ignore the existence and significance of homosexuality in authors' lives and works, even when their sexual orientation is as well known as that of Proust and Gide. It trivializes homosexuality, refusing to see gay and lesbian themes as central, serious, valid in themselves, and is only ready to tolerate them when they can be explained away as metaphors for something completely different. At worst, it is homophobically abusive, representing homosexual characters and their creators as perverted, delinquent, sick, and sexually and morally inadequate. It is easy, for example, to show links between a number of homosexual French writers of the mid-century and pro-fascist or pro-German tendencies, but any implication that there is a *necessary* link between homosexuality and fascism or collaborationism ignores the fact that proportionately a far greater percentage of male writers with such political leanings were heterosexual. This failure of mainstream criticism to deal fairly with homosexuality is not a trivial matter. The intellectually inquisitive reader deserves a body of critical writing which approaches from a non-prejudiced standpoint the problem of how texts reflect the world in general and homosexuality in particular, and which seeks to stimulate debate about issues of special interest to gays.

The question remains, why write a book about homosexuality and *French* literature in particular. The answer is that twentieth-century France is uniquely rich in homosexual literature. As the novelist and critic Dominique Fernandez has rightly observed, it is the only country in the world where creative writers were the first members of the intellectual community – before psychoanalists, sexologists or sociologists – to interest themselves in homosexuality as an independent phenomenon, and to create a tradition of writing on the subject marked by its strength, continuity and diversity of thematic and stylistic approach.[2] But as yet no one, in France or anywhere else, has tried to chart the complexities of this tradition, to look closely at how it has developed, to assess in what respects it manifests unity, in what respects diversity.[3] The richness of the tradition poses its own problems. Since prejudices against historical or thematic approaches to the study of literature have faded somewhat in recent years, it is possible to envisage the subject from such a perspective, but no single approach, no single critical technique, can give a total account of the material.

My coverage is not and cannot be all-inclusive. For reasons of space, I have focused almost exclusively on works with strong homosexual themes by openly homosexual writers, and have largely ignored the impact of sexual orientation on the way other aspects of experience are viewed and recorded, the ways in which closeted gay writers reveal their sexuality in their texts, or the presentation of homosexuality by heterosexual writers. My methodology is necessarily eclectic; some chapters are more historical in emphasis, others more concerned with patterns of writing and what they impose upon the reader. My aim has been to give a sense of the social and intellectual context in which twentieth-century French writers have faced up to their homosexuality, to look at a variety of major issues – self-image; sexuality and religious belief; the impact of AIDS; pederasty; the particular problems of female homosexuals; the idea of a sexual continuum; the ways in which the body and desire are represented – to chart the development of different literary discourses, the recurrence of the motifs and techniques which control our response, as readers, to a given text. In other words, I have tried to open the subject up, bringing home to Anglo-Saxon readers both the parallels with their own literary tradition and the differences from it. For, while there is no particular reason to suppose that the *range* of attitudes to gay or straight issues, to the self, to society is significantly different in France from Britain or the USA, the precise social and intellectual context and the culturally specific influence of the mainstream French literary tradition ensure that the thematic balance and the style and form of expression of literary homosexuality *will* be different in France.

One final caveat. There is a proper place in gay studies for reassessing the value and effect of 'classic' works, whatever the sexual orientation of their writers, just as there is a proper place for identifying works of special interest and value to the homosexual reader. Looking at literature from a gay perspective in the 1990s not only means that authors and texts usually overlooked will take on greater interest and importance; it also means that the shortcomings of works conventionally regarded as beyond criticism will be brought into focus. As Borges implies in *Pierre Menart autor del Quijote*, it is not just the writing of literature which exists in a particular social and intellectual context, but also the reading of it. Inevitably, each age, each generation even, reinvents what it reads – the radical reinterpretations of a classical Greek author such as Homer across the centuries are a good example of the process. The function of academic criticism is in part to provide a perspective on, and further knowledge of, the context in which texts are written, but it is not its job to abolish the evolution of ideas and values between the author and the present, to behave as though there is one eternally valid way of reading. The shortcomings of any attempt to treat cultural phenomenon in this way are only too obvious in the bogus effects obtained by those musicians who pretend to recreate 'authentic' performances of baroque and earlier music. And just as modern audiences have learnt to 'hear' differently from eighteenth-century audiences, so the modern reader has learnt to read differently. This fact has particular reverberations where sexual orientation is concerned, because, like gender, it is an area where values have changed drastically in the course of a relatively short period. Gay readers need to be prepared to take a critical stance towards the presentation of sexuality in earlier texts, regardless of the conventional status of their writers. This is not a question of political correctness. A gay reader cannot give the same reading to, or perceive the same value in, a text which attacks or patronizes homosexuality as a heterosexual reader will; this holds good whether the writer of the text is gay or not. Minority groups seeking to emancipate themselves from majority values must be prepared to look at literature without preconceptions about the 'value' and 'importance' of writers. The value of a text for a given readership is necessarily reduced if the text is based on a negative discourse about that group: *The Merchant of Venice* is as inherently offensive to a Jewish audience as Baudelaire's hysterical misogyny in *Les Fleurs du mal* is to a female readership.

If therefore I appear, in the work which follows, 'disrespectful' about certain writers and texts traditionally regarded as flawless masterpieces, or if I suggest that they should be read in ways other than those normally prescribed, I am not trying to reorder a 'canon', produce a new literary hierarchy; I am merely arguing that there are reasons why 'great' literature ceases to be great – or at least its value is significantly reduced – for a given readership. This has nothing to do with censorship. Though it is a simple fact that *The Satanic Verses* cannot be highly regarded by a convinced Muslim, there is no reason why it should not be so regarded by other groups. Sexual orientation is akin to gender, race and religion in this respect. The way in which we see the world is modified by our particular place on the sexual spectrum. So is the value we put upon what we see. We should not therefore be reluctant to find that the same is true of the way we respond to art, be it visual or verbal.

Notes

1. For a fine, forthright polemic on the topic, see Mark Lilly, *Gay Men's Literature in the Twentieth Century* (London: Macmillan, 1993), pp. xii–xv, 1–14.

2. See Dominique Fernandez, *Le Rapt de Ganymède* (Paris: Grasset, 1989), p. 82.

3. The only work of substance relating to the subject is the volume of essays edited by George Stambolian and Elaine Marks fifteen years ago, under the title *Homosexualities and French Literature: Cultural Contexts/Critical Texts* (Ithaca and London: Cornell University Press, 1979). This offers useful insights into a variety of topics and contains essays which are still classics of their kind, but, as the book appeared at a period when the critical doctrine of the 'death of the author' (i.e. that texts should be considered entirely independently of their context of writing) was at its most fashionable, it declines to deal with many of the issues which particularly interest me.

Christopher Robinson is a university lecturer in French and Senior Tutor in Modern Languages at Christ Church, Oxford. His previous work includes a study of the homosexual Greek poet, C. P. Cavafy.

Here are our bodies. Let them unfold and stretch out for one eternal first time between the sheets of these pages. The scandal is only in the ink, the raw material.

- Yves Navarre, *Le petit galopin de nos corps*

For Paul,
in remembrance of things past

Chapter one

Contexts

'Certainly if society hadn't evolved considerably,
I couldn't have written *The Penis and the
Demoralisation of the West*, I couldn't have revealed
my own values and acts.'

● *Jean-Paul Aron*[1]

LITERATURE exists, by definition, in a social context
with which it has an interactive relationship. The world in which
writers write fashions their values, whether they follow or react
against prevailing ideas; writers address themselves to implicit
readers whose value systems they think they can predict; readers
find their world-view, even their view of themselves, confirmed or
challenged by what they read, but in terms of value debates which
they can recognize as overt or implicit in the world around them. In
the case of homosexual writers, male or female, the special factors
in the social context which affect them range from their status
under the legal system to the various systems of discourse, public
and private, by which society defines them. Not least of these is
literary discourse itself; the literature of any age depends on the
system of language, of patterns and stereotypes which it inherits
from the preceding age, since these define and limit the way in
which a writer can *think* his or her subject, let alone express it.
Equally, readers, whatever their own sexual orientation, are con-
ditioned by the same factors when responding to texts which touch
implicitly or explicitly on gay issues. So, to appreciate the relation-

ship between literature and homosexuality in twentieth-century France, we need to have at least an overview of the forms of discourse which shaped the subject in the nineteenth century, and a general picture of the context of production and reception of gay writing in France in the present century, because it differs from, say, Britain, the USA or Germany in significant ways.

Let us start with the law.[2] Until the French Revolution sodomy was considered a criminal act which could be punished by being burnt alive, a penalty taken over from canon law and symbolic of the hell-fire to which the Church charitably consigned such sinners. But the crime and its penalty were abolished in the first post-Revolutionary penal reforms, under the law of 25 September–6 October 1791. The Napoleonic Code of 1810 maintained silence on the question of homosexuality, but introduced two categories of offence which were to be turned against homosexuals later: a penalty of from three months' to a year's imprisonment for 'affronts to public decency' (public being defined as a place to which a third party had access and where he/she could be an unintentional witness), and a penalty of six months' to two years' imprisonment plus a fine for incitement to debauchery and corruption of young persons under the age of twenty-one. The former provision was to constitute the core of article 330 of the Code, the latter of article 334. In 1810 no distinction was made between homo- and heterosexual infringements under either heading, or under any of the other provisions for sexual offences (e.g. rape, attempted rape or indecent assault with violence). Amendments to legislation on sexual matters in 1832 (the law of 28 April) and 1836 (the law of 13 May), forming the basis of article 331 of the Code, respectively established an age of consent for any type of sexual activity at eleven years, then raised it to thirteen years; the 1836 law also included provision to increase the penalties for public indecency. Article 334 was significantly revised by the law of 3 April 1903. It now prescribed from six months' to three years' imprisonment plus a fine of up to 5,000 francs for procurement, and its first section concerned 'anyone who commits an offence against public decency by habitually inciting, encouraging or assisting the committing of vice or the corruption of young people of either sex under 21 years of age'. Further measures of an evenhanded kind where sexual orientation was concerned were introduced by the law of 11 April 1908, which sought to regulate prostitution by those under eighteen years of age. In all the above legislation there was no attempt to police private sexual activity between consenting persons of the same sex or of opposite sexes, provided both parties were above the age of consent, set in 1836 at thirteen years. The focus of the legislation was on public decency and prostitution.

This position remained unchanged until, in August 1942, under the collaborationist Vichy regime, a law was signed by Maréchal Pétain creating the separate offence of homosexual acts committed with a person under the age of twenty-one, a category added to the provisions of article 334 (the article dealing with prostitution and procuring). This piece of legislation has been variously ascribed to the Vichyite obsession with the promotion of so-called 'family values' (contemporary British readers will recognize the phenomenon), to sympathy with Nazi eugenic theories, which condemned homosexuals as degenerates, or to the determination to find scapegoats for the defeat of 1940 in all possible minority groups. What is much less easily explicable is that, after the Liberation, an edict of the provisional government issued in Algeria on 8 February 1945 and reproducing the substance of the Pétain legislation, became paragraph 3 of article 331 of the Code. The edict prescribed a penalty of from six months' to three years' imprisonment plus a fine of from 60 to 15,000 francs for any indecent or unnatural act committed against an individual of the same sex under the age of twenty-one. To make matters worse, an edict of 2 July of the same year raising the heterosexual age of consent lifted it merely to fifteen. Homosexual inequality was now firmly installed within the Penal Code itself for the first time, without any form of public debate. It is interesting to note ancillary legislation of the same period which could easily be used against homosexuals and suggests increased hostility toward them. For example, employment legislation passed in 1946 decreed that 'no one may be named to a post in the public service unless he is of good morals', a phrase whose equivalents abound in articles of the Civil Code concerned with, for example, the rights of tenants. More directly, on 1 February 1949, the Paris Prefect of Police decreed that in future men were banned from dancing together in public places. The restriction might seem (indeed is) petty, but it contributes to a picture of a public desire to make life difficult for gays.

Things were, however, to get much worse. In July 1960, while the Assemblée nationale was discussing a draft law to enable the government to take measures necessary to combat certain 'social plagues', including alcoholism, prostitution, heart disease and tuberculosis, Paul Mirguet, a right-wing deputy for the Moselle, under the influence of the notorious homophobic psychiatrist Marcel Eck, proposed an amendment adding homosexuality to the list of 'plagues' on the predictable grounds of the 'need to protect our children'. The amendment went through both Houses without discussion and became law on 30 July. The most obvious consequence (the government being apparently more preoccupied with those parts of the new law which obliged it to find ways of reducing the price of fruit juice and of controlling distillers' licences) was the addition of a second paragraph to article 330 imposing much higher penalties for 'affronts to public decency' if the act in question were homosexual. In 1974 the general age of majority was fixed at eighteen, and paragraph 3 of article 331 was amended accordingly, still leaving a disparity between the heterosexual age of consent (fifteen years) and that for homosexuals.

Now we enter the great push-me-pull-you era, when the two Houses of the French legislature shuffled the issue of gay rights between them in agitated debate for several years, taking it in turns to play the role of reactionary oppressor. In December 1977 a proposal was put before the Senate for the removal of all discriminatory legislation concerning homosexuality from the Code – to be more precise, for the removal of paragraph 2 of article 330 and paragraph 3 of article 331. In the Senate debate of 28 June 1978 the (right-wing) government agreed to both proposals. On 11 April 1980 the Assemblée nationale re-established paragraph 3 of article 331; on 22 May the Senate removed it again, but, the Assemblée nationale having replaced it yet again (24 June), the Senate finally gave in (16 October). So, by the end of 1980, the suppression of paragraph 2 of article 330 (the offspring of the Mirguet amendment) was confirmed, but the distinction in age of consent prescribed under article 331 was reinstated (in what had now become paragraph 2 of that article). Then, in 1981, the Left came to power. Already on 19 March of that year Pierre Bérégovoy had promised gay rights groups that if Mitterand were elected, the Socialists would put forward appropriate legislation after consultation with interested parties. On 12 June, the Minister of Health announced that homosexuality would be struck off the list of officially recognized mental illnesses. By 27 August the courts were being advised by the Minister of Justice that, as Parliament proposed an early modification to paragraph 2 (the old paragraph 3) of article 331, it would not be appropriate to bring prosecutions under it except in exceptionally serious cases. And in December of that year a presidential amnesty was announced for all those found guilty under that article who had been sentenced before 10 May 1981.

In February 1982 new legislation amending article 1728 of the Civil Code dispensed tenants from conducting themselves 'as befits good fathers of families', thus removing the potential for concealed anti-homosexual discrimination under that heading. Meanwhile, a proposal to abolish article 331, paragraph 2 was approved by the Assemblée nationale on 20 December 1981, thrown out by the Senate (5 May 1982), re-approved by the Assemblée nationale (24 June) and rejected again by the upper House (8 July), readopted by the lower House (21 July), turned down yet again by the Senate (23 July) and finally and definitively approved by the Assemblée nationale on 27 July, becoming law no. 82–683 of 4 August 1982. Homosexuality had finally disappeared from the statute book. But as an article in *Le Monde* on 24 July 1982, entitled 'The end of the homophobic law', pointed out, silence was not protection enough. What was now needed was to include homosexuality under the anti-racist legislation passed in 1972. In December 1982, the Minister of Justice sent out instructions to the courts asking them to observe the anti-discriminatory spirit of the recent legislation. But it was not until 1985 that article 187, paragraph 1 of the Penal Code was amended to make any form of discrimination (e.g. deprivation of a right or refusal of a service) on grounds of sexual orientation illegal in the same way as discrimination on grounds of gender, race, nationality, religion or family situation was against the law. And, for all that, on 23 May 1991 the Senate, during a debate on the reform of the Penal Code, approved an amendment which sought to re-establish the discriminatory age of sexual majority embodied in the old paragraph 2 of article 331 which had been deleted in 1982. The Assemblée nationale rejected the proposal (22 June). It is easy to understand why the gay press, after the massive victory of the Right in the 1993 elections, began to speculate whether the clock might not soon be turned back for gay rights, and therefore started to urge that the French constitution itself be amended to provide permanent protection for minority groups.

In reality, this long struggle to regain the rights established by the Revolutionary legal reformers of 1791 had been a struggle about *male* homosexuality. For, in practical terms, lesbians remained 'invisible' to the legal eye. At worst they suffered inconvenience from an edict restricting cross-dressing in public, originally issued in 1800 and still being enforced with some severity by the Prefect of Paris at the outset of the twentieth century. Otherwise, French lesbians have suffered that same 'oppression by silence' to which the House of Lords consigned their British sisters in a 1921 debate, during which their lordships patronizingly declined to include lesbian acts under 'gross indecency' legislation on the grounds that to do so would put ideas into the heads of women who had never dreamt of such things.[3] Technically, of course, article 331, paragraph 3 applied to lesbians, and it is interesting that in the Assemblée nationale debate of 25 June 1980 on the suppression of that paragraph, one Socialist male deputy, arguing for the absurdity of the inequality established under existing legislation, deliberately chose a lesbian example to illustrate his point. But neither the public nor the police ever seemed to envisage it in that way. As Brigitte, one of the young lesbians in Dominique Fernandez' *L'Etoile rose*, protests:

> You queers are always complaining that you're persecuted. The laws push you around, Pétain and de Gaulle's decrees set up arbitrary discrimination against you, the second paragraph of article 330 followed the Miranguet amendment. But what about us? Justice quite simply doesn't know we exist. Because we're women, we don't count, in public opinion.

In fact, as we shall see, at certain periods some sections of public opinion were fully aware of lesbianism and vocally hostile to it. But the need to counter their legal 'invisibility' certainly played a part in persuading lesbian militant groups to adopt a higher public profile in the wake of the 'Events of May 1968'. Absence of repression, paradoxically, had as many drawbacks as its presence.

Our first reaction to a review of the history of the legal position of homosexuals in France might be to assume that it reflects a tolerant or indifferent society, which for special reasons becomes hostile to homosexuality after the defeat by the Germans in 1940. This would be a false assumption. Such evidence as we have for public opinion in the nineteenth century suggests a mixture of hostility and contempt toward male homosexuality. But we need to remember that until the last decades of the century there was no concept of homosexuality *as such*. The words *homosexuel* and *homosexualité*, modelled on the terms invented by the Hungarian Benkert von Kertbeny in 1869, only came into common usage alongside *inverti* and *uranisme* at the turn of the century (*Le Petit Robert* dates them to 1967, but examples of their use have been traced from 1891 onward[4]). The proliferation of new terminology at that period indicates, as Jeffery Weeks has argued in the case of Britain, a conceptual turning-point. Previously, when the socialist theorist Proudhon declared in his *Amour et mariage* (1858) that 'the act of sodomy is the sign of incurable depravity', he made no distinction between heterosexual and homosexual anal sex. He was not attacking a condition or criticizing a form of sexual identity; he was simply condemning an *act*. In France prior to the 1870s at the earliest, there is almost no concept of the homosexual which defines who or what he is; there is only terminology describing what he does. I say 'almost' because from the 1830s there is a vaguely formulated notion of the 'queen' which marks the beginning of a process of stereotyping that goes beyond the description of acts as such. Otherwise, in the first half of the century, public discourse observes what is tantamount to a conspiracy of silence. Law reports in the Press play down the homosexual context of offences of 'public indecency' and even of more serious crimes. Scientific discourse itself is loath to tackle the subject head-on. When it does so, as in Fournier-Pescay's article in the *Dictionnaire des sciences médicales* of 1819, its treatment is brief, apologetic and loud in its distaste.

8: Scandal in the Ink

The first sustained study purporting to be scientific, Ambroise Tardieu's *Etude medico-légale sur les attentats aux moeurs* (1857), sets the tone for what is to follow, not only treating its subject in a tone of moral outrage and disgust, but purporting to prove that homosexuals are less than men, a caricature of the other sex, fixed in active or passive roles according to their habitual practices, and even physically deformed by them. Tardieu's work is a product of the arch-bourgeois materialism and conservative morality which characterized the Second Empire. The other important testimony to Second Empire Establishment values is François Carlier's *Les deux prostitutions: étude de pathologie sociale*. Carlier headed the morals squad of the Paris police force between 1860 and 1870, a period when dossiers were established on 6,342 homosexuals, 4,711 exclusively on the grounds of their sexual orientation (despite the fact that this was not in itself illegal). His accounts of surveillance and of what he 'learnt' from it are revealing; he leaves his readers in no doubt that, in his view, homosexual acts constitute a vice which has nothing to do with love or affection but is simply born of greed for sensual pleasures, and that such acts *should be illegal*. He paints a picture of a society in which homosexuals exist in a cross-class (and therefore potentially socially disruptive), exploitative buyer–seller relationship, where they are subject not only to officially tolerated queer-bashing by 'young men who are in high spirits after a good dinner' but to severe harassment by the police themselves, who 'although often at a disadvantage because of the absence of legal provisions' give them as hard a time as possible. Tardieu and Carlier's texts both reflect the way in which Establishment values at the mid-century were firmly tied to the reigning economic model of possession and exploitation, with the family unit as both the microcosm of society and the symbol of its aims. At the same time they also reflect the way in which contemporary official discourse was concerned with classification and control, and their attempts to generalize and categorize are important indicators of the ways in which stereotypes were established in the public mind. The sociopolitical reasons for the marginalization of a 'non-productive' group such as homosexuals are clear, and the terms in which it was done set the pattern for what was to follow.

What might be called 'popular' versions of public discourse

on the subject change very little over the period 1850–1914. The legislature maintained its non-interventionist stance: when the Chamber of Deputies debated the issue of criminalizing homosexuality in 1887, they reaffirmed the view that, where the interest of third parties was not affected, the law had no right to intervene. But there was no reflection of this liberal stance in other aspects of public life. If, for example, we measure the gap in attitudes between the terms of the article on homosexuality in the edition of the *Encyclopédie Larousse* published in the 1860s and those of an article on contemporary literature published in the periodical *La Grande Revue* by the journalist J. Ernest-Charles in 1910, we will find the gap to be nil. The *Larousse* article asks how such a disgusting and ignominious phenomenon as homosexuality can still exist in so advanced a civilization; Ernest-Charles proclaims it a vice repugnant to French morality and to the French mentality. In the atmosphere of fevered nationalism which characterizes the *belle époque* it becomes, by implication, *unpatriotic* to be gay. (Hence French public glee at the turn-of-the-century British and German homosexual scandals, e.g. the Oscar Wilde trials and the scandals involving General Sir Hector Macdonald, F. A. Krupp and Prince Philipp von Eulenburg.) Yet across the same period medical discourse, beginning to absorb the influence of German sexology, moved from treating homosexuality as a crime to looking on it as an illness, and consequently to seeing it not as a series of voluntary acts but as a state or condition for which the individual is not responsible. This is the picture to be gained, for example, from André Raffalovich's *Uranisme et unisexualité* (1896) and Charles Fere's *L'Instinct sexuel, évolution et dissolution* (1899). Raffalovich even goes so far as to make a positive link between homosexuality and artistic genius.

There is, however, little sign of a softening of hostility in the police or the judiciary. Admittedly there is no evidence to suggest that courts were more harsh in penalizing homosexual prostitution or homosexual acts involving minors than their heterosexual equivalents. If anything, statistical evidence suggests that homosexual prostitution may have been pursued *less* tenaciously in the period 1900–10. And certainly there is an indication of complete fairmindedness in, for example, the judgement of the Supreme Court of

9 March 1905, which upheld an appeal against a ruling of the Court of Appeal of Bourges, on the grounds that the fact that the accused had committed repeated homosexual acts with consenting minors could not be held to constitute proof of 'persistent incitement to debauchery' because only on a single occasion had he had sex with two boys at the same time. Yet even here the language of the judgement remains that of a moralizing contempt – 'culpable practices', 'shameful acts', 'depraved instincts' – coherent with that shown by the Tribunal Correctionnel de Marseille in 1908, when it took a strong line on very obvious cruising, declaring that 'the sodomite who, by his demeanour, obscene gestures and words, attempts to pick up men in the streets, is guilty of an affront to public decency' (i.e. in contravention of article 330). Certainly public reactions to trials involving a homosexual element were anything but enlightened. The Press waxed voluble on the Adelsward-Fersen scandal in the summer of 1903, when the wretched young baron was prosecuted over the homoerotic tableaux vivants which he staged in his bachelor apartments in the Avenue Friedland for the benefit (and with the assistance) of schoolboys from the nearby Lycée Condorcet. (He was found guilty of 'encouragement to debauchery' and went into exile in Italy.)[5]

The Renard affair (1908–9) offers a more serious example of public prejudice. Renard, the fifty-year-old butler to a M. Rémy, a banker, was convicted of murdering his employer largely on the grounds that, as a homosexual who admitted having sexual relations with his employer's wife's nephew, he was clearly capable of anything. A journalist commenting on the case in *Le Matin* noted that it had been many years since an accused person had had so much evidence in his favour, but maintained that his conviction and the rejection of his appeal were understandable, since magistrates, jury and the public alike took the view that even if Renard had not murdered Rémy, he was clearly a monster and deserved to be transported (as he was) to a penal colony in Guyana.[6] It was the same form of argumentation that had been used in the Dreyfus case a few years earlier; not for the last time were Jews and homosexuals being considered as equivalent 'lesser breeds without the law'.

Between 1800 and 1914, as we have seen, homosexuality gradually becomes a concept and enters various types of public discourse, some of them evolving, some remaining fairly static in their hostility. The treatment of male homosexuality in nineteenth-century French literature follows a comparable shift to that of science, from silence or relative discretion at the start of the century to a significant opening-up at the end of it. Here it is interesting to contrast the private attitudes of writers as revealed in their letters and diaries with their public attitudes as embodied in works intended for publication. In the early part of the century there is silence. At most, Stendhal, in his correspondence, gives signs of homosexual desire, but there is no evidence that he ever acted upon them. By the mid-century things are changing. Flaubert, in his letters to his close friend Louis Bouilhet from Cairo in 1850, openly describes his escapade with an Egyptian bath-boy and the public way in which such adventures abroad could be discussed with one's fellow travellers.[7] And Gautier, in a letter of the same year, refers to the availability, in Florence, of homosexuals 'who would provide somewhere to stick your willy, for those with the same tastes as Balzac'.[8] But this private openness about homosexual acts is quite at variance with literary practice. With one exception, between 1800 and 1871 male homosexuality as a theme is only handled by the major novelists in minor incidents: a scandal with a coach-boy in Balzac's *La Maison Nucingen*, a reference to the separate housing of homosexuals in prison in his *Splendeurs et misères des courtisanes* and the anecdote of a valet who is sacked for sexual relations with the stable lads in Zola's *La Curée*.[9]

In so far as these episodes tell us anything, it is that male homosexuality is acceptable to the nineteenth-century French heterosexual only in so far as it is *distant* from him. Just as Flaubert can permit himself adventures in Egypt or Gautier can envisage a Frenchman buggering an Italian, so the *Maison Nucingen* episode occurs in England. Where this distance is not geographical it can be rendered in other ways. In *Splendeurs et misères*, the homosexual behaviour is attributed to criminals (i.e. social outcasts) and not just the reader but the *character* (Lord Durham) is specifically kept at a distance from the phenomenon by the refusal of the prison director to take him to the relevant building (the one in which the 'queens' or 'third sex' are housed). In the case of the Zola episode the metaphorical distance is more complex and more important.

There is both a class difference between Renée (to whom the anecdote is recounted) and the valet Baptiste, and a 'moral' distance, the distance between innocence and corruption, which places them worlds apart. The story is so far outside Renée's experience that she can only blush when she hears it, and when she sees Baptiste in the Baron Guiraud's coach later that day, she registers surprise and disgust. But Renée will later commit incestuous adultery with her androgynous stepson, retrospectively abolishing the moral distance between herself and Baptiste. Zola is actually using homosexuality as a marker of what is rotten in the state of France; the distance between Renée and the valet is removed by her own descent into vice. (If anything the text ironically implies that *her* vice is the more socially acceptable.)

In all three cases, then, male homosexuality represents a world separate from the reader's, and one of which the reader should clearly beware. It is only in the case of Balzac's anti-hero, the arch-criminal Vautrin from *Illusions perdues* and *Splendeurs et misères* that we can talk of anything like a major presence or a positive representation of homosexuality, and both arguments require a degree of special pleading. In the first place Vautrin is also distanced from the reader by his criminal status, and his recuperation into society at the end of *Splendeurs et misères* is paralleled by the suppression of the object of his homosexual desire: he becomes a policeman and simultaneously his homophilia ceases to be of thematic importance. In the second place, and more importantly, the texts are anything but explicit about his sexuality. Vautrin is made to represent male power and strength, Lucien de Rubempré whom he adores embodies feminine submission. But the superficial sexuality of the texts is always heterosexual (Lucien's relationships with Coralie and Esther). The Lucien/Vautrin relationship can be read as emblematizing a homosexual relationship of dominance and submission in a way which breaks through the taboos of Louis-Philippard society, but only metaphorically, and the element of creative social disorder which it represents on such a reading is safely neutralized by the eventual suppression of both the sexual and the social threat.

It is from the 1870s onward that a gap develops between official discourse and literary practice, as the range and nature of the representation of homosexual themes in literature begins to change. The explanation for this is complex, but it can best be seen as part of a general phenomenon whereby all the constraints that governed sexual identity and behaviour in *fin-de-siècle* Europe seem to be dissolving. In France we can chart the shift from the relative scandalousness of the presumedly homosexual relationship between Verlaine and Rimbaud in the early 1870s to the much more overtly scandalous (though not necessarily openly homosexual) personal lives of writers such as Rachilde and Jean Lorrain in the 1880s and 1890s. In general, nonetheless, we can observe that even in the 1880s or 1890s overtly deviant writers (overt, that is, in either their lives or the themes of their works or both) belong, socially and intellectually, to closed elitist groups. We can also observe that by and large they belong to what can loosely be called 'Decadence' and 'Symbolism' and were therefore working with currents of ideas that rejected the normalizing doctrines of moral and intellectual certainty, of classification and control, which had dominated the period 1830–70. This was certainly the perception of contemporaries, for example Octave Mirbeau, who launched a fierce attack on the Decadents in 1895, accusing them of poisoning the minds of the young, and reserving his particular venom for homosexual writers, whose heroes 'stink of sodomy, neurosis and syphilis'.[10]

Before 1895 the theme of homosexuality as such is handled relatively rarely by 'Realists'. When Zola received a confession from a young Italian who wanted him to write about 'this terrible sickness of the soul', he passed the material over to his friend. G. Saint-Paul who incorporated it into his book *Tares et poisons: perversion et perversités sexuelles* (published under the pseudonym 'Dr Laupts' in 1896, with a preface by Zola). It is true that Zola's main reason for not wanting to undertake the writing of the 'novel of the invert' was that he was already involved in enough public controversy. But his attitude to the issues is in any case only sympathetic up to a point: 'An invert is an agent of dissolution for the family, the nation, humanity. Man and woman are certainly only here to have children, and they kill life when they no longer do what is necessary to that end.' Even when a Decadent wished to give a positive or realistic account of homosexual experiences, of the kind which Verlaine embodied in his erotic poems *Hombres*, the poems had to be issued anonymously.[11] Indeed, if we look closely at the way in which homosexuality is represented during the period, we find that in a key respect there is no change between *fin-de-siècle* representations and the use of the theme by Balzac or Zola. What I have in mind is the distance between reader and experience, the element which symbolically confirms the essential and (for the heterosexual reader) comforting *otherness* of homosexuality. In this respect the classic representation could be taken to be Jean Lorrain's poem 'Bathylle' (1892), which describes a Thracian dancing-boy performing as an object of erotic desire for sailors in a Roman tavern.[12] The subject is distanced by placing it in antiquity, and within that framework the boy is given an exotic nationality which makes his 'otherness' an object of desire for his fictive audience. This double distancing locks homoerotic desire safely into the world of fantasy, a technique all the more significant in that Lorrain himself, unlike virtually every other author we have been considering so far, was gay.

So far we have only been considering the treatment of *male* homosexuality in nineteenth-century literature. Although in theory attitudes to lesbianism were equally negative, in practice the situation is more complex. It is true that Parent-Duchâtelet, a doctor working in the public health service, adopts an indignant tone over the subject in his treatise *La Prostitution dans la ville de Paris* of 1834. But in general, in the early part of the century, it was possible for public figures to conduct what were at least ambiguous relationships fairly openly, and for writers to feature lesbianism as a major motif in their works. Parisian society in the 1830s and 1840s not only speculated about the sexuality of George Sand and the actress Marie Dorval, it also gossiped about some of its own members, such as the Princesse Belgiojoso and Mme Marliani, without shutting its doors to them. From 1845 onward an obscene poem, 'The Lesbians of Paris', began to circulate and new verses were added every year containing the names of the leading actresses of the day.[13] What we have here is not evidence for the *reality* of any given individual's sexual orientation, but proof of the public's prurient obsession with the topic and of the belief that lesbian behaviour was particularly rife in such 'bohemian' circles as the theatre. This obsession is then sustained in literary terms by the lesbian motifs in the fiction of the period: in George Sand's *Lélia* (1833), where there are what Peter Gay calls 'some heated effusions of lesbian arousal between Pulcherie and her sister'; in Gautier's *Mademoiselle de Maupin* (1835), a novel to which ambiguity of sexual identity is thematically central; and in Balzac's *La Fille aux yeux d'or* (1835), where lesbianism and heterosexual incest come together in a threesome which symbolizes the untamed forces of disorder within society. In the 1830s and 1840s, then, public opinion was ready to accept, even to welcome, lesbian themes in literature.

The Second Empire was to show itself less tolerant: hence the condemnation of precisely those poems in the 1859 edition of Baudelaire's *Les Fleurs du mal* which dealt with such material.[14] It is significant in this context that lesbians under the Second Empire were victims of the same conservative reaction as male homosexuals. In this proto-capitalist society women were valuable possessions, playing an essential role in the 'production' structure of society; hence they were kept under strict male surveillance and control, particularly through marriage. Lesbians threatened the patriarchal principle precisely because they were not susceptible to it, without, as prostitutes did, serving male heterosexual need in any other way. So whereas Second Empire society exorcized its massive indulgence in prostitution by a censorious literature (particularly in the theatre) castigating it, it exorcized lesbianism by censoring it. When literary representation of lesbianism quickly resurfaces in the aftermath of the collapse of the Empire, for example in Zola's *La Curée* and *Nana*, it takes the same voyeuristic form as it had thirty years earlier. So the key to the tolerance of lesbianism as a literary theme before 1850 seems to be a general culturo-economic one. In an entirely patriarchal society such as nineteenth-century France, there is a fascination with what lies outside the male power structure, particularly female sexuality, and a corresponding desire to tame it via the imagination, to reduce it to an object of male power. (It is notable that of all the works to which I have referred so far, only *Lélia* is by a woman, and that is by far the least explicitly lesbian of the examples given.) At the height of the Romantic period, the exercise of power via the imagination was privileged in this way. But at a period when the imagination is no longer privileged by society, in, for example, the highly materialist Second Empire, the sociopolitical threat of untamed female sexuality, particularly in the 'non-productive' form of lesbianism, outweighs the voyeuristic pleasure which imaginative manipulation of it can occasion. As with male homosexuality, it is only in the first decades of the twentieth century that an expression of lesbian themes, *by lesbians* develops, changing the nature of that representation entirely. But the last two decades of the nineteenth century are a complex transitional period which also leave their mark on later lesbian writing.

There are two contradictory factors at work which affect the nature of the representation of lesbianism at the *fin de siècle*. Attacks on male homosexuality are extended for the first time to a serious consideration of its female equivalent. Julien Chevalier's *De l'inversion de l'instinct sexuel* (1885) and Ali Coffignon's *Paris vivant: la corruption à Paris* (1889) present a violently hostile analysis of both male and female homosexuality, which is repeated in Léo Taxil's *La Corruption fin de siècle* (1891). Coffignon's book is sensationalism passing as popular sociology, Chevalier approaches his topic 'from the medico-legal point of view', but both write out of unconcealed homophobia, and both agree that what they call sapphism is dangerously widespread. Chevalier blames equality in the workplace and in the arts, and the desire to compete with men in leisure pursuits and sports, both of which trends in his view had masculinized women. Coffignon pinpoints as causes the overcrowding of girls in the workplace, promiscuity in servants' quarters, boarding schools (for the middle classes), the entrusting of young girls to the care of female servants (among the upper classes), and in particular the influence of a type of 'equivocal literature which excites the woman's curiosity' causing her to experiment with practices of which she would otherwise have remained unaware. But the significant difference between the two writers concerns where the focus of lesbian activity in contemporary society is to be found. Chevalier maintains that it is principally prevalent in café society, the theatre and artistic circles; Coffignon, on the contrary, claims that it pervades all levels of society. Both are clearly more motivated by a desire to discredit than to investigate. Coffignon in particular indulges in detailed accounts of elegant lesbians 'cruising' in their carriages, clutching their secret badge (a well-groomed poodle ...) and in melodramatic tales of across-class seduction which look suspiciously like inventions modelled on the pattern of male homosexual activity.

These male perceptions of lesbianism are prompted by the same desire to protect a rigid social order as had informed the work of Tardieu a generation earlier (and we have to remember that Carlier's *Les Deux Prostitutions*, although written about the Second Empire, was only published in 1887 and thus belongs to the same wave of homophobia as the texts we are now considering). Such attitudes are reflected in literature either at a scandal-mongering level, as in Jean Lorrain's representation of aggressive society lesbianism in *Une Femme par jour* (1896), or in moralizing tales of moral and physical degeneration: the eponymous lesbian heroine of Daniel Bory's *Carlotta Noll, amoureuse et femme de lettres* (1901) ends up in a mental institution, the lovers in Jane de la Vaudere's *Les Demi-sexes* (1896) cling together in a fiery embrace as they are burnt to death – a fate which smacks of the hell-fire visited upon the incestuous brothers in Rachilde's *Les Hors-nature* (1897). Here, then, we have a literature which lends support to the sensationalist approach to lesbianism taken by recent pseudo-scientific work and attempts to take on the socially regulatory function which the law had declined to assume.

At the same time, the voyeuristic/patronizing tradition of representation of lesbianism finds a renewed form in a work which also harnesses that distance between reader and subject which the Decadents had used to make male homosexuality palatable to their readers. I am referring to Pierre Louÿs's *Chansons de Bilitis* (1895), a collection of poems ostensibly by a pupil of Sappho herself, presented as material recently found in a tomb and 'translated' into French, and recounting the triangular relationship between Sappho and two of her pupils, Bilitis and Mnasidika. As well as appealing to his male readers in much the same way as Gautier and Balzac had done, Louÿs develops a whole portrait of 'Greek love' of a richly sensual sort, which was paradoxically to have a very profound effect on poetry by lesbians in the following decade. Louÿs's book in fact has a threefold significance: it panders to the voyeur; it continues the tradition of reassuring its bourgeois readers by link-ing the otherness of its sexuality to a comfortingly distant and exotic otherness in space and time; but it also explicitly revives the classical model of homosexuality as necessary to a process of edu-cation (I do not mean exclusively sexual initiation but also a pro-cess of broadening of experience in a non-sexual sense) deriving from the influence of an older figure upon a younger one. Given that Louÿs was a friend of André Gide, and given the importance of the Greek educational model of homosexuality which dominates Gide's theoretical pronouncements on the subject, it is possible to see the *Chansons de Bilitis* as influencing the growth of a pederastic tradition in general (i.e. by acting as spur to Gide's writing). At the same time the book also served to intensify the interest of lesbian writers in the Sappho tradition and in the applicability of the Greek tradition to *female* writing. Seen in this light it acquires a peculiar dual importance as a transitional text.

With *Chansons de Bilitis* nineteenth-century literature moved decisively out of the limits of portraiture of homosexuality which it had previously imposed on itself. How far Louÿs *intended* this is impossible to establish; what concerns us is the result. Indeed, *Chansons de Bilitis* offers a significant example of the ways in which the sexual affiliations of the *reader* can alter the perception of the text. As read by heterosexual males it belongs to the litera-ture of titillation; as read by the Parisian lesbian group around Natalie Barney and Renée Vivien, it becomes a genuine expression of same-sex female desire. At the same time it provides a rare French contribution to the debate on Greek love which was being conducted in both England and Germany during the same period (notably in the work of John Addington Symonds, Edward Car-penter, Johann Baptiste von Schweitzer and Stefan George), and which is reflected, for example, in Paul Adam's article in the *Revue Blanche* in 1895, apropos of the Oscar Wilde affair, in which the beauty of the mentor/pupil relationship is stoutly defended. This marks the beginning of the third of the currents in homosexual literature – gay male, lesbian and now pederastic – which will develop in France in the following century.

At the outset of the twentieth century, then, we have a largely neutral legal system which, despite a tradition of negatively loaded discourse in the treatment of homosexual acts, has no specifically anti-homosexual legislation, but whose neutrality is in part counteracted by an actively homophobic police force. At the same time scientific discourse is shifting from considering homosexuality as a wilful vice to treating it as an involuntary psychopathological condition. In literature, lesbianism, long tolerated as a source of voyeuristic thrills for heterosexual males, has begun to inspire responses both more positive and more negative; male homosexuality is receiving sustained expression, largely but not exclusively as part of Decadence, but is only tolerated when projected into a distance of time or space; pederasty is beginning to establish a separate identity. There is a clear sense for the first time that the subject will not go away. To observe how these competing discourses defy contemporary attempts to absorb them into a single account of homosexuality, we have only to look at Camille Mauclair's *De l'amour physique* (1912), a classic example of received prejudice masquerading as informed intellectual reflection. Mauclair bases his attitude to male homosexuality on the assertion that sodomy enervates and degrades males and deprives the state of citizens and soldiers (what price the Theban Brigade, classical Greece's army of lovers?). But there is in the work a particularly unpleasant class slant: sodomy between upper-class males might be able to excuse itself on the grounds of exalted friendship or intellectual curiosity(!), but it would be impossible to find anything other than the worst physical and moral ignominy among working-class and lower middle-class sodomites. This snobbery is compounded by the patronizing acceptance of lesbianism: love between poor girls, we are told, 'always involves a certain spiritual beauty' and imposes no dangers on State or family. The socio-economic motives behind this sort of critique are barely concealed, but quite at odds with its concessions to certain aspects of contemporary social and literary practice.

The period that follows is characterized in general by a continued widening of the rift between popular and scientific discourse on the one hand and literature on the other. Scientific accounts of homosexuality are henceforth in the hands of psychiatry, and from the first French contribution to the field, Laforgue and Allendy's *La Psychanalyse et les névroses* in 1924, to Hesnard's

Manuel de sexologie (1959) and Porot's *Manuel alphabétique de psychiatrie* (1960), there is little variation: homosexuality is now an illness, a condition of emotional retardedness. The only professional disagreement concerns whether, and how, it can be cured. In other fields there is no shift away from a hostile public moralizing rooted in the stereotypes of the preceding generation. Yet despite public hostility there is plentiful anecdotal evidence of a greater freedom of action from 1920 onward among homosexuals themselves, at least in Paris. Julien Green in *Jeunesse* (1974) shows the ease with which an inexperienced young man could pick up partners for casual sex in early 1920s Paris; Daniel Guérin in *Son testament* (1979) claims that from his own experience working-class boys in the period 1925–30 were relatively relaxed about taking part in recreational sex with another male of their own age; and according to Michel du Coglay in *Chez les mauvais garçons* (1937) homosexuality was becoming more visible in all classes of French society – there were at least a quarter of a million homosexuals in Paris (with police files on some twenty thousand of them), and a network of gay baths, clubs, bars and restaurants existed which prefigured the modern 'scene'.

It is reasonable to suppose that this opening-up, which stemmed in part from the general relaxation of moral criteria in the immediate post-1918 period, was influenced by the example of artists and writers in their personal lives and by literature itself. Whereas in the pre-war period salon society might have been largely protected from the public gaze and able to operate, as a ruling class, above and beyond the 'rules', the world of the performing arts had always been subject to public scrutiny. If the private lives of homosexual socialites such as Count Robert de Montesquiou or the Prince and Princesse de Polignac remained veiled outside their own social group, it was widely known that homosexuality was common in the circles around Diaghilev and Cocteau. (Matters were more difficult for women, even in the theatre, as we shall see shortly.) As for literature itself, both Proust and Colette openly portrayed and discussed both female and male homosexuality in their works, whilst Gide championed pederasty in *Corydon* (1924) and admitted to his own pederastic experiences in *Si le grain ne meurt* (1926), as well as including more overt references to homosexual relations in his non-polemical writings from *Les Nour-ritures terrestres* (1897) and *L'Immoraliste* (1901) onward.

It is revealing therefore to read Roger Martin du Gard's assessment of public opinion in the 1920s in his *Notes sur André Gide*, where he records his attempts to dissuade Gide from publishing *Corydon* and *Si le grain ne meurt*. Martin du Gard argued that Gide would only cause a scandal which would place decisive weapons in the hands of his enemies whilst alienating two-thirds of his friends, who were willing to tolerate his private life only for such time as it remained *private*. Noting that Gide thought that 'the time was ripe to strike a blow, so that homosexuality can finally take its place in the sun', Martin du Gard expressed the view that Gide was mistaking a surface relaxation of moral codes for a fundamental change of attitudes:

> Homosexuals may benefit provisionally from a more apathetic tolerance; but in fact the homosexual is still subject to the same disapproval as before, and comes up against the same stigmatisation, the same irrevocable condemnation, not just from moralists but from the immense majority of the French.

The justification for his fears is illustrated by the fate, in 1924, of *Inversions*, the first homosexual periodical to be published in France (apart from *Akadémos*, a monthly literary review which appeared for one year in 1909 and was principally homosexual in content), and which was closed down by the authorities before it could get off the ground for offences against morality, pro-contraception propaganda and 'cynical apologia for homosexuality'. The two directors of the review were sentenced to three months' imprisonment apiece.[15]

Martin du Gard's fears are also to some extent justified by some of the replies to an enquiry conducted by the literary periodical *Les Marges* in 1926. *Les Marges* solicited the views of leading writers of the day on homosexuality in literature. The Communist Henri Barbusse declared: 'I consider this perversion of a natural instinct to be an index of the profound social and moral decadence of contemporary society'; and the up-and-coming Catholic novelist François Mauriac (whose youthful propensities were to be outed thirty-eight years later by Roger Peyrefitte in his *Lettre ouverte à François Mauriac*) opined that 'in our pagan society we do not have to tolerate or condemn inverts; in these matters the only tribunal we recognize as competent to judge is the Holy Inquisition'. Unfortunately, comparable cases of crass prejudice are spread across the political and cultural spectrum of the period, from the pronouncement of the Surrealist leader André Breton in 1928: 'I accuse the pederasts of seeking humane tolerance for a mental and moral defect which aims at setting itself up as a system and at paralysing all the undertakings which I respect', to the position taken up by the right-wing arch-Catholic Paul Claudel. He not only criticized Gide in private correspondence for acting in a way incompatible with 'natural reason and Revelation' but also vilified Martin du Gard for his play *Un Taciturne* (1931), attacked Louis Jouvet for directing it, and withdrew a play of his own from a planned collaboration with Jouvet, all because *Un Taciturne* has a homosexual theme. Even a relatively sympathetic study of the literary representation of homosexuality *L'Amour qui n'ose pas dire son nom*, published by François Porche in 1927, insisted that homosexuality is a vice and can have nothing to do with love. Clearly, tolerance in intellectual circles between the wars was decidedly superficial. And if this were the case in intellectual circles, it is unlikely that the rest of the population would have been more enlightened.

What about lesbianism? We have already seen evidence of the conflicting tendencies at work both in public opinion about, and literary representation of, lesbianism in the last fifteen years of the nineteenth century. If there was a new freedom, it was a very limited one. There is no indication that at this period female homosexuality had the same cross-class basis which characterized so much of its male counterpart. Inevitably, less evidence survives for lesbian activity within working milieux than in the upper classes, although Gide records overhearing, at the age of ten, what he much later realized to have been the love-making of their cook and the Swiss maid, and Colette recounts in *Mes apprentissages* how her newly engaged chambermaid wrote obscene verses to all the young female servants in the neighbouring buildings detailing their physical charms, and even tried to buy the favours of Colette's cook for a hundred francs. There *is* evidence of increased lesbian activity in salon society, but even though upper-class women were permitted to amuse themselves with extracurricular same-sex relationships, they were expected to do so firmly within the framework of a heterosexual marriage, and to do so with total discretion. The idea of an independent lesbian relationship was inconceivable. It was only by turning their backs on the social structure that even genuine aristocrats such as the Duchesse de Clermont-Tonnerre were able to give themselves up entirely to their sexual preferences.

Chevalier was probably right in one respect, when he pinpoints the focus of *belle époque* lesbian visibility as café society, the arts and the theatre. Leading courtesans – Liane de Pougy, Emilienne d'Alençon – could be open about their preferences, as could a popular singer like Jane Avril or an actress like Sarah Bernhardt. But while it was acceptable for Liane de Pougy to advertise her love for Natalie Barney in a novel (*Idylle saphique*, 1901), the limits of social tolerance are well illustrated by the case of the Marquise de Belboeuf. When Missy, as she was known, and Colette were involved in 'Egyptian dream', a mime act with definite lesbian overtones, at the Moulin Rouge (3 January 1907), the performance was brought to a halt by the outraged audience, and the Marquise was requested by the Prefect of Police to refrain from taking part in any further performances. As a result of the incident, Colette's husband Willy, who had encouraged her to experiment with lesbianism, found his journalistic contributions to the *Echo de Paris* were no longer required, doubtless a contributory factor in the divorce proceedings which he instituted a fortnight later. Thereafter the two women were no longer socially acceptable: by publicly declaring her sexual orientation a lesbian became an outsider.[16] There were, it is true, salons which served as focal points specifically for lesbians, but if we look at the characterization of them in Colette's *Le Pur et l'impur* we can see that they were mimicking society, rather than part of it. Aside from the issue of sexual orientation, symbols of difference played an important part in their composition: with their cross-dressing, their doubtful titles and claims of exotic aristocratic extraction, these women were, in Colette's words, 'A dying world on the margins of all other worlds'. Lesbians would only be able to transcend the social limitations of their *otherness* by turning it into a specific positive value.

It is not surprising, therefore, that the centre of *literary* lesbianism from 1902 onward, and hence of much lesbian society in Paris in the following decades, was actually in an expatriate group quite separate from Faubourg-Saint-Germain society, and which was not subject, or even susceptible, to the same constraints as those imposed on French women.[17] This was the circle around Natalie Barney, which was to include at various times Renée Vivien, Colette and Lucie Delarue-Mardrus, and which, as I shall discuss later, deliberately pursued what Benstock defines as 'the otherness of womanhood, its difference from the masculine norm'. This predominantly Anglo-Saxon literary world provided a social and cultural context for French lesbian writers right up to the Second World war, at a time when the French feminist movement apparently set its face against any concern with sexual rights at all. From the two *Congresses of Women's Works and Institutions* of 1899 and 1901 onward, there had been a marked absence of discussion in feminist circles (apart from some debate on the issue of prostitution) of such basic issues as a woman's right to control her own body. Between the wars, the feminist groups showed no interest even in rights to contraception or abortion, passively accepting harsh laws designed to prevent even the distribution of literature in favour of such things. The issue of lesbian rights was simply never raised. As Klejman and Rochefort put it, for French feminists of this period 'female individuality stops at the threshold of sexuality'.[18]

If I have dealt exclusively with Paris hitherto, it is for the obvious reason that the centre of both literary and homosexual activity was (and is) the capital. What hints we have of social attitudes elsewhere in France, particularly in rural areas, show them to have been predictably even less tolerant. August Strindberg records in 1886, for example, how two young Danish women, part of the local expatriate Scandinavian artistic community which included himself and his wife, were run out of Gretz by the villagers for seducing a beautiful local girl.[19] This echoes Colette's comment in *Mes apprentissages* that whilst village life did not prohibit close relationships between adolescent girls, it made things difficult for them, made fun of them, and ultimately prevented them. Whatever liberalization of attitudes to homosexuality, male or female, may have occurred in Paris between the wars, outside Paris nothing changed. Dominique Fernandez, describing the experience of growing up gay in northern France a half-century later, sums up the difference between Paris and the provinces precisely: 'It's still very difficult to be a homosexual in Paris, but you can't imagine what it was like to be a queer in Uckville, Moselle'; and he adds: 'I use two different terms deliberately, to indicate two different states of the problem.'[20] He might have said two different worlds. Fernandez characterizes the life of provincial gays in the decade after the war as one of isolation and fear, one where a gay teacher can only protect his career by marrying, and where attempts to set up self-help groups are ridiculed. It is a world where even money provides only limited protection, and blackmail, physical violence, even murder are not uncommon. Inevitably, as a result, sexual activity is clandestine, relationships are virtually impossible, many people refuse to recognize the nature of their sexuality, and those who do are forced by existing stereotypes into 'masculine' or 'feminine' roles. If life in Paris was different, it was because the anonymity of the capital protected the privacy of the individual to some degree, and because the pre-war network of homosexual haunts never completely disappeared despite increased police persecution. This anonymity and a limited mutual 'visibility' were enough to create a significantly less psychologically oppressive environment for Parisian homosexuals than for their country cousins, but the benefits are highly comparative.

If, as the 1950s progressed, the two worlds of Paris and the provinces began to come together a little, at least in the sense of gaining a greater perception of their differences and their common needs, it was through *Arcadie*, a periodical set up in 1954 by André Baudry, a teacher and former *séminariste*, with the backing of Cocteau and Roger Peyrefitte. *Arcadie* came to seem, in the more contestatory spirit of the 1980s, hopelessly timid in its desire to persuade society discreetly of the 'acceptability' of homosexuality, and its consequent desire to play up a somewhat bogus romanticized spirituality at the expense of the physical dimension (Baudry preferred the term *homophile* because it diverted the emphasis from sex to emotion). As one critic puts it:

> In practical terms this struggle in muted – dare I say emascu-
> lated – tones was as effective on behalf of the homosexual
> cause as a group of tarts chatting over a cup of tea would
> have been in promoting votes for women.[21]

But this is to take things out of context. The danger of a more strident approach in the 1950s is well illustrated by the fate of the anti-clerical, pro-homosexual monthly *Futur*, launched two years before *Arcadie*. *Futur* reported on court cases involving homosexu-ality and campaigned for suppression of the discriminatory articles in the Penal Code. It was very quickly banned from advertising or from being sold to those under eighteen; then a case was brought against it for 'affronts to public morality', leading to suspension of publication from March 1953 to June 1954, and it finally ceased publication in the autumn of the following year. The most revealing aspect of the periodical's short history came a year later. *Futur* had made an appeal to the Council of State after the advertising ban. On 5 December 1956 the Council gave a ruling which sums up public attitudes of the period: 'A publication which defends and exalts homosexuality in the name of the absolute liberty of the individual and of liberty of sexual practices is a publication whose aims are contrary to accepted morality.' In such a climate, the decision of Baudry and his collaborators to promote discretion as the prerequisite for progress was only prudent if they did not wish to be put out of business.

For a long time *Arcadie* made no attempt to have discrimi-natory legislation repealed, concentrating instead on creating a cli-mate of informed debate which would allow society to see that homosexuals were just ordinary people of whom society had no reason to be mistrustful. In 1957 Baudry created a meeting place for his Arcadians, the *Club littéraire et scientifique des pays latins*, which organized social evenings, theatre visits and conferences. It was this last activity which in the 1970s was to provide an essential and increasingly radical forum for public debate. At the same time its articles on such issues as the problem of the gay couple, the impossibility of adoption and prejudice in the workplace, together with its presentation of the facts about homosexual experience across France as a whole helped to create a sense of community and joint purpose among French gays for the first time.[22] The effectiveness of *Arcadie* was limited not by its 'softly, softly' policy, but by the fact that despite its discretion it too was banned from advertising, and therefore could not reach more than a fraction of its potential audience (by 1960 it still had only 10,000 subscribers).

The Mirguet amendment of 1960, with its definition of homosexuality as a 'social plague' would seem to indicate that public opinion, contrary to the efforts of *Arcadie*, was hardening. But all commentators agree that there is no evidence for this. On the contrary, the legislation seems to have been received with amused disbelief. In Fernandez' words:

> An enormous, almost unanimous burst of laughter greeted the terms of the new legislation. Homosexuality was beginning to become so established as a part of life that to try to brand it as a social plague suddenly seemed grotesquely comic: as though, in the age of the aeroplane, someone had solemnly pronounced a curse on air travel and preached a return to the stagecoach. The hilarity unleashed by the Mirguet amendment marked the degree of progress accomplished. From now on, there were things which you couldn't say or write without looking ridiculous.[23]

This progress, which can probably be explained in terms of the gradual relaxation of *all* codes of personal morality in France (and indeed in Europe as a whole) under the influence of American ideas and values, accelerated in the 1960s. Sexual sophistication at a conceptual level was spreading in the wake of the Kinsey Report, which had been translated into French immediately after its publication in 1948. Heterosexual literary critics began to write books (Robert Merle on Oscar Wilde, Jean Delay on Gide) which, if still marked by fashionable psychiatric prejudices, were nonetheless markedly more liberal than anything published before. When the first significant opinion poll to raise the issue was taken in

November 1968,[24] the figure for those who thought that homosexuality 'constituted an alarming problem in France at the
moment' was only 32 per cent – a percentage which, though it may
look disturbingly high from the perspective of the 1990s, gave
much encouragement to those hoping for homosexual rights
reforms at the time.

From the end of the 1960s onward, for the first time the
public context of literary production begins to be influenced significantly by homosexuals themselves. The brief but visible presence of
gay and lesbian student activists, under the title *Comité d'action
pédérastique révolutionnaire*, during the 'Events of May 1968' in
Paris, and the example of the Stonewall riots in the USA in 1969,
set the tone for much more aggressive homosexual rights activity in
the 1970s. In 1971 the interruption of an RTL broadcast entitled
'Homosexuality, this painful problem', by a group of young gay
militants, including the future novelist and homosexual theorist
Guy Hocquenghem, marked the birth of the *Front homosexuel
d'action révolutionnaire*, a rather Dadaist organization specializing
in provocative public acts designed to enrage both the Right and the
Left. The FHAR (pronounced *phare*, which in this context trans-
lates roughly as 'beacon') was succeeded in 1974 by an equally
radical but rather more specifically political organization the
Groupe de libération homosexuelle, the core of which combined
former FHAR members with a group of disaffected young ex-
members of *Arcadie*. The GLH, despite splintering into a number of
smaller groups, led the progressive wing of the gay rights movement
between 1974 and 1978. 1979 saw the formation of the *Comité
d'urgence d'antirépression homosexuelle*, intended to orchestrate
campaigns against individual examples of injustice toward gays,
but also responsible for issuing a major manifesto (addressed to the
Health and Social Affairs Commission of the Parliamentary
Assembly of the Council of Europe) which not only demanded the
suppression of anti-homosexual legislation but set out a programme for the protection of homosexual rights in all aspects of
public and private life. Alongside these very politically orientated
groups there also developed less radical organizations, such as
David and Jonathan (founded 1972), a moderate group seeking to
promote the cause of gay Christians,[25] and the *Centre du Christ*

libérateur, which tended to focus on the problems of minorities within homosexuality (e.g. transvestites, male prostitutes, paedophiles) and which stressed the need to 'take the sense of sin' out of all sexual activity.[26]

During the same period there was a comparable amount of activity on the part of specifically lesbian groups, usually more informal than their male equivalents and rarely completely divorced from the wider French feminist movement, which was itself very actively campaigning to improve women's rights. Lesbian groups frequently targeted specific projects, such as the creation of centres for lesbians in Paris and the provinces; their theoretical debates tended to centre on the nature of female sexuality and the attack on all aspects of patriarchism, from the primacy of the vaginal orgasm to the nuclear family as a tool of social control.

The effectiveness of these gay and lesbian organizations in modifying public opinion in general and *political* opinion in particular cannot be doubted. *Le Monde*, after a major demonstration on 4 April 1981, declared: 'Only the existence and development of a homosexual movement has forced the hand of the political parties, obliging them to get to grips with the issue'. Throughout the 1970s and early 1980s conferences and summer schools, film seasons and television debates organized or coordinated by one or another of the rights groups kept the issue in the public eye. The founding of France's first widely available gay paper, *Gai Pied*, in 1979 added to this visibility. The legislative reforms of 1982 and 1985 were the reward.

The legal battle was won, but that did not of course mean that homosexuality had gained real acceptance overnight. After all, there had been no discriminatory legislation against homosexuals for a hundred and fifty years without any long-term improvement in public understanding of it. If we look at the attitudes revealed in parliamentary debates and other public statements made in the period of rights activism we have just been considering – bearing in mind that in so doing we are looking at a relatively highly educated section of the population, with an interest in self-censoring its more obvious prejudices – we find interesting and disturbing evidence that the liberalization of values was superficial and essentially a facet of political allegiances.

There seems to have been little distinction between the attitudes of the extreme Left and the extreme Right: despite, or perhaps because of, the link between many gay rights groups and radical politics, there is no change in the position of the Communist Party on the issue of homosexuality between Barbusse's denunciation of it as a symptom of contemporary decadence in 1926 and an article in *L'Humanité* by Roland Leroy (5 May 1972) which speaks of it as representing 'the rot of capitalism in its declining phase'. Not until 1977 did any leading French Communist make a positive statement about gay rights, and then with the rider that there is no sustainable connection between revolutionary politics and homosexuality. Although one Socialist senator in a 1980 debate described homosexuality as an illness, there was otherwise a straight Left/Right split, with the Left defining homosexuality as simply a normal form of sexual expression and the Right presenting it as a basic threat to family values. Right-wing speakers in debates still regarded homosexuality as a perversion, and pontificated about the need to protect the young from members of their own sex whilst not acknowledging any need to protect them from members of the opposite sex: only one right-wing deputy in 1980 had the courage (and the intelligence) to refuse to vote with his party on the grounds that it was illogical to single out homosexual acts with fifteen- to eighteen-year-olds for condemnation whilst ignoring the possibility of heterosexual manipulation of the same age group. The radical Left view, that the right-wing stance derives less from genuine moral principle than from the economic need to promote the family as the basic agent of control and production in a capitalist society, was confirmed not merely by the family values rhetoric which permeated the debates but also indirectly by the revealing argument put forward by one right-wing deputy in a 1980 debate, that legislation should not be amended because it would reduce the monies accruing to the State from fines.

The language of all the debates revealed that, though only the issue of protection of minors was at issue, a large number of right-wing speakers thought that homosexuality was wrong in itself, a state of sickness or perversion, that homosexuals by definition sought to corrupt the young, and that sexual orientation was a matter of choice. The lack of logical coherence in these positions

– how can you choose a sickness? – seemed not to worry their adherents.

So much for parliamentary opinion. But what of the wider public? Gathering information about an issue like homosexuality becomes easier from the 1970s onward, with the spread of broadly based scientific inquiries and opinion polls. The statistics on the actual *practice* of male and female homosexuality in France in the last twenty years are rather peculiar. If we compare the findings of the Simon report (1970) with those of the major report produced in March 1993 for the National Agency on AIDS Research (ANRS), it would seem that whereas in 1970, 5 per cent of men and 2 per cent of women admitted to having had adult homosexual experience, in 1993 this had actually fallen to 4.1 per cent of men (though the figure for women has risen to 2.6 per cent). Whether or not the figures are reliable, the socio-geographical differences they indicate suggest that conditions in the provinces may not have changed much, relative to Paris, since the period described in *L'Etoile rose*: in rural areas 1.6 per cent of men and 1.2 per cent of women admit to having had adult homosexual experience, as against 5.9 per cent of men and 4.1 per cent of women in Paris. The top figures are all Parisian: 10.6 per cent of men between thirty and thirty-four; 15 per cent of university-educated male Parisians over forty; 14.8 per cent of Parisian women between thirty-five and thirty-nine. But if – and it is a big if – the statistics are right in indicting a stagnation in the liberalization of sexual practice, this is certainly not true of public attitudes towards homosexuality over the same period.

The first really detailed evidence was gathered in a *Société française d'enquêtes par sondage* (SOFRES) poll for *L'Express* in 1975, which suggested that, if anything, public opinion had become more hostile since 1968, 40 per cent now agreeing with the terms of the Mirguet amendment, though 44 per cent rejected that view. The poll revealed, however, a very significant division of opinion according to age, with only 27 per cent of the twenty-one to thirty-four age group agreeing that homosexuality constituted a social plague, as opposed to 53 per cent for those over sixty-five. In the same poll 53 per cent of the respondents described both male and female homosexuality as equally blameworthy, and only 24 per cent saw neither as blameworthy – the same 24 per cent, presumably, who defined homosexuality as 'an acceptable manner of expressing your sexuality', as opposed to the 42 per cent who saw it as an illness and the 22 per cent who considered it a vice (views for which, after all, parallels can be found in French medical manuals throughout the 1970s). Perhaps the most depressing statistic in this poll is the number (72 per cent) who, if they discovered a son of theirs to be gay, would try to get him to change his sexual orientation.

By 1979 an *Institut français d'opinion publique* (IFOP) poll carried out for *Arcadie* indicates a small shift in opinion. Unfortunately the questions were posed in a slightly different form, which prevents direct comparison, but the number of those who regarded homosexuality as an acceptable form of sexual behaviour had risen from 24 per cent to 29 per cent, although only a staggeringly low 17 per cent would have found themselves able to accept a gay son. A SOFRES poll for *Le Nouvel Observateur* in 1980 is much in line, with 27 per cent seeing homosexuality as a 'standard form of sexual expression'. The dramatic change occurs between 1980 and 1986. Despite the growing panic about AIDS, there is no sign of a backlash against gays. In another poll for *Le Nouvel Observateur* (conducted by IFOP) the number of those who consider homosexuality a standard form of sexual expression has *doubled* in 1986 to 54 per cent, while the number of those who see it as a vice has dropped from 26 per cent to 16 per cent. The trend continues in the next IFOP poll for *Le Nouvel Observateur*, in 1988, where those accepting homosexuality have risen to 61 per cent, those castigating it as a vice have been whittled down to 12 per cent. According to a 1991 poll, these attitudes reflect a willingness to accept homosexuals in real, face-to-face terms. When asked how they would feel if they *met* a homosexual, 19 per cent said they would feel uncomfortable, 11 per cent said they would feel sympathetic and 61 per cent said they would feel nothing in particular.

The polls, then, ostensibly suggest a shift of public opinion from widespread hostility in the 1970s to a belief that sexual orientation is no longer an issue. How do the statistics compare with other sources of evidence? It is easy to collect, from the columns of *Arcadie*, from reports by various gay rights groups and even from the general press, examples of hostility to gays and lesbians in all aspects of life in the 1970s. Many of these articles deal with prejudice in the workplace. First, there was the problem of getting a job if you were known to be gay. An article in *Arcadie* reported the story of a young graduate who, having applied for a job with the State railways, was obliged to undergo medical and psychometric tests which involved answers to very personal questions. A month later he received a letter informing him that he was not suitable for the post on grounds of 'sexual deviance liable to prevent the proper functioning of the service'.[27] Then there was the problem of keeping a job once your workmates discovered the truth. In March 1979 the Marseille branch of GLH produced a dossier of cases of prejudice at work: three waiters lost their jobs because of the hostility of the rest of the staff; a sweet-maker who had a nervous collapse as a result of being bullied by fellow workers was dismissed for 'unjustified absence'; and a man was sacked on a trivial pretext after appearing on a television broadcast about homosexuality.[28] The same report also includes material on another major area of potential difficulty, housing: for example, the case of two lesbians cohabiting in Tours who received anonymous letters decorated with swastikas proclaiming, 'We don't like sexual deviance'. A report in *L'Express* in 1978 included a comparable case, that of a fifty-one-year-old man and his lover whose tenancy was not renewed after a campaign against them by neighbours.[29] Private prejudice was rife.

The anti-discrimination legislation of 1985 was designed to eliminate problems of these sorts, of course, but legislation cannot solve more personal problems. Whatever the opinion polls suggest – and after all, at best, they show that one French person in five cannot cope with the idea of a real live homosexual – there is plenty of evidence to show how deeply rooted prejudice still is. On 28 April 1985, for example, war veterans' organizations at Besançon refused to allow homosexual representatives to lay a wreath in memory of their deported comrades on the occasion of the fortieth anniversary of the liberation of the German concentration camps. Except for the very youngest French generation, the damage has already been done. In a broadcast on 12 May 1993 on the newly opened Channel H, a gay cable TV channel, discussing the difficulties of coming out in contemporary France, the cases presented included a forty-year-old female marketing executive whose family cut her out of their wills when she revealed her lesbianism; a forty-four-year-old man trying to balance his relationship with his boyfriend against the claims of his marriage to a wife unaware of his real sexual orientation; and a thirty-eight-year-old former member of the French riot police (CRS) who had been blackmailed by a minor and then lost his job when the truth came out.[30]

The pressures and dangers of going public about one's sexuality may have lessened, but they have not gone away, and for anyone born before the 1970s the legacy of overt social hostility will never be completely shaken off. Despite the progress made, French homosexuals of both sexes, especially outside Paris, are still far from the equals of their heterosexual compatriots anywhere except in the eyes of the law. As Jean-Paul Aron puts it: 'Homosexuality is a form of deviation, of marginality which the social body can tolerate but not endorse to the hilt.'[31] This presumably accounts for the continued reluctance of leading intellectuals to be entirely honest in public about their orientation. Roland Barthes and Michel Foucault are the examples usually cited: Dominique Fernandez attacked Barthes for not mentioning his homosexuality in *Barthes par Barthes*; Jean-Paul Aron criticized Foucault's failure to admit that he was dying of AIDS as a silence born of shame and thereby incompatible with his status as an intellectual. Aron himself was only able to be completely open about his sexuality when he was found to be HIV positive. Even in the inner sanctum of Parisian literary circles self-acceptance is still not easy.

The picture which we can derive from all this of the context of values in which writing about and by homosexuals has been produced in France in the last one hundred years is a complex one. Public awareness of both male and female homosexuality seems to have intensified between 1880 and 1914 and to have remained fairly constant thereafter, until gay rights groups deliberately sought to stimulate public debate in the early 1970s. Neutrality in the legal system from 1791 to 1942 disguised considerable public contempt and hostility, which was fed by a scientific discourse that changed in the late nineteenth century from categorizing homosexuality as a voluntary vice to patronizing it as a sickness, a position still maintained by some psychiatrists to this day.

As we have seen, where gayness and lesbianism in twentieth-century French literature are concerned, the context of writing and reading is really very complex. In the first place, lesbianism, divided between voyeuristic tolerance, brief periods of public indignation and a more general blanket of indifferent silence, is only partly subject to the same constraints as male homosexuality. In the second place, there are a number of discourses – legal, medical, popular – which, although they influence each other, follow different lines of development, and interrelate with pre-existing literary discourse. The nineteenth-century inheritance is itself already heterogeneous, comprising a legal neutrality which disguises a high degree of institutional prejudice reflected in practice in the very language of legal judgements; a popular, thinly concealed hostility born of the desire to exclude everything which risks destabilizing the rigid order of a patriarchal capitalist society; a medical discourse which moves belatedly from the description of perverted acts to the definition of abnormal conditions; and a developing literary discourse of *otherness* shaped and coloured by the very attitudes against which it reacts.

Although the phases of more recent development can be linked to a greater openness of gay and lesbian activity in the period 1890–1914, an apparent public tolerance of such activity in the inter-war years, and the increasingly formalized hostility toward gays in the period after the Second World War, all these 'phenomena' are in different ways deceptive. From 1890 onward once the comforting perception of gay and lesbian activity as *other* in time and space is replaced by an increasing public awareness of the immediate, cross-class presence of such activity in Parisian society, an ever-present latent homophobia asserts itself, is temporarily disguised by a general relaxation of moral criteria, then reasserts itself, only to become increasingly irrelevant as the moral climate once again relaxes. Precisely at the point where the previous evolution of medical discourse, from the language of elective vice to the language of involuntary sickness, freezes in a scientifically unsustainable refusal to recognize homosexuality as a morally neutral natural condition, and where concurrently the law shifts abruptly and arbitrarily from neutrality to hostility, French homosexuals acquire their first vestigial sense of group identity, and begin the process of liberating both themselves and to a limited degree their straight contemporaries from the very same hostile preconceptions which are responsible for the state of medical and judicial thinking. There *is* an evolution in social attitudes, but one which is complicated by the fact that liberalization itself generates a series of hiccups of backlash. As a result, by the 1990s, the French public sees itself (or opinion polls present the French public as seeing itself) as more progressive in theory than it is in practice, but has at least come to accept the presence of homosexuality as an inevitable social reality, rather than relying on neutralizing its threats by a variety of discourses of otherness from the medical to the literary. This, then, is the social context of the writer and the reader. Let us look at what sorts of literary (self)representation it generates.

Notes

1. *Mon sida* (Paris: Christian Bourgois, 1988), p. 30.
2. I have not been able to find a thorough, clear account, in any language, of the history of the legal status of homosexuality in France. My principal sources have been Christian Gury, *L'Homosexuel et la loi* (Lausanne: l'Aire, 1981) and Janine Mossuz-Lavau, *Les Lois de l'amour: les politiques de la sexualité en France (1950–1990)* (Paris: Payot, 1991), ch. V.
3. See Jeffrey Weeks, *Coming Out: Homosexual Politics in Britain from the Nineteenth Century to the Present*, revised edition (London: Quartet Books, 1990), pp. 106–7.
4. See Claude Courouve, *Vocabulaire de l'homosexualité masculine* (Paris: Payot, 1985).
5. For a concise summary of the case see Patrick Pollard, *André Gide, Homosexual Moralist* (New Haven and London: Yale University Press, 1991), p. 133. Fersen's life is the subject of Roger Peyrefitte's novel-cum-*biographie romancée*, *L'Exilé de Capri* (1959).
6. See Pollard, *André Gide*, pp. 133–5.
7. See Gustave Flaubert, *Correspondance*, ed. J. Bruneau (Paris: Gallimard (Bibliothèque de la Pléiade), 1973), vol. 1; the important letters are those of 15 January 1850 (pp. 571–3) and 2 June 1850 (p. 638).
8. Cited by Roger Peyrefitte, *L'Innominato: nouveaux propos secrets* (Paris: Albin Michel, 1977), p. 193.
9. Honoré de Balzac, *La Comédie humaine* (Paris: Gallimard (Bibliothèque de la Pléiade), 1976–81), vol. V, pp. 607–8 and 1055; Emile Zola, *Les Rougon-Macquart* (Paris: Gallimard (Bibliothèque de la Pléiade), 1960), vol. I, p. 591.

10. In an article by Octave Mirbeau entitled 'Des lys! Des lys!', published in *Le Journal*, 7 April 1895: quoted Jennifer Birkett, *The Sins of the Fathers: Decadence in France 1870–1914* (London: Quartet Books, 1986), p. 246.

11. A bilingual edition, with translations by Alistair Elliot, was published by Anvil Press in 1979.

12. The text of this poem is most readily available in Philip Stephan, *Paul Verlaine and the Decadence 1882–90* (Manchester: Manchester University Press, 1974), pp. 41–2.

13. See Antoine Adam (ed.), *Baudelaire: Les Fleurs du mal* (Paris: Garnier, 1961), pp. 411–12.

14. Largely at the prompting of a fiercely moralizing and sensation-hungry Press (a phenomenon familiar to modern readers too), an obscenity charge was brought against the first edition of *Les Fleurs du mal*, and on 20 August 1857 Baudelaire and his editor were found guilty and fined. The court ordered that six poems be dropped from the edition. Of these, two – 'Lesbos' and 'Femmes damnées' – were specifically lesbian in implication. The sentence was retrospectively quashed – three-quarters of a century later.

15. For *Inversions*, see Gury, *L'Homosexuel et la loi*, p. 259; for *Akadémos*, see Pollard, *André Gide*, pp. 251–3.

16. The most accurate account of the events concerned is to be found in Claude Pichois's preface to the second volume of Colette *Oeuvres* (Paris: Gallimard (Bibliothèque de la Pléiade), 1984), pp. xc–xciii.

17. See Shari Benstock, *Women of the Left Bank: Paris, 1900–1940* (London: Virago, 1987), particularly pp. 71–84, 268–310.

18. Laurence Klejman and Florence Rochefort, *L'Egalité en marche* (Paris: Des Femmes, 1989), p. 337.

19. The incident is recounted in Catherine van Casselaer, *Lot's Wife: Lesbian Paris 1890–1914* (Liverpool: Janus Press, 1986).

20. The terms Fernandez actually uses are 'homosexuel' and 'pédé' (*L'Etoile rose* (Paris: Grasset, 1978), p. 89). For a discussion of the French use of 'pédéraste', see below p. 144–6.

21. Daniel Garcia, *Jean-Louis Bory* (Paris: Flammarion, 1991), pp. 197–8.

22. See for example Dominique Dallayrac, 'Dossier homosexualité' in *Arcadie* no. 12, December 1954, which confirms the picture of fear, isolation and petty persecution painted retrospectively in *L'Etoile rose*.

23. Dominique Fernandez, *Le Rapt de Ganymède* (Paris: Grasset, 1989), pp. 119–20, and cf. *L'Etoile rose*, p. 245.

24. See Mossuz-Lavau, *Les Lois de l'amour*, p. 243.

25. The policy of the Catholic Church has shifted so little that the most an officially backed study of *Sexuality and Christian Life* could

offer in the way of succour to homosexuals in 1981 was to suggest that if they were trying to live as good Christians, they ought not to be refused the sacraments.

26. The *Centre du Christ libérateur* was founded by Pastor Joseph Douce, who caused a scandal in December 1979 by celebrating a 'union of homosexual friendship' in a Protestant church in Paris. After a further act of the same sort in Lyons in 1985, Douce was disowned by the French Federation of Evangelical Baptist Churches. He disappeared in mysterious circumstances on 19 July 1990, and in October of the same year his body was found in the woods at Rambouillet. Evidence came to light that he had been under police surveillance because of his work for gay liberation, and suspicions were voiced that officialdom had had a hand in his disappearance and death, but nothing was proven.

27. *Arcadie*, no. 22, June 1972; see also Gury, *L'Homosexuel et la loi*, pp. 137–8.

28. Cited Gury, *L'Homosexuel et la loi*, pp. 143–4.

29. Both cases cited ibid., p. 96.

30. Reported in *Exit* no. 4, April 1993, p. 7. (*Exit* is one of the Parisian free gay papers distributed in bars and clubs.)

31. Aron, *Mon sida*, p. 30.

Chapter two

Looking on the Black Side

'Don't think you'll please them by holding up a mirror
to them; there's nothing they hate more.'

● *Dominique Fernandez*[1]

GIVEN the permanent predominance of heterosexual
stereotypes in all aspects of life, and the role this predominance
plays in enforcing a sense of isolation and inferiority on homosexuals, one of the most significant issues in writing by and about gays
is inevitably the question of self-image. To understand how images
of homosexuality developed in twentieth-century French literature,
we need to begin by asking what traditions of portraiture helped to
form modern literary discourse on the topic in France. As we saw in
Chapter 1, the only theoretical model for a positive account of any
aspect of homosexuality was that provided by contemporary English and German defences of an idealized Greek pederasty, a model
which also provided lesbians with an alternative to the literature of
guilt. But the main literary inheritance derived from two ostensibly
disparate nineteenth-century traditions which significantly overlap
on this issue, one of which was heavily influenced by the prevailing
scientific discourse: Decadence and social and psychological realism.

As we have seen, late nineteenth-century works on medicine
and psychology had begun to assert that sexual orientation was not

a matter of choice, and that homosexuals should not therefore be *blamed* for the nature of their sexuality. Even this view represents a sort of negative tolerance which encourages a self-image of inadequacy. To make matters worse, most such theorists still presented homosexuality as a form of degeneracy, and linked it with criminality. Realist novels of the *fin de siècle* refer to it in terms of the contemporary medico-legal orthodoxy: Paul Bonnetain's *Charlot s'amuse* (1883) links masturbation and homosexuality to degeneracy; Lucien Descaves's *Sous-offs* (1890) includes an unsympathetic portrait of a sodomite, Laprevolte, who is caught having illegal sexual relations with minors in Le Havre; in Zola's *Verité* (1902) a choirboy is raped and murdered by a priest. In this kind of treatment, homosexuality is at best a sickness, at worst a vice, and is certain to lead its adherents to personal and social destruction.

The particular contribution of the Decadents included the Romantic motif of the artist as social and moral outcast, particularly in its Baudelairean form of the artist as condemned to explore evil in order to transmute it into beauty. This evil is defined in terms of a deviant sexuality (especially male homosexuality) which associates the text with corruption and disaster: in Joris-karl Huysmans's *A rebours*, the Decadent bible, the implicitly homosexual relations between Des Esseintes and Auguste accompany the former's attempts to turn the latter into a criminal; in Rachilde's *Monsieur Vénus*, Jacques is feminized into a transvestism and incipient homosexuality which lead to his death, whilst in her *Les Hors-nature* the fraternal incest ends in symbolic hell-fire; the hero of Jean Lorrain's *Le Vice errant*, the physically and morally ruined Noronsoff, dies while frantically searching for partners for his uncontrollable homosexual desires.

The visual arts produced or admired by the Decadents reflect the same vision: Huysmans, contemplating a fifteenth-century *Virgin and Child with Saint Quentin* by Francesco Bianchi, reflects on the 'dizzying signs of Sodom' which the anguished androgynous beauty of the saint suggests to him;[2] Jean Lorrain chooses Gustave Moreau's *Les Prétendants*, in which all the slaughtered suitors of Penelope are represented as sensuously displayed, debauched adolescents, as the painting the contemplation of which will turn the repressedly homosexual Monsieur Phocas (in the novel of that name) into the ultimate artist-pariah. There is in all these works an inescapable link between the homoerotic, degeneracy and death, which only the gifted artist is destined to transcend – a situation offering no solace to the ordinary gay reader. At the same time, as we saw in Chapter 1, the Decadents often sought to pacify the heterosexual reader by a process of distancing, placing the homosexual 'threat' at a safe distance in time and space, a technique which only serves to increase the *gay* reader's sense of alienation. As I suggested earlier, the two disparate literary traditions of Decadence and social and psychological realism curiously converge in their presentation of homosexuality. The moral offered by both to the contemporary gay reader and the aspiring gay writer must have seemed clear enough: homosexuality = perversion = destruction; it will always be punished literally or symbolically and can only find justification in art.

Not until Binet-Valmer's *Lucien* (1910) do we find a novel which, while representing current social attitudes accurately, balances them with any positive element.[3] On the one hand Lucien's homosexuality is linked to inadequacy – he is effeminate and physically degenerate – on the other, the attempts of his father, a famous doctor, to 'cure' him are shown as barbarous and misguided. The shock element of the novel comes in its ending: Lucien's suicide is a feint; he and his lover Reggie are not dead but enjoying themselves in a new, free life in Italy. Not surprisingly, the novel caused a storm of protest from moralizing critics, who considered that Lucien had not met his just deserts. It was thought not to be the task of novelists to broach such issues, especially when in so doing they managed to attack the medical profession and the sacrosanct role of the father in the same breath. As the reviewer in *Le Temps* pontificated: 'Some topics should be left to treatises on pathology or to handbooks intended for the guidance of confessors'. Yet to read the novel in this way is to overlook the element of wish-fulfilment in the conclusion of *Lucien*, which can be compared with the same element in the finale of E. M. Forster's *Maurice*. The flight of Adelsward-Fersen or Krupp to Capri hardly offered a realistic pattern of self-realization for the contemporary gay reader.

Lucien was an exception among novels (whether by heterosexual or homosexual authors) prior to 1914, the majority of which generally present a negative view of adult male 'inversion', or attack the physical exploitation of the young by unscrupulous perverts. The only other work of substance reflecting a positive discourse, one defined by the contemporary debate on pederasty, is Eekhoud's *Escal-Vigor* (1899). However, here too there are limitations in the treatment of the subject. In this novel, characteristically *fin de siècle* in its theatrically imprecise temporal and physical setting, Eekhoud portrays the idealized passion of a highborn artistic dreamer for a young lad from a poor family. Despite the evident sensuality underlying the relationship, all the emphasis is on spiritual love. The hero defends himself in terms of the noble homophilic passions of the past, communicated to him through art and literature; the physical, in the form of sodomy, is specifically rejected. And at the end of the novel the ill-starred couple are attacked and killed by an uncomprehending mob, dying (like Rachilde's incestuous brothers) on an eternal kiss. Society's hostility toward gay love is represented as implacable, however disembodied the emotion.

At the same time, there is also in Eekhoud's work another strand of homophilic writing, whose sexual significance is for the most part only expressed implicitly: the theme of the superiority of the 'other' defined in terms of social class. The boy Guidon's class origins in *Escal-Vigor* are a 'fact' but are not emblematically represented in the boy's character or person. He is as much the typical artist, submissive and a dreamer, as his lover. Elsewhere, particularly in *Le Cycle patibulaire* (1892) and *Voyous de velours* (1904), Eekhoud focuses on social misfits and criminals, whose energy and beauty contrast with the lifelessness of the bourgeois society which has marginalized them. That these outcasts are all, at a certain level, symbols of sexual difference becomes clear in *Le Cycle patibulaire* in the final story, 'Le Quadrille du lancier'. For, here Eekhoud abandons the lyricized social realism which he has used throughout the collection in favour of a gothic nightmare. The subject of the story, a handsome young soldier, undergoes at its outset the humiliating ritual of *degradation*, as he is expelled from the army for an unspecified but easily intuitable 'offence against morals'. This physically violent expulsion, symbolizing the exclusion of the homosexual from society, is then paralleled by a scene in a dance hall where he gets his revenge on the straight world which has betrayed him. In a classic scene of homosexual wish-fulfilment, by encouraging all the women present to reduce themselves to lusting animals who strip and tempt him, he induces disgust in their husbands and lovers, whose desire is turned instead onto himself. Eekhoud cannot escape the clichés of his period: despite the young man's male beauty, his homosexuality implies an inner femininity which the author communicates by defining him as 'the androgyne' at the moment of his final conquest. Furthermore the vocabulary of sin and hell-fire dominates the final moment, when the ravening maenads have bled him to death only to find their menfolk caught in the flames of perdition created by their mystical union with this 'fallen archangel'. But despite this concession to the literature of the pariah, Eekhoud's image of otherness does transfer guilt firmly from the rejected to the rejecters.

If we look more closely at Eekhoud's work, we find that the value system underlying the stories of *Le Cycle patibulaire* and explicit in 'Le quadrille du lancier' is not unique. *Voyous de velours* has something of the same pattern, with its portrait of a renegade bourgeois, Laurent Paridael, who exiles himself from his class in the pursuit of the company of young ruffians. The homoerotic nature of his feelings is obvious from the outset. The very sensual descriptions of these adolescents and young men appeal to the sense of touch as much as to the eye, and the scene in which he is inveigled into wrestling with the half-naked Bugutte allows the frank expression of physical desire, translated into aesthetic images. Contemporary clichés again abound: Paridael eventually shoots himself in yet another Romantic death scene, and the vocabulary of his desire is frequently idealized through religious terminology – ecstasy, devotion, idolatry, the religion of love. But, as in *Le Cycle patibulaire*, the focus of blame is effectively shifted onto a society which cannot value the *voyous* or understand Paridael's love for them. The episode in the reformatory at Poulderbauge, in which Paridael sacrifices his job and his reputation to save the maltreated Warre, only to see the lad shot in the succeeding riot,[4] perfectly establishes the issue of moral right and wrong at precisely the point at which Paridael's desire is most overt: 'We wanted so badly to embrace each other for a first and last time. Our lips desired each other', he writes as he evokes the moment when the authorities separate him from Warre for ever. Homosexuality in Eekhoud's work is ill-starred, but it has right on its side.

Although Paridael represents a classic exposition of the homosexual as misfit, whose passions, destined to frustration within a hostile society, lead to his destruction, Eekhoud's firm attribution of blame to that society, coupled with his appreciation of working-class male sensuality and his frank rendering of inter-male desire, somewhat modify the negative associations of homosexuality in his works. This positive element in his treatment is particularly obvious if we contrast it with the completely different way in which similar themes of low-life milieux, adolescent sexuality and criminality are presented in Francis Carco's *Jésus-la-caille* (1914). Reverting to the medical stereotype of the period, Carco's eponymous young gay hero, like Binet-Valmer's Lucien, is characterized by his femininity, and lacks the intense maleness of Eekhoud's street-boys. This equation of homosexuality with effeminacy is heightened in Carco's racy portrait of drag queens (a motif he was to develop separately in his *Dialogues des courtisanes* of 1928). For Eekhoud's doomed but justified pariahs, Carco substitutes a bohemian picturesqueness which panders to heterosexual prejudices about the unmanliness of homosexuality in a rather sentimental way.

Unsurprisingly, then, given the scientific and literary discourse which contributed to its formation, the immediate legacy of the generation which came to maturity in the final decades of the nineteenth century was, in its main lines, twofold: a gay male literature of guilt and an incipient literature of pederastic apologia. At the same time, the foundations are laid down for a third stream of writing: a fascination with the otherness represented by young working-class masculinity, and a willingness to explore the hitherto forbidden literary area of male sensuality. The development of modern gay writing in France reflects these divisions precisely. Pederastic writing is immediately taken over and refashioned by Gide, to form a tradition which we will examine separately. The first phase of gay male writing proper, running from Proust to Genet via Cocteau, reacts to, and is moulded by, the medico-psychological discourse of inadequacy, but seeks to transcend it through reworked images of the artist-pariah and through the parallel lyricization of the social outcast.

Let us begin by looking at the presentation of homosexuality in Proust's *A la recherche du temps perdu*.[5] Proust's own sexual orientation was clear. It is interesting to read Gide's comments on the subject in his *Journal*. In an entry for 14 May 1921, he writes of Proust: 'Far from denying or concealing his uranism, he reveals it; I could almost say, boasts about it. He says he has only ever loved women spiritually and has never experienced physical love except with men'. The passage goes on to discuss a surprising assertion by Proust that Baudelaire must have been a practising homosexual. Gide finishes his entry on the topic: 'I hope he is right and that homosexuals are even more numerous than I initially supposed. In any case I had no idea that Proust was so exclusively homosexual'. This factor might be assumed to account for the importance given to the topic in his novel but does not automatically explain the way in which it is treated. In the first place, the narrator Marcel is made heterosexual and events from Proust's own life are transposed into heterosexual terms; in the second place, key episodes are devoted to a negative representation of homosexuality.

Another entry in Gide's diary, recorded a few days after the above, throws some light on the issue. According to Gide, Proust reproached himself for the hesitation which had caused him to transpose the positive aspects of his sexual memories into a feminine context, leaving only 'the grotesque and the abject' aspects to be treated in the *Sodome et Gomorrhe* volume of the novel. At the same time he had been so greatly put out when it was suggested that he intended to *condemn* homosexuality that Gide had come to the conclusion that 'what we find ignoble, ridiculous or disgusting does not seem so repellent to him'. It has to be said, however, that it is difficult to believe that Proust was unaware of the full extent to which he had reduced his portrait of homosexuality to the purely negative, in view of the evidence offered by his own notebooks, which contain some explicitly pessimistic passages on the subject. Nor is the negative approach one which Proust adopted belatedly. In 'Avant la nuit', a story he published in the *Revue Blanche* in 1908, Proust presents suicide as the inevitable end to homosexual experience, and in 'Violante ou la mondanité', a story included in his collection *Les Plaisirs et les jours* (1896) he uses lesbianism as a symbol for human depravity in general.

One explanation for this negativity is pragmatic. Given that Proust sets his action in contemporary Paris, he is limited both by the reality of contemporary values and by the limits of his putative readers' tolerance. In Peter Gay's words: 'It was, in short, easier to publish an account of homosexuality if it conveyed pain rather than pleasure'.[6] Another argument links this 'self-punishment' of a part of the author with the equivalent negative account of another important part of himself, Jewishness, and it is indeed significant that Proust makes direct comparisons between the problems of homosexuals and Jews in contemporary society. Neither argument, however, is quite enough to account for the number of extended set pieces – Mlle Vinteuil and her lesbian lover in *Du côté de chez Swann*, Charlus and Jupien at the beginning of *Sodome et Gomorrhe*, M. Nissim Bernard and the hotel boys in the same volume, Jupien's male brothel in *Le Temps retrouvé*, to name but a few. Nor do such arguments suffice to explain the importance given to the Baron de Charlus as a character, and to account for his relationship with the violinist Morel, or for the extraordinary number of characters who turn out to be, or become, homosexual during the course of the novel– Albertine, Gilberte, Robert de Saint-Loup, for example. Ideally, then, we need an explanation which accounts simultaneously for both proliferation of homosexuality and negative presentation of it.

To understand the negative presentation, we should note first that the Greek love/master–pupil defence of homosexuality is not one in which Proust is interested. Indeed his narrator specifically states that it is a dead concept with no relevance to modern times. Yet it is the only existing model for a positive literary account of homosexuality at that period. On the basis of his experience of salon life, the realist in Proust leads him, as does the nature of his own particular sexuality, to emphasize male homosexual desire as a pursuit of an otherness which can indeed be found in youth – lift-boys and page-boys in the novel are almost universally and often amusingly portrayed as 'on for it' – but is more often translated into class difference. Charlus has sex with Jupien, falls in love with Morel (although here, as we shall see, we have the ambiguity of the combination lower-class yob/artist), and is eventually reduced to finding pleasure of a sado-masochistic kind in a brothel with young men who pretend to be hardened criminals in order to increase his thrills. All the aristocratic homosexuals mentioned – Saint-Loup, the Duc de Châtelraut, the son of the Prince de Foix – have liaisons with their social inferiors. Proust's narrator even generalizes the point into a principle: 'For in this anachronistically fairy-tale existence, ambassadors befriend convicts, and princes, with that freedom of behaviour which aristocratic education bestows and which a trembling bourgeois would not possess, go off for tête-à-têtes with young toughs.'

In this respect Proust is in fact producing a homosexual equivalent to the fascination with across-class *hetero*sexual relations to be found in the novels of Zola (notably *Nana*), and he is doing it in a very different way from Eekhoud, in whose work the lover aspires to the status of his beloved by trying to lose or transcend his upper- or middle-class identity. For Proustian characters the *frisson* comes in part from the very existence of the gulf; they have no desire to eliminate it. But fascination with an unobtainable 'other' symbolized in class difference is at the same time, on a different level, a frustrated pursuit of a more fundamental otherness. Proust's account of homosexuality also has its roots in contemporary German sexology, as originally expounded by Karl-Heinrich Ulrichs and later embodied in the work of Kraft-Ebbing, Hirschfeld and Havelock Ellis, in that it sees homosexuals as 'spiritual hermaphrodites', people who possess the soul of one sex in the body of the other. It is clear from Proust's correspondence that he regarded this particular scientific theory as *true*, and it lies at the centre of his long disquisition on, and exemplification of, homosexuality at the beginning of *Sodome et Gomorrhe*. The epigraph to the book reads: 'First appearance of the men-women, descendants of those inhabitants of Sodom who were spared by the fire from heaven.' Proust thus simultaneously introduces the idea that homosexuals are a third or inter-sex, men-women, and at the same time endows this idea with a mythological status conferred by the use of the biblical reference.

The 'scientific' element is developed in the episode of

Jupien's seduction of Charlus, where the courtship is represented in an elaborate botanical metaphor of bee fertilizing flower. The logic of Proust's double imagery is inescapable. Homosexuality is a part of the scientific order (the word 'heredity' occurs often in this context in Proust), but it is the equivalent of a mythological curse. Thus the narrator follows his analysis of Charlus as a man-woman – 'He belongs to the race of those beings, less contradictory than they might seem, whose ideal is manly precisely because their temperament is feminine' – by describing the social curse under which this race lives. The ultimate element of that curse, in Proust's eyes, is that the man-woman by definition must desire a man who has no female element in his make-up, but that such a man will not be an 'invert' and therefore cannot love another man. His equation thereby makes homosexual love, or at least the true fulfilment of homosexual love, impossible. The only positive element in this situation is the acknowledgement that where some kind of communication is genuinely established, the result is an exceptionally *special* relationship: Proust talks about 'fécondation morale', spiritual impregnation, and emphasizes the value of one individual passing to another 'his music, his passion or his perfume'. Here, then, is the value of Morel as artist, and of the relationship between Morel as violinist and Charlus as his accompanist. But in that relationship, too, the perfect balance cannot be achieved, and ultimately the relationship is self-destroying.

Proust's account of homosexuality *is* depressing: firstly, because all the images he uses for it suggest an inescapable and ill-starred condition; secondly, because he presents it as creating structures within society which, by cutting across normal social boundaries, undermine society, and therefore make it a phenomenon which society must *inevitably* oppose. Hence the comparisons with freemasonry and Jewishness, which he also presents as subversive agents. The spread of homosexuality as the novel progresses is part of the metaphor of the dissolution of society: the social promiscuity of Jupien's brothel in *Le Temps retrouvé*, for example, simply prefigures the equally disguised social promiscuity which Marcel will find at the Princesse de Guermantes' matinée. The problem for the gay reader is that the inverse holds good. The portrait of homosexuality comes to seem more negative as it becomes more widespread precisely *because* it is being used as a metaphor for decadence. The gay reader is being offered an image of him or herself as an agent of corruption in the broadest sense. At the same time, the very negative portrait of love in the novel, and indeed the whole sense of the unknowability of the 'other', clearly stems from the particular image of the homosexual temperament which Proust held, thus re-enforcing the equation between homosexuality and isolation. The one apparently unavoidable positive (if elitist) argument to be expected from a novel which is essentially about art and the artist is the connection between homosexuality and artistic genius embodied in the Decadent tradition of the artist-pariah and given respectability by Raffalovich in *Uranisme et unisexualité*. But Proust declines to use this argument; all his artists are in some sense outsiders but *not* sexually so. At best one can conclude that his portrait absolved homosexuals of moral responsibility: a fate is not a vice. It is therefore difficult to disagree with Eric Bentley's claim that the negative self-image in Proust is such that there would be a case for banning his work, were censorship not a bad thing in itself.[7]

Proust's view of his own sexual orientation is very much the product of his period, and the metaphorical uses to which he puts this view merely intensify the negative aspects of his self-image. Many of the same elements recur in the work of his younger contemporary Jean Cocteau, whose image of homosexuality, although more ambivalent in at least one key respect, is ultimately equally destructive. Homosexuality for Cocteau is, as for Proust, congenital, inescapable, but also a mark of difference which constitutes a source of guilt. Despite the semi-public nature of his attentions to a series of variously talented and often very handsome young men, from the adolescent writer Raymond Radiguet to the actor Jean Marais, Cocteau never acknowledged his sexuality in print any more than Proust did. Indeed, as late as *La Difficulté d'être* (1947) he still felt obliged to protest that people 'misinterpreted' his interest in the young, going so far as to suggest that, past a certain age, any form of sexual activity is disgusting. Apart from some light verse celebrating sailors, published under the title *Escales* (Ports of call) – a special private edition of which contained a 'secret museum', a section of erotic poems and drawings – he produced nothing for public consumption that was clearly homoerotic. To be more precise, he produced nothing *under his own name*. For in 1928 he allowed Maurice Sachs, a young homosexual would-be writer and member of his entourage, to arrange the anonymous publication of *Le Livre blanc*, a short autobiographical novel specifically about homosexuality, which was widely known to be by Cocteau himself. (In his *Journal* entry for 11 October 1929, for example, Gide wrote: 'Read Cocteau's *Le Livre blanc*, lent to me by Raymond Saucier, since I am still waiting for the copy Cocteau promised me'.) The second edition in 1930 contains mildly erotic illustrations of young men unmistakably by Cocteau, but it was still anonymous. And even in 1957, when Cocteau wrote a preface for the re-edition of the work, he sustained the fiction of the author's anonymity, and refused to be identified even with the book's sexual orientation:

> In several previous editions I have indeed ... illustrated the text with drawings which are clear evidence that, even if I do not specialise in a taste for my own sex, I do nonetheless acknowledge one of the helping hands which Mother Nature is in the habit of slily extending to mankind.

The anonymity is just a silly game; the refusal to admit his own sexual identity reflects a more deep-seated malaise, a form of self-rejection.

Le Livre blanc is in fact an essential key to the image of homosexuality, which Cocteau projects in codified form or translated into heterosexual symbols, in his other works. Ostensibly it is a plea for social acceptance, finishing proudly on the words: 'But I will not agree to be tolerated. Toleration damages my love of life and liberty'. But the text itself is much more negative in its implications than this suggests. In its descriptions of the narrator's love for boys and young men, the emphasis is constantly on unhappiness. The idea that his condition is imposed on him by fate is established by the hint that it is genetically determined – his father is described as latently homosexual – but the inevitability of his unhappiness then by no means derives exclusively from society's inability to accept homosexuality. Each episode ends in death, or in a separation which equates with, and is as painful as, death: his love is thwarted by timidity; by a difference of class, beauty and values; by his inability to cope with his partner's bisexuality; by his inability to face his own real sexual nature. The impression left overall is inevitably that homosexual love is doomed to disappointment, failure or destruction.

A certain amount can be attributed to social pressure, as when the other adolescents begin to experiment with female prostitutes and the narrator has to falsify his own nature to hide his difference. A certain amount more plays on the attraction of the 'otherness' created by class difference – the pimp, the sailor, the working-class boys in the bathhouse-cum-male brothel. But the failure is more often represented as inherent in homosexuality itself. The image of Narcissus recurs: the boy who commits suicide 'was in love with himself. In loving me he was unfaithful to himself'. He dies leaving the grease-mark of his lips and the blurred mist of his breath on the wardrobe mirror. The otherness of class difference is not a metaphor for the difference between 'real' men and men-women as in Proust, or for the 'reality' which middle-class culture has erased in men as in Eekhoud (although elements of both ideas are contained in the feelings and attitudes represented), it is simply an image of unattainability. The homosexual is seeking an impossible union with himself, and the nearest he can get is a mutual mirroring of the sort described in the bathhouse episode. A masturbating youth, 'a Narcissus who was pleasuring himself', kisses what is, unbeknown to him, a two-way mirror, whilst the unseen narrator returns the kiss on the other side of the mirror and brings himself to an equivalent climax. There is a superficial fulfilment but no communication. The value of the experience is limited to the individual.

Le Livre blanc offers the only extended study of homosexuality in Cocteau's work, but not of course the only reference to it. Many of his writings incorporate specific references to homosexuality as a passing motif, from *Le Grand Écart* (1923) with its lesbian scene and its portrait of the sexually ambiguous young Englishman Peter Stopwell, to the defence of the undifferentiating blindness of the sex instinct in the chapter 'On customs' of *La Difficulté d'être*. The passage in the latter work reiterates the belief, also alluded to in *Journal d'un inconnu* and *Opium*, that at an instinctual level it is natural for a man to find sexual gratification with any person or object, exclusive heterosexuality being by implication merely the product of a social taboo. Inevitably, the most interesting and important texts are the poem cycles written for, and under the influence of, Radiguet: *Plain-Chant* (1923), written at the height of their relationship, and *L'Ange Heurtebise* (1925), an opium-induced fantasy about passive love and the creative processes inspired by the memory of his beloved. In his earlier collection, *Vocabulaire* (1922), there are hints of Cocteau's sexual orientation, not least in an amusing allegory about a water sprite and a rose-bush, designed to warn young men of the destructive sexual power of women and brimming with Freudian imagery:

> 17 Dans le fleuve de verre
>   Bouge l'ondine
>
>   Qui mollit les bâtons
> 20 Et les montre cassés
>   Si on l'agace.

(In the river of glass/moves the water-sprite/who makes sticks go soft/and shows them as broken/if you upset her.)

The poems of *Plain-Chant* are actually less direct:[8] when grammar demands it, they transpose the beloved into the feminine gender (even if only to the eye, as most such references are ambiguous to the ear). They are very tender love poems, expressions of desire, of pleasure in sleeping together with limbs entwined, and of creative submission to the inspirational power of love. But it is difficult not to notice the Baudelairean suggestion of the corruptness of the flesh. Love, however sweet, is the 'mud' of reality, even if this is in part redeemed by the fact that the beloved is also the angel, the agent of the Muses, who helps the poet to transcend that reality, turning the 'mud' into art:

> Notre boue a des douceurs
> Notre humaine, tendre boue
> Mais tu me couches en joue

Ange, soldat des neuf soeurs. (pt 1, st. 17)

(Our mud has its pleasant qualities/Our human, tender mud/But you get me in your sights/Angel, soldier of the nine sisters.)

L'Ange Heurtebise explores in greater detail, and much more startlingly the parallel of love and art. With brutal duality it represents Cocteau being literally buggered by his angel (Radiguet), and more generally the poet being fertilized by his muse in a metaphorical description of sexual possession and fecundation which leads to the birth of the poem.[9] Even read metaphorically the second poem of the cycle clearly rests on an image of male rape:

> L'Ange Heurtebise, d'une brutalité
> Incroyable, saute sur moi. De grace
> Ne saute pas si fort
> Garçon bestial, fleur de haute stature.

(The Angel Heurtebise, with unbelievable/brutality, jumps on me. Please/don't do it so hard/Bestial boy, flower of great stature.)

And toward the end of the cycle (no. XIV), having accepted Heurtebise and whatever, as a representative of beauty, the angel does to him, the poet reiterates the moral ambiguity of the experience:

> Qu'il est laid le bonheur qu'on veut
> Qu'il est beau le malheur qu'on a.

(How ugly is the happiness one wants/How beautiful the unhappiness one has.)

Homosexuality is a burden to be tolerated, its positive contribution to art bought only at the price of submission to its negative associations.

If we take the direct portrait of homosexuality in *Le Livre blanc* and the indirect one in *Plain-Chant* and *L'Ange Heurtebise* together, we can see a pattern emerging. Like Proust, Cocteau transfers the positive aspects of homosexuality into non-gay images. Even the traditional form and classical metrics of the poems of *Plain-Chant*, for example, help to insert them into the mainstream of French heterosexual love poetry. What is left for the portrait of homosexuality is the love = destruction equation, a Proustian doubling of the scientific and mythological (in that homosexuality is a congenital defect, the beloved an angelic force of both destruction and creation) and a host of negative details. Like Proust, Cocteau uses the motif of class difference in *Le Livre blanc* (though its otherness has a different value for him), and he also includes in it two motifs which look as though they have been directly borrowed from *A la recherche*: (1) homosexuals as a subversive social subgroup in which 'pederast knows pederast as Jew knows Jew. They sense each other beneath the mask'; and (2) an emphasis on sado-masochism – the clients at the baths, like those in Jupien's brothel, want to be insulted, to be chained up or to watch 'a Hercules killing a rat with a red-hot needle'. The point at which Cocteau goes beyond Proust is in making the link between outcast-status and artistic creativity, so dear to the Romantics, rest on *sexual* difference, the potential connection which, as I noted earlier, Proust deliberately denies himself by making his narrator and his artist-figures resolutely heterosexual.

Three of Cocteau's works invite gay readings which establish this equation artist = outcast = sexual otherness: *Orphée* (both play and film), the film *Le Sang d'un poète* and the ballet *Le Jeune Homme et la mort*. Although, when decoded, all three serve to confirm the negative self-image of homosexuality which we have already identified in *Le Livre blanc* and the poems, at the same time they extend the theme of the importance of homosexuality to the creative artist: in both *Orphée* and *Le Sang d'un poète* mirrors are used to suggest the artist's need to escape convention via an erotic relationship with the self (echoing the motif of the two-way mirror in the bathhouse); in all three works an equation is constructed between the artist (in the first two a poet, in the third a painter), love and death. The fact that the various works give death a different gender (a beautiful woman in *Orphée* and *Le Jeune Homme et la mort*, the masculine Angel of Death in *Le Sang d'un poète*) is not significant. In the ballet death is merely a mask worn by the beloved, literally identifying passion with destruction. And Cocteau himself indicated that he envisaged death in *Orphée* in terms of the beautiful transvestite trapeze artist Barbette, on whom he wrote several articles.

In practice, then, death is essentially an *androgynous* figure (picking up the motif of the dangerous androgyne from *fin-de-siècle* literature). What *is* significant is the equation death = beauty. In Cocteau's works, death derives its power from its relation to beauty, and specifically to the beauty of young men. Picking up a motif sketched as early as *Le Grand Écart* – 'The vague desire for beauty kills us' – and linking it to Baudelaire's injunction from the end of the 'Death' section of the *Fleurs du mal* to travel 'To the depths of the unknown, in pursuit of the new', Cocteau is emphasizing the complete submission of the artist to beauty and his willingness to pursue it into the unknown territory of real or metaphorical self-annihilation. The snowball fight episode of *Le Sang d'un poète*, repeating the same scene from *Les Enfants terribles*, is the clearest expression of this image of the 'wound of beauty'. The handsome Dargelos inflicts a fatal wound on his (male) victim, whose body is then absorbed by the angel of Death in a convincing imitation of the sexual act. But in parallel with the beauty = death equation, Cocteau also connects beauty and sexual possession. He often produces theoretical definitions of beauty in just such terms: for example, beauty for him is 'an erection of the soul', the appreciation of art 'a moral erection'.

To equate beauty with both ultimate destruction (death) and the source of creation (sex) might seem paradoxical, but there is in fact no gap between these two ostensibly disparate classifications. Playing with the baroque conceit of *la petite mort* (the little death), in which orgasm and the consequent collapse of the penis are represented as the moment of death, and with the identification of the death spasm with that of orgasm (an identification which also occurs in the imagery of *Le Grand Écart* and the poem 'L'endroit et l'envers'), Cocteau can suggest that what kills, fecundates. What is more, he challenges the traditional associations of fertility and womanhood by using images and vocabulary of *male* sexuality for both purposes. The other episodes of *Le Sang d'un poète*, introducing the image of the mortal danger posed by the Hermaphrodite (the perilous androgyne again), and that of the Mexican executed by the firing squad who rises to face execution again, continue the same set of sexual metaphors, all within a film defining (as its title indicates) the lifeblood of poetry. The poetic trance in which creation occurs is a passive condition, a necessary 'death' from which the poet will return, just as the lover 'recovers' from his post-orgasmic death. The artist-pariah thus transcends the emotional/social destruction to which his deviant sexuality condemns him, through the creativity for which this same destruction is a prerequisite.

We can, as I suggested earlier, move outward from these relatively lightly coded works to see the transposition of the same ideas into more or less completely heterosexual images throughout the rest of Cocteau's work. Outsider motifs abound, notably in the figure of Thomas, the social outsider in *Thomas l'imposteur*, and in the theme of 'shutting out the world' which lies at the heart of *Les Enfants terribles*. But perhaps the classic statement of the impossible pursuit of otherness occurs in *Le Grand Écart*: 'From childhood he [Jacques] had felt the desire to *be* those he found beautiful, and not just to make them love him'. Doomed sexuality is represented by incest in *Les Enfants terribles*, *Les Parents terribles* and *La Machine infernale*. The wound of beauty occurs in a slightly different form in the image of the 'diamond race' which inevitably marks 'the glass race', the Stopwells of this world who scar the Petitcopains without the fertilizing effects which Dargelos will have in his various incarnations (*Les Enfants terribles*, *Le Sang d'un poète*, *La Fin du Potomak*).

The effect of the repetition of these interwoven motifs is to emphasize that, however fruitful the effect of homosexual passion is for the artist, it is a fruitfulness born of the masochistic frisson of guilt and despair. Indeed, Cocteau's only-just-averted conversion to Catholicism owed itself, as Robert Merle perceptibly noted in his 1954 study of Oscar Wilde, to the desire to reintegrate himself into the human community (from which he felt banished by his homosexuality) via a religion which would *punish* him for being something over which, by his own admission, he had no choice. Once we start to give gay readings to Cocteau's work, we are faced with a self-image which, whilst it insists on the centrality of the writer's sexuality to his creativity, links both inexorably to pain and destruction. Although it may seem a less negative self-image than that of Proust from the writer's point of view, it offers nothing to the *reader*, who is not granted the saving grace of artistic genius.

The connections between Proust and Cocteau may not seem very surprising: the shift between *fin-de-siècle* values and the aesthetics of the inter-war years is not always as large as people assume, and both authors had their feet firmly planted in both the modernist and the Decadent camps. To connect either writer with Genet might look a lot less likely. For a long time Genet was seen as the real mould-breaker in the literary treatment of homosexuality. He had broken out of the apologetic mode; he had challenged his readers by presenting homosexuality not even as a simple fact of existence, but as a source of pleasure equal in value and status to heterosexuality; he had exploited homosexuality as a source of material which, however morally negative in conventional terms, could be transformed into positive aesthetic worth through literary creation. Furthermore, Jean-Paul Sartre's monumental study of Genet's life and work, *Saint-Genet, comédien et martyr*, which appeared in 1952, consecrated the view that Genet's homosexuality was an act of defiance against a world which had denied him love and security. As early as 1946 Sartre had written, in a publicity leaflet for *Miracle de la rose*, that 'Proust has shown homosexuality as a destiny, Genet claims it as a choice'.[10] Linking Genet's status as a foundling to his awareness of social rejection, Sartre posits a Genet who, as a child, 'solved' the problem of identity through the antisocial act of theft: he had stolen, he was labelled a thief, he reacted by taking on the permanent condition of thief – in Genet's own words: 'I decided to become what crime had made me'.

For Sartre homosexuality was only the logical extension of Genet's consequent need to turn all normal values inside out; although the older Genet might be a thief because he was a homosexual, the young Genet had become a homosexual to reinforce his outcast status as thief. This merely inverts the terms of Genet's own pronouncement in his 'autobiography' *Journal du voleur* (1949), that, abandoned by his family, he had found it natural to aggravate his isolation by loving boys, to aggravate that love by theft, and theft by other forms of crime, such that he could turn the world's rejection of him into his rejection of the world. For our present purposes it does not matter whether Genet's sexual orientation was inborn or acquired. The significant fact is that for a while Genet became a symbol of the rejection of bourgeois values in general and an embodiment of the frank expression of homosexual desires and acts in particular.

Yet by the late 1980s, shortly after his death, Genet's view of homosexuality had come to seem to a younger generation at best obsolete, at worst as pandering to heterosexual prejudice. Dominique Fernandez in *La Gloire du paria* (1987) makes Marc, his representative of contemporary youth, express the first of these ideas explicitly. Commenting on Genet's death Marc observes:

> Jean Genet's death is not just the end of a writer or an individual. Several idols of the history of mankind end with him today. He was the last of his species left. None of the things which he talks about and which are what give substance to his books actually exist any longer.

Marc argues that Genet was the last witness to a period in which the choice of a homosexual lifestyle obligatorily constituted an act of revolt which marked the rebel as delinquent and evil in the eyes of society at large. Whilst the equation of sex with violence, of love with death, of beauty with malediction in Genet's work was explicable in terms of the author's own personal experience, it had no relevance to the changed moral perspectives of the 1980s. Two years later, in his study of homosexuality and the arts, *Le Rapt de Ganymède*, Fernandez repeated the same general sentiments in his own voice and in a more hostile tone. This time he focused on Genet's fondness for transvestite characters, attacking it as chosen to coincide as closely as possible with the negative image of gays as woman-substitutes so dear to heterosexuals: 'a policy of self-vilification, in a sense, whose aim is to attract onto himself the maximum reprobation'. Similarly, for Fernandez homosexuals in Genet lay claim to every vice not because they possess them, but in order to discourage others definitively from showing indulgence or pity toward them. On this reading the importance of homosexuality for Genet lies exclusively in its power to shock, to arouse hostility. In support of this argument, Fernandez very relevantly points to a passage in *Journal du voleur* in which the narrator can see no point in theft in a context where stealing has no power to upset society, a context where it is not accorded the status of evil.

Seen in this light Genet is not really an innovator; he is the zenith of the whole post-Romantic tradition of the outcast, particularly in the Decadent form of the sexual transgressor. In bringing together aspects of Lautréamont's association of homosexuality with evil, Proust's self-hatred and Cocteau's obsession with 'accursed' love as a vehicle for death, to present a profoundly negative self-image, he is guilty of pandering to, intensifying, even giving new life to, the traditional heterosexual view of homosexuality as abnormal, morally depraved and socially destructive. Fernandez' charges become more significant, perhaps, when we find them echoed by a gay activist of the same period with whom he has little in common, Renaud Camus. Camus, in his *Notes achriennes*, denies that Genet was a pioneer liberator, on the grounds that his version of homosexuality 'too closely resembles that which its worst enemies imagine and depict', in particular the use of the transvestite to equate gay males with femininity and the identification of homosexuality with evil.

The charges of Fernandez and Camus have some point. A number of critics claim to perceive change and development in Genet's presentation of homosexuality. Edmund White, for example, in his excellent biography, relates such changes to Genet's own emotional problems and in particular to his experience of writer's block.[11] But it is possible to see a constant underlying view of homosexuality as a curse, right from Genet's first novel *Notre-Dame des Fleurs* (1944). For this reason I do not think it unfair to take as a key text the *Fragments d'un discours* (first published in 1954 and intended as part of a wider text on homosexuality to have been called, symbolically, *La Mort*), even though its exceptionally pessimistic treatment undoubtedly derives, as White has shown, from Genet's circumstances at the time of writing, a period when he was suffering from an unrequited passion for a young Italian male prostitute and concurrently from a sense of artistic sterility. *Fragments d'un discours* effectively sums up the sense of isolation and guilt which his sexual orientation had created in Genet from early on:

Homosexuality is not a factor I could adapt to. Apart from the fact that there is no tradition to come to the aid of the pederast, to hand him down a system of references – except for lacunae – or teach him a set of moral conventions deriving exclusively from homosexuality, this very nature, either acquired or inborn, is experienced as a subject of guilt. It isolates me, cuts me off from both the rest of the world and from every other pederast.

How do this isolation and guilt manifest themselves in Genet's writings? Primarily in the sense of unfulfilled otherness which haunts his characters. For Genet, what a man seeks in sexual union with another man is a confirmation of his own essence: the act is narcissistic. Hence the importance of mirror images and doubles in his work: the sailor who dances with his image/double in the ballet libretto *'Adame Miroir*; the close physical resemblance between 'Genet' and Divers in *Miracle de la rose*; and that between Querelle and his brother Robert in *Querelle de Brest*. But paradoxically, since what the homosexual in a Genet text is pursuing in the sex act is the confirmation of a masculinity in which he is deficient, the pursuits of the 'real' (i.e. active) male by the homosexual (i.e. passive) pseudo-male leads not to a sense of fulfilment but to a heightened sense of otherness. To be a homosexual for Genet is not merely a question of having sex with another man – almost none of the characters in *Querelle de Brest* or the play *Haut Surveillance* who desire or perform sex acts with other men are considered homosexuals. Homosexuality is *passive* sexuality, associated with submission, softness, defeat and martyrdom. Not surprisingly, then, one of the first things we notice about the male characters in Genet's novels is that they are sharply divided into active and passive sexual roles which are largely equated with 'masculine' and 'feminine' characteristics. Interestingly, this is a division which Fernandez acknowledges as realistic in France in the 1950s. In his novel *L'Etoile rose*, after describing the division of the gays of Luxemburg and Sarrebruck into 'gonzesses' (bimbos) and 'mecs' (blokes), his narrator expresses astonishment at this desire, taken to the point of obsession, to reproduce the division of the sexes and to emphasize their respective roles:

What is the good, I said to myself, of putting oneself on the margins of society and its laws, if you slavishly copy all that is most mutilating in it. I recalled the novels of Jean Genet. I would have preferred not to have to acknowledge how closely they correspond to reality.

The division in Genet's first novel, *Notre-Dame des fleurs*, is deepened by making the central 'feminine' character Divine a transvestite, and by emphasizing her complete subordination to sex and sexual subordination to her masculine partners. Thus Divine and her 'mec' Mignon are defined as the ideal couple, although for Mignon Divine is 'barely even a pretext', whereas for Divine Mignon is everything. The subordination is literal in scenes where Divine services a male partner, as when she is face-fucked by the soldier Gabriel. It is also presented as part of a hierarchy or pecking order: when Divine attempts to take an active role with the young Notre-Dame (later the passive partner of the negro Gorgui), she finds herself automatically having to submit to his adolescent masculinity.

The pattern repeats itself within the prisons of Mettray and Fontevrault in *Miracle de la rose*, where a group of good-looking younger males services the group of older 'toughs'. It becomes more evident still in the pseudo-autobiography *Journal du voleur*. Here 'Genet', the only acknowledged homosexual character, services the heterosexual Stilitano, and his sexual passivity is a key element in the series of degradations around which the book is centred. It is only a small step from presenting homosexuals as degraded (*Journal du voleur*) and marked for martyrdom (*Notre-Dame des Fleurs*) to Genet's position in *Fragments d'un discours*. There Genet defines the passive male, paradoxically represented by the active participle *l'aimant*, as a dead, empty figure who transfers onto *l'aimé*, the active beloved, the task of living for him. While Genet himself could be said to have attempted to live through some of his younger, basically heterosexual lovers (notably Lucien Senemaud and Jacky Maglia), in *Fragments* this 'life' is to be interpreted not as real existence but as the literary translation of existence, the lover as reproduction of the myth of *La Dame aux camélias* (alluded to more than once in the text) and of the *fin-de-siècle* Decadent writer

Villiers de l'Isle-Adam's injunction that living is a task to be deputed to one's servants.

A second ingredient in the creation of a sense of guilt and isolation is the inextricable link in Genet's works between homosexuality and criminality. Following the pattern of their creator's own life, the heroes of his novels break both the legal code and the social code, and their sexual desirability depends on and is enhanced by their consequent outlaw status. At the most innocent level there is a particular stress on theft; in *Miracle*, for example, most of the desirable boys in both Mettray and Fontevrault have committed theft in some form. At this level the thematic links are strengthened by a metaphorical identification of theft with the emergence of homosexual desire, expressed in frequent references to the desire of younger, passive boys to take/take on the active masculine qualities of an older male. In *Miracle* the narrator finds the strength to fight Charlot by 'stealing' it, in his imagination, from his beloved Villeroy. In the same novel he describes his need, in his formative period, for subjugation to any male with a powerful, sturdy body as the inability to be at rest unless he could 'take his place, take his qualities, his virtues'. Significantly, the same masculine essence which the narrator seeks to steal from his sexual partners is provided for him, when he takes on the role of real thief, by the jemmy, suggestively described as a steel penis. But theft is hardly more than a basic qualification for homosexual desire. The real objects of desire are murderers like Harcamone and Querelle. Hence, in *Miracle*, if Bulkaen, the beautiful burglar, is 'the finger of God' for the narrator, Harcamone *is* God.

Transgressions of the law are linked to other forms of transgression: the narrator in *Journal du voleur* mugs other homosexuals and betrays his accomplices, as does Mignon in *Notre-Dame des fleurs*; Querelle shops Gil Turko; Stilitano is a coward; Pierrot in *Pompes funèbres* denounces the leaders of the prison rebellion to save his own skin; Erik in the same novel is a member of the *Waffen SS*. The connection is typically summed up by the narrator of *Journal du voleur*:

Treachery, theft and homosexuality are the essential subjects of this book. There exists between them a relationship which, if not always apparent, at least seems to acknowledge a sort of vascular exchange between my taste for treachery and theft and my love affairs.

Genet builds a network of connnections between homosexuality and all that is conventionally taboo, thereby creating the equation: homosexuality = evil.

The connection between homosexuality and evil is perhaps most perfectly constructed, and most shocking, in *Pompes funèbres*. Genet constructs this text around the narrator, 'Jean Genet', and his response to the death of a 'lover', Jean D. There are recurrent references to the young man's death and to his funeral throughout the work, rooting it firmly in the literature of love-as-death: 'under the aegis of this death I place my story, if you can call "story" the prismatic decomposition of my love and my pain'. Genet emphasizes from the outset that this is a homosexual passion (despite the fact that Jean D. was straight) by his use of erotic images which link Jean D.'s 'bronze eye', the anus which he only allows the narrator to penetrate once, with the door of the church, the 'black hole' which has to be penetrated at the start of the funeral. This hole in turn contains and reveals the figure of the handsome Erik, Jean's mother's lover, here described as 'this arse-fucked member of the Tank Corps, the God of my night'.[12] What makes this opening section of the novel more than merely the usual mixture of homosexual passion and death is that it is set against the fall of Paris to the Allies, Erik is a German soldier, Jean D. a Resistance worker. The criminality with which homosexuality is to be associated is not merely theft or even murder: it is the genocide perpetrated by the Nazis. Similarly the motif of betrayal is not merely the betrayal of criminal accomplices but full-blown treason: Jean D. is killed by a young collaborator, a 'milicien' whose identity the narrator projects via his imagination under the name of Riton, and on whom, in his own act of treachery, he bestows his love.

Genet thus carefully interrelates homosexual desire and the most serious forms of social and personal treachery. At the same time the book develops, in parts, into a hymn to masculine brutality and blood-lust as a source of sexual attraction: the narrator

imagines that Erik as a youth has had sexual relations with the
Berlin public executioner (picking up the traditional association of
execution and orgasm); his scenario provides for the rape of Riton
by a German soldier and for the boy's subsequent anal submission
to Erik on the rooftops; in particular he creates a fantastic extended
account of a sexual assignation between Jean D.'s brother Paolo
and Hitler, in which the former sexually dominates the latter. It is
possible, of course, to argue that by allowing Paolo to fuck Hitler,
Genet is creating an image of the subordination of Germany to
France, but this does not override the fact that the episode creates
an inescapable association of homosexuality with ultimate evil. It
offers a complete antithesis to the argument put forward by Fernandez in *L'Etoile rose* that the Nazis, by discrediting the cult of
masculinity, have made it easier for people to accept the implicit
reconciliation of masculinity and femininity in homosexuality.
Genet has *eliminated* the feminine element: when the executioner
submits sexually to the young Erik, or Jean D. to the narrator, even
passivity has become masculinized. Genet wants his readers to be
faced with an inescapable association of sex, violence and evil, his
excuse being the purely Baudelairean one (expressed in a passage
shot through with Baudelaire's own terminology) that the poet's
task is to extract beauty from evil:

> As my art consists in exploiting evil, given that I am a poet,
> no one should be surprised that I interest myself in these
> things, in the conflicts which are the characteristic features
> of the most pathetic of epochs. The poet deals in evil. It is his
> role to perceive the beauty which lies in it, to extract that
> beauty from it (or to add to it the beauty which he desires?)
> and to make use of it.

Now, it can justifiably be argued, as Fernandez does, that this
approach to homosexuality is negative and panders to heterosexual
prejudice, the ultimate and unintended self-betrayal in fact. Genet
can only cope with his own sexuality by devouring the objects of his
desire and turning them into art, justifying his position by an appeal
to Baudelaire's ethic of the flowers of Evil. Like Proust, Genet is
arrogating to himself as the artist-pariah the right to rise above

morality through art whilst damning his fellow gays in the process. It is arguable, however, that this assessment does not do full justice to the complexities of his portrait of homosexuality in the first three 'novels' or of the extension of those complexities and ambiguities in *Querelle de Brest*. The further the reader delves into the presentation of homosexuality in these texts, the more inconsistencies he will find. The boundaries of femininity and masculinity, for example, are not as neatly defined as at first appears the case. In *Notre-Dame des fleurs* the transvestite Divine refashions the heterosexual Mignon to the point at which Mignon cannot find sexual satisfaction with a woman because he expects his 'feminine' partner to have an erection. Some of the 'male' heroes in *Miracle de la rose* have shifting sexual roles: what the narrator is to Bulkaen, Bulkaen is to Rocky, without loss of masculine prestige. Above all, in *Querelle*, as Edmund White puts it, 'the strict masculine-feminine (or father-son) role-playing in sex is replaced with actual or potentially reversible and reciprocal sadomasochism',[13] such acts representing the ultimate in stereotyped masculinity.

But even, or perhaps especially, in *Querelle*, where Genet has created in the eponymous hero a character beyond guilt, who murders a fellow sailor for profit and escapes unpunished, the issue of *sexual* guilt is not completely eradicated. In the first place, all the men who actually commit homosexual acts are 'straight'; the one homosexual, Lieutenant Seblon, is tortured by repressed desires and finally martyrs himself for Querelle by accepting responsibility for a crime committed by the latter. To Seblon's feelings Genet applies the familiar vocabulary of femininity and self-abasement: 'The more I love Querelle, the more clearly the woman in me is defined,' Seblon reflects, 'I should like to throw myself at his feet for him to trample me'. And when Querelle makes a deliberate decision to be buggered by Nono, he does it to expiate a crime and to acquire a new essence, changing him from 'murderer' to 'homosexual'. Thus in this novel Genet is yet again portraying homosexuality as an inferior, passive state, and yet again is linking it to guilt and evil.

One further repeated element in the novels contributes significantly to the pariah status of the homosexual: the theme of imprisonment, the traditional punishment for criminality but at the same time also a familiar literary symbol of isolation. Genet plays on both these elements. *Miracle* is entirely staged in prison or reformatory; substantial prison scenes occur in the other texts, particularly in *Journal du voleur*; there is an episode of prison revolt in *Pompes funèbres*. There are also other scenes of enforced confinement: for example, seven German soldiers are trapped with Riton in the final housetop battle in *Pompes funèbres*. And the spectrum of the motif extends to the theme of confinement with the self, reflected in such phrases as 'my homosexuality ... which already kept me in an unhabitual solitude'. Admittedly, Genet presents prison as a haven of security, a place to dream, a mythical space. But when he does so, he does it in the form of a paradox: 'Prison offered me my first experience of consolation, peace, friendly confusion: I found them in its vileness.[14] So much solitude had forced me to make a companion of myself, for myself'. The outside world is an alien space, continually making Genet aware of his otherness; prison, by contrast, forces the isolated self into a creative self-acceptance, which in turn allows free reign to the imagination. And the imagination in its turn will 'assimilate' the outside world:

> I have the cheek to think that Bulkaen only lived in order for me to write my book. So he had to die, after a life that I can only imagine as daring and arrogant, a slap in the face for all the pale figures he encountered on his passage through it.

In describing this assimilation Genet constantly uses the vocabulary of devouring. Just as in *Pompes funèbres* he 'devours' Jean D., 'contains' him, then 'embodies' him in the text, so in *Journal du voleur* the emprisoned narrator 'swallows' the outside world and regurgitates it as literature. This motif of eating and assimilating derives from *fin-de-siècle* gay writing. Thus Eekhoud makes Laurent Paridael, in regretting that modern painters do not preserve the beauty of the contemporary 'young tough', express his own response to such men in a vocabulary of digestion: 'They will have become part of my substance ... I absorb them, I devour them, I breathe them in aesthetically'. But Eekhoud is devouring *beauty*; Genet is digesting *evil* and regurgitating it as beauty. He adds the motif of assimilation, which is positive enough in itself, to a blend of two Romantic traditions: the Stendhalian prison, which in shutting in the elite individual shuts out the world which is threatening to destroy that individual (an image peculiarly applicable to the relationship between the world and the elite homosexual artist); and the Proustian artist, who can create aesthetic meaning from the meaningless material of personal experience. Neither of these traditions offers an optimistic view of life. Accordingly, in the context of the prison/homosexuality relationship, they reinforce the negative associations – isolation and criminality – whilst suggesting that these can be transcended *only* through the accident of artistic genius.

Genet's negative portrait of homosexuality is, of course, justifiable on historical grounds, but his negative attitude to his own sexuality as revealed in *Fragments d'un discours* and his use of it to create a niche for himself in the post-Romantic tradition of the artist-outlaw are more disturbing. I should emphasize here that I am not concerned with the wider aesthetic or intellectual interest of his work: to these I shall give consideration elsewhere. At the same time it would be absurd to suggest that there was *no* potentially positive dimension to his work for a gay reader in the 1950s. The extent to which Genet does go beyond the pure negativity of his predecessors in the portrait of homosexuality is clearer if we compare his approach with that of an author working on the topic contemporaneously with Genet, Roger Martin du Gard.

Martin du Gard had previously included a few timid references to the topic in his long novel cycle *Les Thibault* (1922–40) and had made it the central topic of his 1931 play *Un Taciturne*. But it seems to have been in the 1950s, while working on *Mémoires du lieutenant-colonel Maumort*, that he compiled a substantial dossier on homosexuality, with the specific aim of showing that it was a natural condition.[15] The resulting text is nonetheless well rooted in existing literary traditions in such a way as to subtly modify the import of the content. The school episodes of Maumort himself belong firmly to the 'literature of youth' and I shall mention them again in that context. The study

of adult homosexual desire is confined to the story of the relationship between a young junior officer, Xavier de Balcourt, and a
seventeen-and-a-half-year-old bakery boy, Yves, whom he meets
whilst on manoeuvres, an episode which constitutes a self-suf-
ficient inserted narrative entitled 'The Drowning'. Now, although
Martin du Gard was writing this part of the novel in the 1940s
and early 1950s, he did not envisage the novel's publication
during his lifetime precisely because he thought the subject of
homosexuality too daring; at most he considered the possibility of
a private edition of the chapters relating to sexual education. Yet
neither the content nor the expression of 'The Drowning', surely
the most 'daring' section of the novel, is designed to shock. It
constitutes a straightforward study in forbidden sexual desire in a
socially hostile context. Furthermore, Martin du Gard inserts the
story into the long literary tradition of impossible love and love-
the-destroyer: Xavier's ill-starred assignation with Yves leads to
the boy's drowning and his own eventual suicide. Admittedly,
Martin du Gard's handling of the relationship is progressive in the
sense that he paints a picture of a directly physical homosexual
desire which is not 'justified' by a romantic context: Xavier is
only in Aulnay briefly, he meets an attractive male and he wants
to have sex with him, something which the text conveys without
any hostile moral overtones.

Society's *implicit* hostility is, of course, indirectly responsible for the tragedy, in that it forces the two men into a secrecy
which leads to a fatal misunderstanding. But the only overtly
homophobic character, Honoré, is barely a mouthpiece for that
hostility; indeed he gives every sign of a jealousy deriving from his
own heavily repressed sexuality. Rather, as is underlined by the
symbolism of the last encounter, with Yves on one river bank and
Xavier on the other, it is the relationship itself which contains its
own insuperable divisions, the Proustian barriers of age and class.
And by eliminating the lovers, however poetically touching their
unfulfilled idyll, the author reinstates the conventional values of
the heterosexual bourgeois reader. As at the end of *La Dame aux
camélias*, emotion is given full play without the demands of social
normality being disturbed. What is true of the content is equally
true of the verbal treatment, which is discreet in the extreme. In

the lyrical description of Yves' body the nearest thing to eroticism is an evocation of the young man's nipples as 'those two patches of mauve, like two flower petals', and an even more restrained reference to his penis: 'the virile secret of this body: a pale shadow barely crowned with a touch of russet'.

Superficially the attitudes to homosexuality in Martin du Gard's treatment seem no less backward-looking than Genet's, and just as rooted in existing literary tradition. But in one respect his *is* more progressive. Like Fernandez or Renaud Camus, he believes in the normality of homosexuality: once it is fully accepted socially it will cease to be of significance. Genet, on the other hand, does not believe that homosexuality is normal. What links Martin du Gard principally to his literary predecessors is his use of the literary motif of homosexuality as ill-starred; what links Genet to them irrevocably is his underlying self-hatred. Yet on any reading of the two novelists it is Genet who appears the more daring. This is because what separates him from the earlier tradition is his strident eroticism. Whereas Martin du Gard, however progressive his willingness to represent homosexual desire as valid in itself, describes that desire only very allusively, Genet confronts it head-on. Whereas the former infuses his descriptions of the contact between Yves and Xavier with so much conventional lyrical intensity that the reader forgets that what is being described is not love but basic sexual attraction – much as Gide seeks to disarm the heterosexual reader by his lushly Romantic treatment of his seduction by young Ali in the dunes at Blidah in the second part of *Si le grain ne meurt* – Genet, by contrast, rubs his reader's nose in the physical realities of oral and anal sex between males, constructing his lyricism out of, and around, violent colloquial language. He challenges preconceived notions of the borderline between eroticism and pornography by insisting that the details of sex acts between males are admissible in literature and that such descriptions can be both explicit and beautiful. If we remember that the only other explicitly homoerotic text of the period, Marcel Jouhandeau's apologia for anal sex, *Tirésias*, only appeared in an anonymous private edition confined to 150 copies, the significance of this aspect of Genet's writing is put into perspective.

As we have seen, the self-image projected in the first half of the century by three of France's major homosexual writers, Proust, Cocteau and Genet, derives directly from a number of features of *fin-de-siècle* discourse. The figure of the androgyne, used to suggest the power of the feminine within the male in an essentially macho context in Eekhoud's '*Le Quadrille du lancier*', gives rise to the men-women of Proust and the transvestites of Genet, with a consequent slide into stereotypes of effeminacy and inadequacy. Thematic associations with isolation, alienation, corruption and destruction, both personal and social, are constants: homosexuality is an agent for the dissolution of society in Proust, an agent of death in Cocteau, a symbol of all that is conventionally evil in Genet. And, as in Decadent writing, the only saving grace for the writer is the ability to extract beauty from the ugliness of experience and to turn it into art. The Romantic figure of the artist-pariah thus finds redemption for his sins of sexual otherness by devouring the world and regurgitating it as metaphor.

At the same time, the whole question of otherness becomes much more complex than in nineteenth-century texts. The use of distance in time and space as a technique for 'protecting' the reader more or less disappears. Spatial difference more often becomes a symbol of shutting out the 'normal' world and creating a protected space for homosexuality (as in Genet's prisons) or for whatever other form of sexual otherness is being used to symbolize it (e.g. incest in Cocteau). Otherwise, spatial and temporal differences are replaced by an increased use of social class, age and sexual role as symbols of difference. Moreover, the symbolic functions of these elements shift from author to author: class and age difference in Proust work together to symbolize sexual otherness (the gap between man and man-woman) and to motivate social dissolution; in Eekhoud, on the other hand, inverting the Proustian argument they work together to redefine what is sexually and socially desirable. And whereas both Proust and Eekhoud intend the pursuit of otherness to be taken as a genuine desire for what is *not* in the self, Cocteau uses the motif inside out, as it were, presenting the pursuit of otherness as a narcissistic fascination with *sameness*, an attempt to abolish difference.

A comparable complexity occurs in the representation of sexuality itself. In general Proust, Cocteau and Genet all work to the same stereotype of maleness, one which by definition consigns the homosexual to an inferior 'feminine' role. But Genet considerably complicates matters by separating sexual essence from sexual acts at certain points in his work, in such a way that sexual roles have more to do with power structures than with sexual orientation. At the same time Cocteau and Genet suggest that only the artist can transcend sexual difference, linking the feminine (aesthetic creativity within the self) with the masculine (the sexual presence of the beloved), and justifying sterility of sexual practice by aesthetic fecundity, a solution not available to Proust's heterosexual narrator.

So, in the writers we have been looking at, difference is no longer a fixed measure of inferiority or superiority but a shifting factor linked with both the positive and the negative; its only constant is its importance as a stimulus to the artist. Admittedly this ambiguity seems a sleight of hand. The broad lines of the picture still emphasize that the ordinary homosexual, not saved by the grace of art, is fated to unhappiness, rejection and destruction, and can at best, Genet-style, make a virtue of rebellion itself. But there are aspects of the detail of the picture which can be read differently. In particular, the poeticization of masculine beauty in Eekhoud and Cocteau, and of all-male sex acts in Genet, is susceptible to two readings. At one level it confirms for the heterosexual reader – indifferent to, or even repulsed by, the material used – the capacity of the artist to transmute material coventionally not regarded as poetic; but at another level it creates for the *gay* reader, who has a positive response to the material itself, an identification between homoerotic desire and aesthetic worth which runs counter to the negative images elsewhere in the texts. In this small but significant respect art offers us a chance to self-revaluation equivalent in kind if not in scale to the redemption of the writer.

Notes

1. *L'Etoile rose* (Paris: Grasset, 1978), p. 298.
2. See the last essay in Huysmans's collection of art-critical essays, *Certains* (1889).
3. The best critical account of *Lucien* is to be found in J. E. Rivers, *Proust and the Art of Love* (New York: Columbia University Press, 1980), pp. 141–4.
4. The episode has been compared with Genet's treatment of Fontevrault in *Miracle de la rose*, just as Eekhoud's portraits of *voyous* have been described as forerunners of those of Jouhandeau and Hervé Guibert.
5. Rivers, *Art of Love*, constitutes an excellent, if sometimes contentious, full-length study of this topic.
6. Peter Gay, *The Tender Passion*, vol. II of *The Bourgeois Experience: Victoria to Freud* (New York and Oxford: Oxford University Press), p. 201.
7. See 'We are in History', in George Stambolian and Elaine Marks (eds.), *Homosexualities and French Literature: Cultural Contexts/ Critical Texts* (Ithaca and London: Cornell University Press, 1979), pp. 122–40.
8. In any case, the application of the poems to Radiguet is only deducible by the initiated, from a reference near the end of the second section to the relative ages of the lover (thirty) and the beloved (nineteen).
9. This motif can be seen as the extension of the Baudelairean theme of literary procreation as an inversion of biological processes: in the prose poem 'Les Veuves', for example, the poet is 'fertilized' by his female subjects. In Cocteau the fertilizing agent is male, but it is still the subject which, by a process of inversion, fertilizes its own creator. Cf. also the creation/procreation motif in Guy Hocquenghem's *Eve*, ch. 5 below, p. 139.
10. An idea consonant with psychological thinking of the period – Claude Elsen in a 1949 article on Genet claimed that homosexuality has no basis in heredity or biology, but is an act of subconscious choice involving neither reason nor the will. The article is in 'Les Masques d'Uranus', *Table Ronde*, July 1949.
11. White shows how, at certain periods of Genet's life, a sense of creative sterility coincides with an obsession with the non-procreational nature of homosexual sex. See Edmund White, *Jean Genet* (London: Chatto & Windus, 1993), in particular ch. XIV.
12. I have translated *enculé* (which literally means 'sodomized' but is usually used as an empty expletive, in the same way that 'fucking' is frequently used in English) by the awkward neologism 'arse-

fucked', because in this context the word does not merely function as negative padding; its *literal* sense is activated by the image-chain of anal references in which it stands.

13. White, *Genet*, pp. 335–6.

14. There is a pun here. The word which Genet uses for vileness – *l'immonde* – looks like a negation of the word 'monde', meaning *world*. Prison is vile, but because it is a non-world, not 'the real world', it offers new possibilities for self-realization.

15. For evidence of Martin du Gard's research on the subject, see the notes by André Daspre to the Pléiade edition (Paris: Gallimard, 1983), pp. 1148–52, 1156–62.

Chapter three

A Season in Hell

'Physical relations between two men are not
compatible with the Bible and cannot be accepted by
the Church.'

● *Mgr Henri L'Heureux, Bishop of Perpignan*[1]

THE 1950s and 1960s represent an uneasy transitional
period for the gay self-image in French literature. Hitherto, adult
male homosexuality had been more or less exclusively represented,
however defiantly, as a defective condition; texts denying this
tended to remain unpublished, to appear in limited private editions
or anonymously. Since, in the face of the threat of new repression
represented by the anti-homosexual legislation of 1945 and 1960
the reaction of some gays was to look cautiously for ways to project
an 'acceptable' face to the straight majority while at the same time
creating some sense of group solidarity (the founding of *Arcadie*
and the policies pursued by its editors typifies this approach), it is
not surprising that some novels of the early 1950s project the same
spirit. Wim Gerard's *Chvoul* (1953), for example, recounting the
experiences of a French student in Germany as he comes to realize
the nature of his sexuality, makes its hero Raoul reflect on the
strength and joy he will draw from the invisible army he is about to
join.[2] But there was still a particular area of opposition to the
validity of gayness which literature had hardly faced: religion. The
intellectually neanderthal nature of the response of the Christian
Churches in general, and of the Roman Catholic Church in particu-

lar, to the issue of sexual orientation is notorious. It is therefore significant that the major literary development of the period 1950–69 from a gay point of view is precisely the appearance of writing reflecting on the religio-moral implications of gay sex.

I left out of my consideration of the social context any reference to the attitude of the Church precisely because, whilst the continuing anti-homosexual stand of the Roman Catholic hierarchy is only too well known, the patchy nature of the phenomenon of religious belief in modern France makes it very difficult to assess the impact of the Church's attitudes on French society as a group, as opposed to its effect on individuals. Nonetheless it is important that, whereas in Italy hardly anyone lets their Catholicism interfere with the realities of personal life, in France, at least until the 1960s, the interrelation of religion and morality was an issue taken seriously by many people, whether Catholics, Protestants or non-believers. Many homosexual writers in the first half of the century had been very sensitive to religious issues, but their resulting attitudes were disparate. Only the heterodox Gide really faced up to the issue of sexuality fairly and squarely, defending the right of every man to explore his own nature on the grounds that God is immanent in all experience. More conventional thinkers such as Max Jacob, Cocteau and Maurice Sachs had all sought refuge in conversion to Catholicism without debating the sexual implications of such a move. Indeed, Robert Merle has interpreted the phenomenon of conversion, in the case of Cocteau and Sachs, as an attempt on the part of men who felt themselves outlawed by society on account of their homosexuality to rejoin the human community and expiate their sense of guilt by adhering precisely to that system which most rigidly rejected their sexual orientation.[3] By becoming Catholics they hoped to be *saved* from their sexuality. The fatuity of such an exercise is obvious. Jacob, it is true, seems eventually to have been successful in suppressing his sexual desires, but he had age on his side.[4] Cocteau's failure is translated into an episode in *Le Livre blanc*, whilst Sachs records his in *Le Sabbat*.[5] In any case, these isolated case histories do not construct a coherent debate on the issues they raise. Such a debate required the stimulus of a general questioning of the parameters of social and individual ethics such as the proponents of Existentialism were to prompt.

Not surprisingly, therefore, it is only in the early 1950s that we meet texts which, implicitly or explicitly, denounce the destructive effect of Catholic moral dogma on young gay males. Marcel Guersant's *Jean-Paul* (1953), for example, is cited by Fernandez as 'the first public affirmation, the first cry of revolt, the first protestation of innocence from a race persecuted for a lot it has not chosen'.[6] If Jean-Paul dies young, it is because society has condemned him to find his natural sexual fulfilment furtively, cottaging or cruising around Pigalle and the Boulevard de Clichy, until almost inevitably he is seriously beaten up. Roger Peyrefitte describes the same phenomenon in more general terms a quarter of a century later in his *Propos secrets*:

> Homosexuality, because it is not accepted by society ... tries to live by night. Many such men will be done to death in the early hours of the morning. Victims of their fellows, these adolescent or adult males would not have suffered this appalling fate if 'the others' had not drawn a line of dishonour around them.

The prime manifestation of 'the others' in the case of Jean-Paul is the Church. He can neither accept the emasculation represented by the chastity which the Church seeks to impose on him and his like, nor can he shake off his Catholic upbringing and accept the love which he finds with young Philippe, momentarily and too late. Like Eekhoud in 'La Quadrille du lancier', Guersant uses the tradition of homosexuality = death only to deny that it is a necessary equation. The novel is very much a transitional text, linking a classic pattern of anguish and destruction and a realistic portrait of male prostitution with a lyrical account of young love (the Philippe episode) and a frank eroticism based on direct vocabulary (cock, knob, get a hard-on, wank, etc.). The self-rejection of pre-1950s fiction is thus at least questioned and an uneasy attempt made to offer some aspects of positive experience to the gay reader.

Jean-Paul, which caused a critical stir when the avant-garde Editions de Minuit brought it out, provides a good departure point for a study of the basic issue of the relationship between sexual orientation and religious morality in more established writers of the period. Guersant focuses on the social and psychological issues in a realistic way and in so doing asserts the naturalness of his hero's condition, the fact that it is fundamental to his character and one over which he has no control. The significance of this is heightened if we consider the date of the novel's publication (1953). The appearance of a literature of this sort at this moment has, in fact, more to do with the post-war French debate on the nature of ethics sparked off by Sartrean Existentialism than it does with religious issues as such. The previous year Sartre had brought out his monumental study of Genet, *Saint-Genet, comédien et martyr*, in which he made great play with the notion that Genet had *chosen* his sexual orientation. Although in the context of Existentialism this notion of choice has a very particular meaning, in the context of homosexuality it offered potentially dangerous ammunition to homophobes, particularly in the Church and the medical profession, who continued to preach the possibility of 'cures'. If a homosexual could choose his orientation, he could ostensibly choose to change or reject it. *Jean-Paul* can be seen as part of an essentialist reaction, an insistence on the *involuntary* nature of sexual orientation, which at the same time contributes to the continuing debate on the relationship between the nature of man and the nature/existence of God.

Gay Christian writers in the 1950s had, then, to reconcile a number of different literary traditions and prevailing ideas. As models for the representation of gayness they had to hand only the same negative tradition as anyone else. Furthermore, French Catholicism itself had a long tradition of hysterical rejection of sexual pleasure of any sort, from Léon Bloy to Paul Claudel and Georges Bernanos. And as far as the essence-versus-existence debate was concerned, although there *is* a strand of Christian Existentialism in French thought, in the work of Gabriel Marcel, for example, French Catholic writing was by and large essentialist by definition. The two most revealing examples of gay Christian writing for our purposes are to be found in the work of Marcel Jouhandeau and Julien Green,[7] because the patterns of the evolution of their self-images, stretching across the period 1920–70, show comparable developments despite the very different nature of their personal lives, beliefs and modes of literary expression. It may seem slightly perverse to represent the development of the gay self-image in the 1950s and 1960s through two Catholic writers, both of whom had established their literary reputations in the pre-war period. But I find them interestingly representative of the curious atmosphere of that period when, for the first time, there were legal sanctions against homosexuality and yet, also for the first time, there was a consistent attempt among gays to foster a positive attitude toward homosexuality both within themselves and in a wider public. It was a period of facing guilt and going beyond it. Although the literary links between Jouhandeau, Green and the previous tradition of homosexual writing are clear, neither writer consistently or unambiguously represents his sexuality as a defect in itself in the way that Proust does. The trend in their work, however stumbling and hesitant, is toward self-acceptance. In *that* sense they are very fit representatives of the 1950s and 1960s.

Jouhandeau's writings were, from the outset, firmly rooted in an essentialist conception of human nature. It is central to his view of man that each individual exists in a predetermined form which is revealed to him only when he starts to act: in his own words, 'Being precedes our soul within us, and we only discover our personality at the moment of acting freely for the first time.'[8] Yet despite the importance of this divine imposition of man's personality, Jouhandeau did not openly face the issue of sexuality as a part of human 'essence' in his fiction from *La Jeunesse de Théophile* (1921) to the *Chroniques maritales* (1938). This is all the more striking in that Jouhandeau combines his essentialist view of the psychological status of man with a concept of his metaphysical status which has its roots in Romantic revolt as defined in the works of Hugo, Baudelaire and above all Lautréamont, and which therefore relates closely to the tradition of the gay outlaw already present in earlier twentieth-century writings. In Jouhandeau's version of the myth of the Romantic pariah, in giving man total freedom God grants him the possibility of setting himself up as the rival of God; to fulfil himself (and thereby paradoxically to fulfil his creator's aim) man must beat God at his own game, by striving for his own absolute. Logically one thinks of an absolute as a fixed state, but for Jouhandeau what man aspires to is a process rather than a state, a process which cannot be evaluated according to

conventional categories of Good and Evil but whose validity lies in
its intensity. In other words, for Jouhandeau a man comes closer to
God the more intensely he lives his own essence to the full, regardless of conventional moral judgements of that essence. Evil for
Jouhandeau is therefore not what is conventionally regarded as
vice, but 'the negation of being' (cf. Baudelairean spleen), the refusal to take up the challenge to man posed by his creator.

The implications of this characteristically Romantic view of
man for the individual who has been predetermined as a homosexual are obvious: he should pursue intensity of experience through
sexual outlawry. But in practice, despite the implications of his
beliefs, Jouhandeau was very slow to face up to the challenge of his
own sexuality. Not until the anonymously published *Traité de l'abjection* (1939) did he actually tackle the issue head-on, illustrating
his argument with personal confession and proposing that rejection
by both God and society, in exiling a man definitively, both physically and spiritually, is a prerequisite for spiritual exaltation:

> Only passion or vice casts you into the same destitution as
> Holiness, and I think that it is only at the point at which man
> finds himself thus utterly abandoned by everyone and every-
> thing including himself that he is the closest to Grace, by
> which I mean the closest to being worthy of Grace.

So, up to the Second World War the values underpinning
Jouhandeau's image of the homosexual cohere fairly closely (at
least as far as their negativity is concerned) with those of Proust and
Cocteau, and have their roots in the same literary traditions. Not
surprisingly, then, in *De l'abjection* Jouhandeau is still projecting a
view of the homosexual-as-pariah which makes concessions to the
idea of vice. In particular the end of the first part of the treatise
distinguishes between heterosexual passion, which is merely obey-
ing a law of nature, and homosexual passion, which Jouhandeau
represents as wilful and unnatural:

> A man who loves a man only loves Man, and he is lost,
> because it is his own nature which he prefers to the whole of
> Nature and because, in seeing the rest of nature as inferior to

his own, he not only prefers himself to the work of God, such as God has created it, he prefers himself to God, he prefers his specifically human nature to the nature of God.

He then defends the value of this voluntary assumption of outlaw status on a purely individual basis: what is a defect in itself will provide him personally with a key to salvation. It seems that he was still coming to terms, at this relatively late stage in his life, with conventional moral evaluations, preferring to defend his own personal homosexuality rather than homosexuality in general.

Across the 1940s and 1950s he begins to publish a series of texts – but almost all anonymously or in private editions – which mark a new openness and a gradually less ambiguously positive position. The immediately public aspect was his frank celebration of male beauty. He had already defended the value of the body in *Algèbre des valeurs morales* (1935, re-edited 1954): 'The body has its part in the destinies of the soul and in the pride of the Eternal'. In the fourth volume of his *Mémorial*, entitled 'Apprentices and lads' (1953), he describes young men with the evident sensual pleasure of an Eekhoud, but without any of the sense of otherness created by the awareness of class difference (Jouhandeau himself was a butcher's son). *Tirésias* (1954) faces up to the negative implications of the Proustian man-woman myth by eulogizing anal sex as the release of the feminine element within the male, allowing a man to transcend the limitations of conventional masculinity. At the same time, like Genet and Guersant, Jouhandeau insists, through his lyrical evocations of his young partners and of the mutual pleasure achieved, on the validity of the sex act itself in both life and literature. In this acknowledgement of the power of beauty and the pleasures of the body, Jouhandeau reveals his first real break with preceding traditions, both gay and Catholic.

Alongside this reassessment of the validity of physical experience, other less 'private' texts were looking at the emotional and spiritual dimensions of homosexuality on an equally autobiographical plane. Initially this is still done very much within the limitations of the negative self-image laid down in *De l'Abjection*. In the *Chroniques maritales* Jouhandeau had dealt obliquely with the problems of a married homosexual through the character of his *alter ego* M. Godeau. He handled the same problems directly in *Chronique d'une passion* (private edition 1944, public edition 1949), where the autobiographical element is underlined by the use of his own wife's name, Elise, for Godeau's wife. What *Chronique d'une passion* does is to represent the issues debated in *De l'Abjection* in a concrete form, translating Jouhandeau's theories into the complexities of an experience of homosexual passion and the crisis of values which it precipitates. By 'in a concrete form' I mean that the reader is faced with an intricate puzzle to untangle which acts as a metaphor for the puzzle faced by the characters (and biographically by the author). The first-person narrator has to reconcile his sexual and emotional commitment to Jacques with his commitment to marriage. In attempting to do so he has to come to terms with Jacques' permissiveness and promiscuity. The text seems to suggest not just that Jacques is a difficult object for love but that he may be in some sense an inadequate one. Yet this very inadequacy seems to make the narrator's attachment more, rather than less, noble. In the end he has to cope with his wife's violent rejection of the possibility of compromise and with his own sense that the relationship threatens his spiritual destiny.

But Jouhandeau, in presenting his material, avoids passing judgements upon homosexuality, preferring to subordinate conventional concepts of ethics to an ethic of intensity. The justification lies in the fact that what is experienced is a *passion*, which separates the elite individual from the destiny and duty of others, endowing him with an ethic – or in Jouhandeau's terminology, an aesthetic – incompatible with the rest of the world and thus creating 'his own delectable Hell'. However, the passion is so strong that the narrator feels his own identity to have been dissolved by it, a situation which threatens what can best be defined in Baudelairean terms as his 'conscience dans le mal', an awareness which can only be returned to him by the inner solitude imposed on him by his marriage. The text implies that the value of the whole experience lies in the contemplation of the eternal damnation to which the narrator aspires and the achievement of the aesthetic stimulus which has given rise to the book.

In terms of homosexual self-image, therefore, the text offers a series of unreconcilable abstract images. At the one extreme, it preaches an exalted idealism, extolling Jacques' love as 'saving' the narrator from the destructive carnal excesses of 'easy' love affairs: 'Love is not only the emulator of Grace, it is the source of heroism and of Prowess, it is the quality most closely resembling Holiness.' At the other extreme lies sinister damnation, as in the hell-fire metaphors of the following passage:

> Oh that burning June afternoon in an attic crowned with storms and stuffed with roses, close to that naked man stretched out on that bed of iron and fire like an Apollo struck by a thunderbolt, his hand hanging down, and the lemon ice which gave us such delight as we stroked it across our calcinated lips.

And in between are only maxims of cynical self-interest:

> If there is anything in love other than love, anything in pleasure other than pleasure, it is the attraction of conquest, of an obstacle to be overcome, a challenge to be taken up, a rape to carry out, a crazy adventure to be undertaken at the risk of one's life, of one's honour, sometimes even of one's eternal life.

In a portrait of homosexual relations which spans these extremes the Romantic desire to parade one's evil and the underlying temptation of sexual self-rejection are still only too evident. This affinity with the existing tradition betrays itself in, for example, the recurrence of the same image of 'the beloved as mirror' and its concomitant theme of narcissism which we found in Cocteau and Genet. Jouhandeau is playing the role of the Romantic outlaw as defined for him by his predecessors, using his sexual orientation as one of the masks appropriate to the part.

In *L'Ecole des garçons* (1953) and *Du pur amour* (first version 1955, expanded edition (1969) Jouhandeau re-examines the same problems in a new light. *Du pur amour* takes us a decisive step further away from the moral ambiguities of *De l'Abjection* than does *Chronique d'une passion*. It, too, recounts a triangle: the narrator's love for both Elise and Robert, a young clarinettist in a military band. To be more precise it recounts three interlocking triangles: the narrator, Elise and Robert; the narrator, Robert and their mutual friend Henri; and the narrator, Robert and Brigitte, the girl he marries. At the same time the whole text interlocks intertextually with *L'Ecole des garçons*, the letters of Jouhandeau, Henri and Robert (a text which briefly becomes a subject of discussion in part VI of *Du pur amour*). It is significant that both texts shift the subject to a more openly autobiographical plane. The narrator is now Marcel, he is the author of texts recognizable in the reader's world (the anonymous *De l'Abjection*, the named *L'Ecole des garçons*). [9]

At the same time the focus of the text also shifts towards 'real' experience, social and psychological, and away from the religio-metaphysical debates which dominate the second half of *Chronique d'une passion*. Gone is any sustained sense of homosexuality as morally wrong; although the basically heterosexual Robert has phases of difficulty in his physical relationship with Marcel, this still survives as an inevitable part of the relationship, a form of gift made by the beloved to the lover in recognition of the fact that such intense emotion imposes a need for physical expression. As Jouhandeau puts it in the closing pages of the book, for them sex becomes something other than itself:

> the concrete sign of a total mutual adhesion, like the signature of a form of unanimity, a perfect accord only resulting from the slow pursuit and eventual achievement of a physical and moral unity, when in the beginning, everything seemed to divide us, above all our sex and our age.

The terms in which Jouhandeau analyses love are no longer in any way particular to homosexual relations. He makes a threefold division into *pleasure*, *passion* and *love*, sex/pleasure being a separate activity in itself, or a concomitant of either passion or love. Casual sex (in Jouhandeau's case gay, in Robert's straight) is tolerated but despised in both cases as catering to a mere passing physical need. The distinction made between passion and love is the key one. Passion is no longer viewed simply in terms of its intensity, but as an attempt to act as God, to take total power over another human being; pure love is self-abnegation, the aspiration to total sacrifice for the beloved: 'The happiness to be found in love lies in love itself, in so far as it achieves the intensification of purity, delicacy, disinterestedness, abandon, fervour, and exclusive fide-lity.' No less intense than passion, true love is not condemned to self-destruct from satiety but constitutes an absolute, an eternal in which the lovers can install themselves – Jouhandeau's language is significantly that of religious bliss. The book thus proffers, to some extent, a warning against casual sex (which still carries the flavour of hell-fire) and against passion as redefined by Jouhandeau, but makes no moral condemnation of homosexuality as such. On the contrary, it sets up the 'pure love' of two adult males, a relationship in which the physical side is an accepted, symbolically necessary ingredient, as far superior to heterosexual marriage (Robert's mar-riage is no more successful than Marcel's). This must be one of the earliest Catholic-based texts in which gay male French readers were offered a model (albeit a very particular one) of adult homosexual happiness as a desirable and possible facet of ordinary life.

By the 1960s, both aspects of Jouhandeau's treatment of love – physical and spiritual – take root in the mainstream of his writing. This is particularly true of the autobiographical chronicles-cum-reflections which he started to publish in 1961 under the title *Journaliers*. In volume XIX, *Un Second Soleil* (published in 1973), for example, we find, amongst other things, reflections on the re-lationship between the love of God and gay love; an account of a passionate spiritual relationship with a twenty-year-old and the masturbatory fantasies which it engenders; discussion of the author's physical attraction toward two other young men; rejection of Christianity's negative attitude to the flesh and Jouhandeau's own assessment of the importance of the beauty of the naked male body; observations about the normality of masturbation and the abnormality of chastity; reflections on the relative claims of the spiritual and the sensual in love; and an examination of the idea that if all men were gay there would be no more violence. Although few readers are likely to share Jouhandeau's highly personal meta-physics, there is an encouraging sense, in these late works, of a man at peace with his sexuality despite his social context.

In Jouhandeau, then, we meet the paradox of a writer who harnesses the most negative aspects of the post-Romantic gay self-image (homosexuality = evil, and therefore cause for rejection by both God and man) to the positive assertion that it is through the passionate pursuit of his ability to love his fellow man, physically as well as spiritually, that the writer's personal fulfilment, and therefore his salvation, lie. Whilst Jouhandeau never seems to separate himself totally from the masochistic implications of Decadent Catholicism, in which the pleasure to be derived from the consciousness of being sinful is the spiritual equivalent of ejaculating under the stimulus of physical pain, his texts become both more open about his own sexuality and more assertive of the worth of the experience across the 1950s and 1960s.[10]

As first a Protestant, then a Catholic, Julien Green approaches the problems of the Flesh and the Devil from a very different angle; but if we compare him with Jouhandeau, we can see similar signs of a move toward greater self-comprehension and self-acceptance across the 1950s and 1960s which tend to suggest that such a development represents a general intellectual trend rather than an isolated phenomenon. Green's earliest fiction portrays a cruel and hopeless world, in which neither family life nor social contacts can remedy the sense of total solitude, a world condemned to lovelessness and non-communication by an undefined, invisible, malevolent destiny. Adrienne Mesurat, in the novel of that name (1927), kills her father and goes mad; Guéret (*Léviathan*, 1929) commits rape and murder; in *Epaves* (1932) Philippe, Eliane and Henriette coexist in an atmosphere of guilt and aimless lassitude. These novels are generally seen as the work of a writer with an acute religious sensibility who is at the same time unable to find any sort of divine purpose in the pattern of life which he observes.

The works which follow, from 1934–49, all add a more overt metaphysical element, but they are still haunted by motifs of annihilation and suffering, intensified by the feeling that unhappiness is predestined, that it derives from a personal essence over which individuals have no control. Although the metaphysical dimension to Green's work is clear – what he describes in the preface to *Si j'étais vous* (1947) as 'the dual anguish of being unable to escape one's private destiny or the harsh necessity of death, and of finding oneself alone in an incomprehensible universe' – it is equally possible to read all these works as projections of a writer whose tortured homosexuality, an essence imposed on him by a 'malevolent' destiny, locks him into a sense of isolation and guilt when confronted with a world which condemns him to the position of outcast. The viability of such a reading is confirmed in two ways: first, by an isolated and neglected text, the novella *L'Autre Sommeil* (1930), in which solitude, guilt and death are evoked in the context of a specifically homosexual passion; and secondly, by Green's works of the 1950s and 1960s, the period in which he begins to confront, cautiously but systematically, the issues of sexuality in general, homosexuality in particular, and eventually, his own homosexuality.

My preamble may have suggested that Green's image of homosexuality, as his texts came openly to grips with the topic, was to be an unremittingly negative one. The facts are not so simple. What the early novels (even *L'Autre Sommeil*) disguise is the extent to which Green's whole conception of life is based on a Baudelairean duality of flesh and spirit as inseparable but incompatible. On the one hand, as he wrote in his *Journal* (2 January 1949), talking of the equal and opposing presence of spiritual energy and passionate emotion within man:

> Nothing is completely pure, just as nothing is completely impure ... the madness of passion only makes complete sense and is only absolutely comprehensible if we see it as containing an element of the divine and of a yearning for the divine.

Yet on the other hand, within this duality the flesh is frequently identified with the Devil. As Joseph, the puritan hero of *Moïra* (1950), whom Green has admitted is a projection of himself, puts it: 'I hate the sexual instinct. ... That blind force is Evil'. What Green expresses is thus, at least superficially, an attitude to sexuality in general rather than to homosexuality specifically, and although it may be possible to argue that his ethical and metaphysical views are born of, or coloured by, the nature of his own sexual experience, the fact remains that the texts themselves, unlike Jouhandeau's *De l'Abjection*, make no distinction between types of sexuality.

This inability either to dismiss or to welcome the role of the physical creates an ambiguity in the emerging image of homosexuality which Green's works project in the post-war period. Across the 1950s we find the developing portrait of a gradually more explicit homosexuality. In *Moïra*, the theme is still submerged: Joseph never understands the passion which leads Simon to commit suicide, or what Edmund Killigrew is trying to make him comprehend about himself; and the nature of the attraction (unconscious on the part of the former, conscious on the part of the latter) between Joseph and Bruce Praileau is not articulated, although it expresses itself in a classic scene of Lawrentian male bonding, the fight by the edge of the pond. Rather than a specific condemnation of homosexuality what emerges from the novel is a sense of the sinfulness of sexuality in general, combined with a conviction that purity and spirituality are ultimately linked. Joseph murders Moïra because he cannot cope with the desire which she provokes within him.

The same tension between sensuality and spirituality is at the centre of both the play *Sud* (1952) and the novel *Le Malfaiteur* (1955), but again the question of gay self-image is obscured. In *Sud* the relationship between Lieutenant Wicziewski and Erik Mac-Clure *is* the central issue, but the language of the play is sufficiently oblique for it to be, in performance at any rate, easily misunderstood. And the first edition of *Le Malfaiteur* omitted the whole 'Confession de Jean' section (only included for the first time in the 1973 edition). This transformed the novel from an expression of the destructive power of homosexuality into the tragedy of a woman who loves a man who cannot respond to her affections, without the reason for that inability being clear, let alone evaluated. Only with *Chaque homme dans sa nuit* (1960), a novel principally about heterosexual excess, did Green face the issue of homosexuality head on: Wilfred, the frenetically active heterosexual, and his two homosexual counterparts, lucid, rational Angus and instinctive, unbalanced Max, all throw further light on the problem of integrating sexuality into the human condition without destroying the capacity for religious fulfilment. Ostensibly, then, as homosexuality emerges as a subject in its own right, it remains tied to the general rejection of the dangers of the flesh which characterized Green's earlier works.

Can we, in fact, say that for Green sexual orientation is simply a morally neutral aspect of this general human problem of flesh versus spirit, that homosexuality as such is not a particular barrier to salvation? The answer, I think, is no. For when we look closely at these works of the period 1950–60 we can perceive a concealed negativity in the presentation of homosexuality which contradicts the claim that Green is rejecting all sins of the flesh with the even-handedness which he purports to show. First homosexuality is consistently the agent of death: Joseph's repression of his desire for Praileau is a cause of his inability to suppress his desire for Moïra – by then he just needs *sex* – and this in turn is the source of the violence which expresses itself in the act of strangulation; homosexual desire leads Ian Wicziewski to provoke the duel in which he intends to kill Erik and in which he decides to die himself; Jean, in *Le Malfaiteur*, commits suicide; Max kills Wilfred because he desires him and that desire is not reciprocated. Not only is Green offering us yet another version of the love = death equation, but to it he adds the equally traditional motif of the homosexual as outsider. Joseph is a redneck, coming to the University of South Carolina from a small town in the hills; Wicziewski is a Pole, alien to the North/South divide of an America on the brink of civil war; Max is a Slav. Lastly, the one character who finds a way to achieve the combination of sexuality and faith which Green is pursuing is Wilfred, an unashamed heterosexual. In practice, then, the neutrality of the pre-1950 works on questions of sexual orientation is broken in those published in the 1950s; it is precisely at the period when the issue of homosexuality is gradually becoming more explicit in both the novels and the plays that the question of sexuality as a barrier to salvation also becomes explicit. The connection is hardly a coincidence.

Having brought himself in the 1950s to confront in fictional form the issues which he saw as central to man's spiritual problems, Green finally took the step, in the next decade, of tracing the same itinerary on an openly personal level, in his autobiography. The pattern here confirms what we have already found in his fiction and plays, which is hardly surprising given their highly autobiographical nature. The portrait of his childhood in *Partir avant le jour* (1963) insists on the extreme puritanism of his upbringing and how this led him to reject the body in general and the sexual in particular: 'The flesh was anarchy, it was the horror which cast a shadow over people's faces. To this very day I hate its inexorable force which subjects men to its all-powerful whims.' Accordingly, if the boys who eventually initiate him into masturbation are associated with images of darkness and the Devil, it is because all carnality is evil, not because homosexuality as such is.

At the same time, right from the first volume we find fore-tastes of a Coctelian 'wound of beauty' – Green's admission of his susceptibility to the physical charm of Frederic's blue eyes, or the perfection of Roger's white skin, dark eyes and oval face. It is in the third volume, *Terre lointaine* (1966), recounting his time at the University of South Carolina, however, that the effect of masculine beauty on both his senses and his emotions really comes to the fore. Green here emphasizes the motif of difference with which he has endowed himself by presenting himself as seeing this male beauty in terms of Greek art, and as feeling himself to be the sole survivor of pagan antiquity, misplaced in time and space. The image of homo-sexual desire is here projected in divided form – a cerebral passion for the beautiful Mark and a fierce sensual desire for another boy called Nicolls, a desire which he makes no attempt to translate into action, because 'Physical love was surrounded by a barrier of disgust'. But again, he qualifies this by saying that of one thing he was certain, because the Bible said so: sin resided in sexual pleasure itself, whatever the sex of the partner. It is significant that Green intended his 'confession' to stop with this volume; he has much to say in the third volume about the intensity of his love for Mark and even leaves the reader wondering whether Mark himself might not have responded, if Julien had ever given him the chance. But the emphasis of the account is on the destructive tension between religious moral belief and pagan love and desire.

The changed climate of the early 1970s encouraged Green to go further. In 1973 he allowed the self-censored 'Confession de Jean' to be inserted into its rightful place in *Le Malfaiteur*, and thus brought to a head the issue of 'telling all' (to which I shall return shortly) in a text which, for the first time, places onto society much of the blame for the distortions experienced by homosexuals:

There is no harsher punishment for an individual than a

sexual inclination which society rejects; it reduces him to a choice between dissimulation and scandal, and if he lacks the inner strength to 'come out', he is unjustly obliged to live the life of a hypocrite.

In 1974 he brought out a fourth volume of autobiography, *Jeunesse*, which, in recounting his years in Paris immediately after his return from the USA, finally constituted an avowal of his sexual *activity*. From the perspective of the 1990s this might seem a trivial extension, but it was evidently a major step as far as Green was concerned. If anything he is even more insistent in this volume that '*it was sexuality in its entirety that I was rejecting*, whether or not it was the sexuality of the majority' (Green's italics). Gide's defence of the spiritual and emotional value of homosexuality in *Corydon* seemed irrelevant to him because he could see no difference between his own physical experiences and those of a promiscuous heterosexual. It is now sex *without love* which is being targeted. However, for the first time, Green makes two substantial concessions. First, that sexual desire is a madness or intoxication which renders men non-responsible for their actions, without lessening the element of evil; second, that it is useless to preach morality at the young, who are by definition unable to overcome their inner contradictions. *Jeunesse* does not change the equation flesh = evil, but it does expound the need for a young man to accept himself for what God has made him, whilst striving to go beyond the natural limitations of the human condition.

All this might lead one to interpret the portrait of homosexuality in Green's autobiographies as morally neutral (i.e. no better or worse than heterosexuality). Such a judgement needs a little modification. Just as I indicated a covert slanting in the texts of the 1950s, so it seems to me that there is a further slanting to his work as a whole which is revealed by the texts of the 1960s. The fact is that, prior to the 1970s, it is not true to say that Green sees homosexuality as no more sinful than heterosexuality. What reveals his real feelings on the subject is the motif of 'confessions' in his work. From *Moïra* onward there appears a motif of 'the unavowed', of an attempt to confess something which is not in fact achieved. Green himself, in *Terre lointaine*, lists such failed avowals from Praileau to Joseph (*Moïra*), Ian to Erik (*Sud*), and Angus and Wilfred alternately in *Chaque homme dans sa nuit*, Paul in *Le Voyageur* and the handsome boy in his only pre-1950 homosexual text, *L'Autre Sommeil*. The motif occurs centrally in the autobiographies themselves, in Julien's own inability to speak out to Mark in *Terre lointaine*, an episode re-represented in *Jeunesse*. What this motif emblematizes is Green's own inability to make a public avowal, to confess to the reader. The motif of the *completed* avowal, represented tentatively in the confession made by Angus in *Chaque homme dans sa nuit*, and which Green finally manages to publish in a full form for the first time in the 1973 edition of *Le Malfaiteur*, he himself only brings to realization in a personal form in *Jeunesse*. By 'completed avowal' I mean not just that the confession is made but that it is an admission of carnal desire as well as of love. Ian in *Sud*, like Julien himself in *Terre lointaine*, deceives himself into seeing love and desire as separate (indeed incompatible). By *Jeunesse* Green has come to admit the element of sensuality buried within the apparently spiritual passion for Mark. This he confesses to himself in the midst of his first admission of carnal experience to his readers. *Jeunesse* is thus the first of his texts which the gay reader can interpret as an unambiguous acceptance of the inevitability of his own sexual desire and its practical physical implications. This explains why the sense of torment disappears from the novels of the 1970s and 1980s, and why, in an interview in *Le Figaro* in July 1988, Green was able to answer the question, 'Do you feel at ease with your homosexuality?', with an unqualified yes.[11]

Notes

1. Quoted J. Mossuz-Lavau, *Les Lois de l'amour: les politiques de la sexualité en France (1950–1990)* (Paris: Payot, 1991), p. 243.
2. As I have been unable to find a copy of this text, I rely for my account on Edmund White's summary in *Jean Genet* (London: Chatto & Windus, 1993), pp. 445, 772. The title is a French transliteration of the German *schwul*, meaning 'homosexual'. The novel would seem to offer interesting potential comparison and contrast with Francis King's account of an English student in similar circumstances, *Punishments*.

3.   In an article in *Les Temps modernes* in 1954.

4.   For Jacob's life, see Pierre Andreu, *Vie et mort de Max Jacob* (Paris: Table Ronde, 1982).

5.   Sachs played the role of devoted hanger-on to both Gide and Cocteau; the lesbian Violette Leduc later entertained an improbable and fruitless passion for him. *Le Sabbat: souvenirs d'une jeunesse orageuse* (first published posthumously in 1946) was the first French autobiography confessing adult homosexuality (as opposed to Gide's declaration of pederasty in *Si le grain ne meurt*). It is a very interesting example of an obsession with authority which is both thematic (father-figures, Catholicism) and textual (the desire to shelter behind the 'authority' of previous writers).

6.   Dominique Fernandez, *Le Rapt de Ganymède* (Paris: Grasset, 1989), p. 110. Not everyone shares this view of *Jean-Paul*. In particular, Renaud Camus, in *Notes achriennes* (pp. 215–16) denounces it fiercely as a book which, together with Maxence van der Meersch's *Masque de chair*, helped to poison his adolescence by the repressive sense of guilt and sickness which they propagated. In his view the 'viscous moralising' of the two books is about as healthy as the stagnant liquid in a urinal.

7.   It is an interesting reflection on the hidden prejudices which go to make up the 'canon' of academically and critically 'approved' writing, that the twentieth-century Catholic writers of good standing are the extremely unpleasant right-wing homophobe Paul Claudel, the fanatical opponent of the flesh Georges Bernanos and the middle-brow but respectably closeted François Mauriac. Green and Jouhandeau, both much more interesting writers from an aesthetic point of view than Bernanos or Mauriac, and lacking the crazed extremism of Claudel and Bernanos, have been critically marginalized. There are no prizes for guessing why this should be the case.

8.   'Being' here is not simply a matter of physical existence in the Existentialist sense but existence in a divinely preordained form.

9.   The comparison to be made is not so much with Proust (despite the coincidence of names) as with Colette's *La Naissance du jour*, where the boundaries of autobiography and fiction are also made to seem irrelevant to the task of self-exploration.

10.   It is nonetheless noticeable that Jouhandeau never allowed *Tirésias*, the key text of his erotology, to be published under his own name during his lifetime.

11.   Cited by Roger Peyrefitte, *L'Innominato: nouveaux propos secrets* (Paris: Albin Michel, 1989), p. 205.

Chapter four

From Self-defence to Self-assertion

'A homosexual is just a heterosexual who likes boys.'
● *Jean-Louis Bory*[1]

FROM the tentative self-acceptance which characterizes much 1950s and 1960s gay writing, the next step, and a much smaller one than it sounds, was to writing which presented homosexuality as a fact rather than an issue (using it at least in part to explore other problems), or which focused on the problems imposed on gays by the outside world, or which examined the positive potential of being gay. In other words, writers began, in essence, to take homosexuality for granted, in the sense that they treated it as a norm to be embraced and explored by literature. By the late 1960s texts were appearing which no longer saw self-defence as a prerequisite. Jean-Louis Bory's *La Peau des zèbres* (1969), for example, falls into the first of the above categories. It no longer places gay life in a private or twilight zone, nor does the text function as a set of symbols of otherness and guilt. It centres on the effects of the break-up of a relationship, studying the interplay of social and psychological pressures in exactly the same way that other writers have studied the pressures deriving from race, creed or gender. It concerns itself with two couples who exist as couples in public, known for what they are to their families, their friends, even their work colleagues, without there being scandal or surprise. The novel focuses *outward* from gayness rather than inward upon it. It studies the difficulties of sustaining long-term gay relationships in contemporary society, against a portrait of the state and values of French society at the time of de Gaulle's referendum of autumn 1958. It also reflects the tentativeness of emerging gay consciousness, and in doing so it emphasizes the diversity of sexual and emotional temperaments, of social and aesthetic credos, which exists as much among gays as in the heterosexual section of a community. Bory is making a statement which lays the ground for his gay rights struggles of the 1970s; he wants the individual to accept his own normality, and to assume public responsibility for his sexuality without any sense of shame but without any aggressive desire to impose it on others, let alone to proselytize. As such, his position is perfectly summed up by the poker-faced definition attributed to him in the epigraph to this chapter.

Bory's quip could equally well stand as the epigraph to a novel by Christiane Rochefort which appeared in the same year as *La Peau des zèbres*, and which presents a complementary dimension of contemporary sexual awareness. It may seem odd to invoke the work of a woman writer in a chapter devoted to the gay male self-image, but, as might be expected from a writer whose theory of polysexuality abolishes such distinctions as 'gay male', her *Printemps au parking* perfectly represents the moment at which sexual orientation ceases to be seen as a black and white opposition of homo- and heterosexuality and is redefined as a spectrum of possibilities. The concept of same-sex love is therefore no longer an issue, a stage prerequisite for the 1970s debates on the implications of a homosexual identity for civil rights and lifestyle.

At the centre of *Printemps au parking* is a sexual relationship between an adolescent and a university student, the former in flight from the distorting effects of the repressive structure of the conventional family unit. But it is important that neither of them can be labelled 'homosexual' – indeed they stand in contrast to Thomas's brother Fabrice, who is so labelled. The narrator, Christophe, a sixteen-year-old from the suburbs, is a perfectly ordinary, non-delinquent type who is not succeeding in school, feels oppressed and rejected at home, and, on a whim, runs away. His capacity for heterosexuality is not questioned – he has been having sex with girls since he was thirteen, he has successful casual sex with a girl within the first few pages of the novel, and he revels in his explicit seduction of an older girl later in the novel. But he meets Thomas, an ordinary middle-class student from a slightly zany progressive family, not misogynistic, and himself also heterosexual. They start to talk, and the acquaintanceship leads gradually to sexual passion. In Rochefort's words: 'Neither of them wants it, God knows; but they end up by really giving in to it. And the scene that is described, the sexual scene, I don't think it could be categorised as erotic or pornographic.'[2]

Again, we are dealing with the opening-up of individuals, the release of aspects of themselves which, it is implied, can only be achieved through intimate communion with a member of the same sex. What Christophe has discovered, as he says to his friend Nicolas in the closing pages of the novel, is that the interdicts of society shut the individual off from his own possibilities: 'They hid the whole earth from me with their cloud of shit, and they'll go on doing it if I don't watch out'. The 'spring' of the title is a metaphor akin to 'Prague spring' as applied to the Czech uprising. The defiant chorus of 'shit' delivered by the two boys in the parking lot is itself the real symbol of the arrival of a spring whose natural counterpart is excluded by the absence of trees, flowers, birds. Rebellion, including the refusal to be sexually categorized and constrained, is the symbol of hope for the future. Just as Bory's novel inserts homosexual relationships into the 'normal' structures of society, so Rochefort's inserts homosexual acts and emotions into the spectrum of 'normal' relationships.

Without wanting to overstress the significance of the 'events of May 1968',[3] I cannot help but observe that these two novels of the following year confirm how sharp a shift in French social values the events had precipitated. Homosexuality was no longer a problem *for homosexuals*; if society had difficulties with it, that was society's problem. On the contrary, homosexuality was now assumed to have the same power to act as a metaphor for society's wider problems as heterosexuality had traditionally had, and indeed, because of its association with youth and rebellion, was thought of as having a privileged power to convey the new spirit of the times. Consequently, for the first time gay French readers could see themselves mirrored in texts freed from all negative associations and owing nothing to the tradition of literary homosexuality established in the period 1830–1950.

It would be easy to underestimate the importance of this eradication of negative associations. On the surface it looks like a mere change in literary fashions. But the potential consequences of a literature which presents an exclusively negative picture of a section of society are very serious. Writers like Fernandez and Renaud Camus make it clear that until the 1970s many French homosexuals found their negative self-image damagingly reinforced by literary stereotypes. I have defined these stereotypes in terms of the association of homosexuality with the outlaw, social destruction, crime, sickness, evil, the equation of love with death. These motifs occur, in varying forms, in Proust, Cocteau, Genet, and to some extent in Green and Jouhandeau too, on a symbolic/mythical level. Clearly it can be objected that similar negative images have always proliferated in straight literature too, and that there is no evidence that heterosexuals have been damaged by reading *Anna Karenina* or *Madame Bovary*. There are two answers to this objection. (1) whilst the notion that heterosexual *men* have been adversely affected by the way that they are portrayed in literature may seem absurd,[4] the problem of the negative self-image acquired by *women*, from art in general and nineteenth-century literature in particular, is indeed a serious one, to which feminist studies have paid considerable attention (see for example Cathérine Clément's *Opera or the Undoing of Women* for the sense of fascinated betrayal provoked by the operatic presentation of women from Mozart to Puccini). (2) the question of male self-image involves one of reading context. The heterosexual male lives in a society which promotes a positive image of him at all levels: a negative literary image would, if it existed, play only a small part in his self-evaluation. For gay males, in the repressive social context of France from 1870 to 1968, literature was one of the few places where they might have hoped to find any positive evaluation of their sexual orientation. Where literature, too, projects images of isolation and guilt, it only serves to intensify the pressures of the social context. Unfortunately, since literature is by definition the product of a social context, it can only evolve *with* a society, and the relevant evolution was delayed until the end of the 1960s.

Rather than being surprised by the persistence of negative self-images, we should be amazed at how far the French gay community in the 1950s and 1960s managed to work itself free from those images, as it moved from symbolic/mythical self-rejection to realistic self-assessment. In the first place, the issue of masculinity, i.e. the stereotyping homosexual = feminine = inferior, ceased to exist in gay writing (the stereotype remains important, of course, in *heterosexual* representations of gayness, as in the success of *La Cage aux folles*). When macho/effeminate stereotypes occur in 1970s gay literature, they usually form part of a debate about forms of self-assumption *within* a gay 'society'. In the second place, there was a growing willingness to shift the blame for the difficulties experienced by homosexuals onto society itself. Thirdly, there was a broadening of the attempt to give aesthetic value to homosexual sex itself, of which Genet is the forerunner. And fourthly, a debate begins within gay writing about the relative values of sexual pleasure and homosexual *love*, with or without physical expression, a debate which is in essence the natural extension of the existing debate on the same issues in 1960s heterosexual literature. The final emergence at the end of the 1960s of a literature liberated from both self-repression and the embedded prejudices of tradition had marked a watershed for gay self-esteem.

This is not to say that the issue of self-image had simply vanished overnight. In the first place, aspects of the old tradition persisted in many writers; in the second, even for progressive writers the problem of self-image had simply changed focus from one of identity to one of lifestyle. Not surprisingly, self-image in the 1970s and early 1980s is a far more fragmented concept than in the preceding period. Whilst individual writers remained cautious about naming their sexuality openly – even Bory managed to write his autobiographical narrative *Ma moitié d'orange* in 1937 without using the word homosexual so much as once – and such leading figures of the intellectual world as Roland Barthes and Michel Foucault never officially 'came out', the assumption behind almost all gay writing of the period is that sexual orientation is now a non-issue for gays themselves. The fragmentation to which I referred results from competing theories of how a gay identity should be lived, whether it is by definition the assumption of a revolutionary position in a repressive society, and whether gays have the right to follow heterosexual life-patterns or the duty to seek to overthrow them.

The most 'representative' theoretical text of the period is in a sense *Comment nous appelez-vous déjà?*, precisely because it simply juxtaposes two accounts of homosexuality, by Bory and Guy Hocquenghem, which are based on fundamentally different conceptions of human nature and social processes. Bory's stance is humanist and pragmatic, seeking the sexual liberation of the individual within the framework and terms of the contemporary social structure. Hocquenghem's follows the radical position established in his earlier essays, from *Le Désir homosexuel* (1972) onward.[5] For him the cordoning-off of homosexuality into a separate identity is an aspect of capitalism's need to focus all human energy on production (in this context *procreation*), and to replace the previous unstructured communality of human relationships (including the sexual) by the policing structure of the bourgeois family unit. (Renaud Camus is working from the same angle, in *Chroniques achriennes*, when he states that the reason why homosexuality is not subject to the same arbitrary taboos as heterosexuality is that it is not tied by issues of inheritance and the continuation of the race.) Hocquenghem wants to liberate the forces of desire which he sees as intrinsic to human nature, as a prerequisite for breaking down the artificial fixed roles and identities which, following a divide-and-rule policy, modern capitalist society has imposed on its members. The point had previously been made by Freud, of all people, that 'homosexual love is far more compatible [i.e. than heterosexual love] with group ties, even when it takes the shape of uninhibited sexual impulsions'. Hocquenghem inverts Freud's point, suggesting that this greater compatibility with group ties exists *because* homosexual desire takes the form of uninhibited sexual impulsions. It is, he argues, precisely because homosexuals are free to experiment, unlike heterosexuals, with the unfettered 'plugging-in' of organs – i.e. their sexual practices do not impose a fixed or hierarchical pattern of acts or relationships – that they have a special potential for radical subversion of arbitrary received values. Hocquenghem's position shares common ground with that taken by Michel Foucault in an interview in *Gai Pied* in 1981, where he puts forward the view that the question of homosexuality is not one of individual identity but of asking what relations can be invented, multiplied and modulated *through* homosexuality.[6] For all these writers, unlike Bory, the body corporate ceases to be a political metaphor and becomes the basis of personal relations too. They redefine homosexuality as a continuing process rather than a condition, a new way of experiencing and remodelling the world.

In creative writing of the period (I use the term simply in opposition to polemical theoretical essays) the difference between Bory on the one hand and Hocquenghem and Co. on the other corresponds, crudely speaking, to that between 'conventional' representation of the social and psychological problems of a homosexual condition and 'experimental' texts celebrating pleasure as an end in itself, or at least promoting it as a primary means of relating to others. The work of Renaud Camus illustrates this second sort of writing. His will to abolish the self is obvious. In his early texts he 'abolishes' the author not only by the pseudonyms and variations on his own name under which he writes, but by producing texts made up from fragments of other authors or from passages taken from his own previous writings. Later he cultivates the fragment itself as a literary form in *Notes achriennes*, his text passing rapidly between criticism, chronicle, maxim and poem and still incorporating passages from existing writings of his own or by others, with the aim of preventing the subject of the text, homosexuality, from fixing itself as a form of speech, and thereby as a code or doctrine. In order not to be bound by heterosexual concepts of homosexuality he even refuses the customary vocabulary of sexual differentiation, substituting the word *achrien* for gay and insisting on sexuality as a single spectrum by using an anagram, *hinarce*, for straight.

His gay-centred texts – *Notes achriennes* and *Chroniques achriennes* – and the various travelogues (the term is approximate since any attempt at generic categorization of his work is a distortion) all exemplify this rejection of predetermined qualities and fixed effects by their interweaving of sexual and textual experience and their juxtaposition of physical and cerebral pleasure. Taking at random a sequence in *Notes achriennes*[7] we find: (1) a fragment from Suarès' *Voyage du Condottiere* reflecting on the eternal sense of being an outsider in Florence; (2) a passage from Camus's own work *Travers* attacking homosexual intellectuals and artists for only offering a picture of homosexuality which conforms with the dominant repressive ideology of their period; this is followed by further reflections occasioned by the passage on the still greater unwillingness of gays in politics and the performing arts to compromise their public image by at least allowing their sexuality to colour their public lives; (3) an example of an Italian singer who dedicated a love song to a man, but then retreated from the implications of his action; (4) a brief sexual anecdote dependent on a pun; (5) attacks on homosexual writers whose works he read when an adolescent and which poisoned him with their tortured guilt and moralizing; (6) a graphic account of sucking off a young man in the cellar room of the Crisco club in Florence: Camus, having on this occasion accepted his partner's refusal to treat him as more than a pleasuring agent, reflects on the loss of the conventional sense of individual identity which the encounter created and of the intense pleasure which he experienced as a result.

This series of fragments, typical of the work as a whole, depersonalizes the author, from the metaphors of otherness to a precise sexual experience of the abolition of the self, and passes the focus to the unfolding subject of gayness itself. At the same time all this is placed in the context of social reflections on the status and communication of gayness which invite the reader to measure the text that is being read against the texts/artists criticized. Camus's sexual anarchy, his personal form of adherence to Hocquenghem's 'plugging of holes without law or rule' is thus made part of a highly provocative invitation to the reader – consonant with Camus's dictum about the need to avoid reducing homosexuality to a fixed discourse – to create his or her own image of the potential of homosexual experience out of what is being read. We are a long way from the social and psychological neo-realism which, despite its use of fragmentation, lacuna and other techniques of the *nouveau roman*,[8] is at the heart of Bory's presentation of homosexuality in *La Peau des zèbres*. Yet both Bory and Camus could be said to project a sense of their sexual orientation as a source of what they see as positive experience. They simply differ profoundly as to what constitutes that positiveness.

Given such incompatible models of 'gayness' and how to record it, there are considerable complexities and ambiguities in talking about positive or negative gay male self-image. The difficulties are well illustrated by the work of Yves Navarre. Navarre has been held up as a classic example of a writer projecting a negative image of homosexuality, and ostensibly with some justification. It has been suggested that in his early novels, whereas the heterosexual characters in *Evolène* (1972) and *Le Coeur qui cogne* (1974) achieve meaningful relationships, the three homosexual novels, *Lady Black* (1971), *Les Loukoums* (1973) and *Killer* (1975) all emphasize isolation, violence, destruction and the love = death motif (most perfectly represented in the grotesque scene of mass necrophilia in a New York funeral chapel in *Les Loukoums*). This is all perfectly true. Indeed, it would be easy to add a list of other motifs drawn from the existing outlaw tradition, e.g. *the gay as outsider*: Rasky in *Les Loukoums* is half-Romanian, half-Turk and Luc is a Frenchman in New York, whilst for long stretches of *Killer* the eponymous hero is an anti-*ingénu* in England; and *effeminacy*: the central character of *Lady Black* is a transvestite, as are three important figures in *Killer*, whilst in *Les Loukoums* there are repeated vignettes of New York life in which queens abound and are described in the feminine.

In Navarre's defence it should be pointed out that these are *ghetto* novels. They invoke the intensity of the pursuit of promiscuous gay lifestyles in the early period of liberation in a realistic manner, and in so doing they run into the same problem that faced Zola and Maupassant in their attempts to record the underside of heterosexual reality a century earlier. Even when Navarre is quoted in an interview as saying that homosexuals seem to him to have a gift for unhappiness and that in the long run they tend to withdraw into egoistic indifference and narcissism,[9] themes well illustrated by the mutually destructive relationship of Tony and Killer, we have to see his remarks in their temporal context. It can be argued that, particularly in the early 1970s, when gay rebellion was expressing itself very openly in the rejection of the heterosexual couple as a model for relationships, the difficulties of creating positive alternatives were very considerable. To provide a critique of current alternatives Navarre uses *as symbols* those elements of contemporary gay life which represent the objectification and exploitation of others which he found present in this experimental period. In painting a negative picture of the gay ghetto, these early novels are simply making a critical contribution to the debate on lifestyles launched by novels like *La Peau des zèbres*.

A text is not negative simply because it insists on the shortcomings of a given homosexual lifestyle, any more than it is positive simply because it insists on the negative aspects of heterosexuality. Underlying mythology is more important than surface realism. Take Michel Tournier's *Les Météores* (1974) for example.[10] It contains three ostensibly positive portraits of homosexuality, in the individual characters of Alexandre and Thomas and in the incestuous relationship between the identical twins Paul and Jean. These portraits are set in the context of a constantly negative account of heterosexuality, at least in the voices of Alexandre and Paul: homosexual aesthetic creativity is promoted as superior to the merely physical (pro)creativity of the heterosexual; heterosexuals are portrayed as impotently jealous of the recreational nature of gay sex; the heterosexual majority is derided for creating a caricature of the homosexual minority and attempting to force it to conform to that distorted image of itself. If we judge *Les Météores* exclusively by the politically correct pronouncements of its gay characters, it would seem to be a classic 1970s progressive text. If, however, we look at the *symbolism* of the text, we get a very different reading.

The problem is that Tournier's view of homosexuality is in a major respect identical with that of Proust, a point confirmed by the author himself in the section on *Les Météores* in Tournier's collection of essays *Le Vent paraclet*. Proust describes his men-women as looking for a totally 'masculine' other half. Tournier sticks closer to the Platonic myth of the androgyne as found in the *Symposium* but modifies it by the kind of narcissism described in Navarre's *Killer* (i.e. the pursuit of the self in the beloved). For Tournier, identical twins represent the perfect form of otherness because the other is *identical* with the self without losing its identity as difference. Homosexuality, although an advance on the ill-matched pattern of *hetero*sexuality, is, like incest, only an imperfect approximation of this perfect coincidence of two selves:

> Should one talk of them in terms of homosexuality or incest? Definitely not, for these two terms are too weak even taken together to communicate the reality of twinship. Too weak because homosexuality and incest practised by individuals are only two rough and imperfect approximations of twinship.

The true homosexual, as represented by Alexandre,

> shares in the nature of both twinship and singleness. He is single, having been born without a twin. But he refuses to accept his condition and demands the privileges of twinship. Instead of marrying and having children, he searches *sorrowfully* for a twin brother who does not exist (my italics).

For all Tournier's comparisons of Alexandre with Vautrin and Charlus, and his insistence on the daring he shows as author in making a homosexual the main voice of the criticism of heterosexual society, the fact remains that the condition of homosexuality is defined as *per se* inadequate or failed. The homosexuality of the twins is merely an incidental accessory of the perfect state of twinship, and the nearest a mere gay can come to this is the provocatively defined 'spiritual' homosexuality of the relationship which Alexandre's friend Thomas implies that he has achieved with God via the penetration of the Holy Spirit. This underlying negativity is reflected in details of the surface structure of the text. Alexandre may be a flamboyant homosexual, but he is also a sewage engineer; his sexual preference and his occupation both represent what society rejects. Such an image risks suggesting that, since society has reason to reject the latter, perhaps it has equal reason to reject the former. When we look closely at Alexandre's defence of homosexuality, we find that it is not markedly progressive. His praise of promiscuity, for example, is conducted not in terms of a new communality but of the old individuality, the homosexual as 'free and solitary wolf'. And in other respects, the values of heterocracy are merely turned on their heads, asserting that homosexuals possess the very qualities which heterosexuals deny them. Perhaps the most revealing retrogressive motif of all is that of the desire for sex with straight men: 'Making love with a heterosexual is incomparably delicious, you know. Heterosexuals are our women.' What Tournier offers us is really only a form of conservative 'revenge' literature, equivalent to Rachilde's inversion of male/female relations in *Monsieur Vénus* and *La Marquise de Sade*.[11] Its underlying symbolic structure is rooted in a vision of gayness as inadequate, even defective, which is far closer to pre-war literature than to that of the 1970s.

Negativity in Tournier is, then, of a different kind from the negativity of Navarre's early novels. For Tournier, although gayness is preferable to heterosexuality, it is still an imperfect state. For Navarre, it is not gayness itself which is a negative condition – it would be surprising if it were, given his work in the media for gay rights – but certain ways of *living out* gayness. If sex is a meaningless, banal, often violent and ephemeral pleasure in *Les Loukoums* or *Killer*, it is not because the characters are gay but because they choose to experience sex at that level. For Navarre this sort of promiscuity is barely different in kind from the violent temporary pleasure obtained from prison rape (a basically heterosexual pastime) in *Portrait de Julien devant la fenêtre* (1979). The key novel for an appreciation of Navarre's *positive* position on gayness and its values is *Le petit galopin de nos corps* (1977), the post-liberation answer to Jouhandeau's *Du pur amour*. For this novel is a poetic hymn to the homosexual *couple*, and at the same time a first contribution to Navarre's reflections on an issue which finds its ultimate expression in his AIDS novel *Ce sont amis que vent emporte* (1991, see below pp. 134–6): the relationship between homosexual love and artistic (pro)creation. The novel presents the lifetime love of Roland and Joseph as emotionally and physically fulfilling, whatever the personal and social difficulties which it faces. The key thematic and symbolic element in this exploration of the positive experience of gayness is nature. The two men take for granted that their love is natural; they express both their emotion and their desire in images of nature; they make love in the open air in the rain; Joseph writes what is in effect an extended prose poem to

Roland with the refrain, 'You have the body of the days and the seasons', emphasizing the sense of change within continuity which links them to the rhythms of the world around them. And both to emphasize the idyllic tone and to make the link with the theme of preservation of experience in writing, the reader is invited to make an intertextual reading with the Virgil of the *Eclogues* and the *Georgics*.[12]

If we look back to *Les Loukoums* or *Killer* we can see that what Navarre rejects in the ghetto society of the early 1970s is the *use* (even mutual) of human beings as objects, an abuse which he sees as no different in kind from contemporary bourgeois materialist exploitation. But his response is not to idealize disembodied emotion. On the contrary, love in *Le petit galopin* could not be more physical. When Roland writes, in the closing stages of the book, 'the real great voyage of our lives was to explore our bodies, all around and within them, diving deep', he is referring not merely to sex, the endless mutual exploration, inside and out, which is lovingly recorded throughout the narrative, but also to the sense of physical twinship, of wearing each other's skin, to the metaphors of eating and drinking each other, to the extreme *corporeality* of their emotional and spiritual union. For the Jouhandeau of *Du pur amour* 'pleasure' is a symbolic extra; for Roland and Joseph the experience of body and soul is a single one, lived under the pagan sign of classical pastoral and untouched by any Christian sense of tension between flesh and spirit.

Navarre's handling of this theme is in no way simplistic. The pressures of normative society are not avoided: eventually the lovers marry, to conform, although in marrying sisters they find a secret way of making their own union 'official'. At the same time, emotional fulfilment is not treated as a panacea for deeper problems. The text is haunted by the question, 'What do our lives mean?', by the literal and metaphorical presence of a death which risks negating the meaning of lived experience. Their love is shadowed by death from the outset – the accidental death of the sixteen-year-old Sicilian Sandro from whom they learn how to express their sexuality freely – just as the narration itself is shadowed by the death of Joseph, which has occasioned Roland to write. Roland is constantly disturbed by his sense of the unfinished.

Even the important assertion that the justification for their lives is the *way* they have 'lived' their desire is not a solution to the problem of death. There is no simple contrast between heterosexuality and homosexuality. On the contrary the sense of the unfinished and of imperfection is far stronger in the lives of conventional couples. And in a sub-theme, heterosexual violence – its macrocosm the Great War, its microcosm the butcher Antoine who murders his wife and children – is paralleled by a *potential* for violence in Roland and Joseph which they overcome.

Inevitably, the answer to death is the continuity of literal and metaphorical paternity. The issue of fatherhood offers a particular complexity of treatment. Again there is no simple equation between sexual orientation and good or bad fatherhood. Joseph, who had no real contact with his own father, is quite at ease with his own children: Roland is not. But their real fatherhood lies elsewhere, in a joint venture: they have a spiritual son, Martial, whom they formed, teaching him not just to read and write but to find himself mentally and physically, a form of paternity which seems deeper and more lasting than mere procreation (see Chapter 6 below). Yet Martia, like all children, has to break free of his father's influence at a certain point, his release into independent adulthood being symbolized by a spontaneous sexual initiation whose taboo-breaking character emphasizes the special nature of the triadic relationship. The meaning Martial can contribute to their relationship, though profound, is only a partial one.

The real answer to death, then, in so far as there is one, lies in writing itself. Navarre leaves us in no doubt that physical paternity, even in the spiritualized form of the 'fathering' of Martial, is far less important than creative paternity, the fathering of the text. Roland's text is composed from earlier texts, mostly by Joseph: mutual portraits, declarations of love, letters, records of incidents – attempts to 'embody' their lives which are digested and recorporealized by Roland into the final work. The process is emphasized by a recurrent image of the text as body (e.g. the skin of the notebooks), of insemination and fertilization, just as the textuality of their lives is emphasized by references to the poetry of their actions. Roland grasps his pen as he used to grasp Joseph's erection; their bodies stir and stretch between the written pages; the text is described in terms of self-fecundation and gestation. This leads to the paradox that the completion of the book will be the moment of 'real' death for their lives but the moment of birth for the preservation of the meaning of their lives. Nothing is asserted as definite, but the moments of doubt are outnumbered by the belief in the possibility of achievement.

If we put together the effect of the poetry inherent in the record of the relationship itself and the belief in the power of the text to embody that poetry in a form which will cheat death, we find a novel which projects a uniquely positive image of homosexuality and its value in life and art. Not even the fact that Navarre has set the relationship in the period 1899–1935, thereby apparently hinting that the contemporary world may have no room for such idylls, can destroy the impression that it can be good to be gay. *Le petit galopin* throws out of the window all the paraphernalia of the doomed Romantic artist-outlaw which had dominated a century of French gay writing, answering the obsessions of that tradition point for point. It offers a relationship-based, positive gay image which Navarre sets up in contrast with the dead-end sexual consumerism into which, in his eyes, the exploration of the body as tool of communication often degenerated in the post-liberation ghetto society of the 1970s and early 1980s.

The shift to positive writing in 1970s France was not as firmly established as I may have implied. Paradoxically, both the conflicting approaches which I have identified as characterizing the positive dimension of the 1970s debate about gayness – Renaud Camus's promiscuous fragmentation and Navarre's poeticization of the couple – tend, in the hands of other writers, to slide back into the negative images of the previous generation. Even the experimentalists do not seem able to emancipate themselves totally from the traditional myths. The motif of a causal connection between love and death proliferates in the fictions of Herve Guibert, for example, well before AIDS becomes their focus. From his first novel *La Mort-propagande* (1977), themes of violence, sexual aggression and non-communication abound; *Chien* (1982) records in minute detail the sado-masochistic practices of the author and a group of his friends; in *Des aveugles* (1985) wife, husband and lover kill each other. Perhaps the fullest example of a retreat into negativity is

Fou de Vincent (1989), the story of a passion for an adolescent, told in reverse chronological order from the boy's drug-induced death-fall backwards, as though struggling to identify and resurrect the impetus which initiated the relationship. The result, however, is an exercise in cancellation. The text alternates images of affection and rejection, desire and hatred, interweaving them with images of sickness; passages of poetic eroticism are countered by passages of expressionless pornography. The 'rerunning' of the affair simply highlights the non-communication which is at its heart, the same ultimate impossibility of communication which characterizes the unbridgeable 'otherness' of lovers in Proust or Cocteau. Thus Guibert's work reveals the extent to which the pursuit of pleasure as a meaning in itself, when it fails to lead to the restoration of a different kind of human communality as envisaged by Hocquenghem and to a certain extent as ostensibly experienced by Renaud Camus, creates the very isolation which it is seeking to supplant.

On the other hand, if we turn to novels by a 'defender' of the couple, such as Dominique Fernandez, we find that, despite the portrait of love fulfilled and the twin triumph over the age gap and social prejudice in *L'Etoile rose* (1978), Fernandez manifests a growing dissatisfaction with the personal possibilities of domesticity, exemplified in *Une Fleur de jasmin à l'oreille*, and a growing conviction, articulated openly in *Le Rapt de Ganymède*,[13] that homosexuality is only a creative subject for literature when it is the object of contestation. Whilst the same argument could be advanced about heterosexual relationships (i.e. that thwarted love provides the best literary inspiration), Fernandez' position leads him to appear to welcome AIDS for its restitution to gays of the status of outlaw (in *La Gloire du paria*, see below, pp. 126 and 128–9), thus taking us right back to the self-image of the outsider and the association of homosexuality with sickness and death.

It is difficult to prove that Fernandez is wrong to think that homosexuality is only a fit subject for literature in which it is oppressed. It seems to me, however, that he was addressing himself to the wrong issue. The significant question is surely whether gay writing in a post-liberation climate can not only be positive in image but at the same time address itself to broader issues, whilst fruitfully absorbing much of the previous literary tradition in the process? The proof that it can – whilst contriving to be more intellectually challenging and less inward-looking than most metropolitan gay French literature in the 1970s and early 1980s – is to be found in the work of the French-Canadian novelist and playwright Michel Tremblay. Tremblay's work is concerned with three levels of identity – sexual, social and cultural – and he treats each in some sense as a metaphor for the others.[14] He is gay, he was born in a working-class suburb of Montreal, he is a French-Canadian: each of these elements represents a separate level of oppression, but each is treated as having a positive value in itself. In particular, the issue of cultural oppression is very complex, since he has to deal with the spectre of English Canada and the USA on the one hand and with France itself on the other. Whilst distancing himself from alien Anglo-Saxon models, he tries, through complex intertextual reference, to tame the overbearing influence and image of metropolitan French culture and to draw on it for strengths in his own work, without allowing the latter to become imitative or constrained by external models and critical criteria. In the same way his exploration of homosexuality traces the difficult path between servile acceptance of heterosexual models and facile rejection of them, between conforming to heterosexual images of gayness and rebellion for the sake of it. To see how his treatment of sexuality fits into the general scheme of his writing and is affected by its place in that scheme, we have first to face the aggressively challenging way in which Tremblay uses the figure of the transvestite in his early works.

Tremblay's use of the transvestite is an excellent example of the way in which he tackles two fronts at once, whilst defusing the negative power of a symbol previously used *against* gays. The monologue *La Duchesse de Langeais* (1969) and the duologue *Hosanna* (1973) dramatize the issue of gender-linked identity in a deliberately shocking way, intended to criticize the oppressive structures of a society which compels people to *lay claim* publicly to basic aspects of their own identity rather than just have them quietly accepted or assumed. There is no question of pandering to conventional images of homosexual effeminacy or colluding with heterosexual ridicule of the sort which Genet openly and masochistically invites. Tremblay stridently asserts the right of the male to qualities and experiences traditionally labelled feminine, thus attacking the prejudices of both heterosexual convention and post-liberation gay machismo together.

The theme is expanded in a more overtly realist context in the novels, *La Duchesse et le roturier* (1982) and *Des nouvelles d'Edouard* (1984) (the third and fourth volumes in the five-volume cycle, *Chroniques du Plateau Mont-Royal*). Edouard, in adopting the transvestite identity of the Duchesse de Langeais, makes not merely a sexual protest but a *social* protest, the protest of a man born in a poor district of eastern Montreal against the social domination exercised by Outremont and the western suburbs; and a *cultural* protest against the marginalization of French Canada, laying claim to the status, within the text, of the Balzacian heroine whose name he usurps. The social issue is more thoroughly explored in *La Duchesse et le roturier*, while the cultural issue emerges in Edouard's brief trip to France in *Des nouvelles d'Edouard*. At each level of the novels it is the outcast, the 'other', who struggles against the constraints of the role to which he is condemned by society. Edouard unhesitatingly seizes on dream, pretence and lies to sustain his illusions, to create an alternative reality – something which, Tremblay suggests in his play *Le Vrai Monde?* (1989), is inherent to the writer's profession.[15] As Claude, Tremblay's alter ego, says at the end of that play: 'Lies. I've tried, through lies, to tell the truth. Worse still, I reckon I've succeeded up to a point, because I reckon what I've written is good.'

At the same period Tremblay looks at homosexuality in a more conventional form in two more narrowly focused works, the play *Les Anciennes Odeurs* (1981) and the novel *Le Coeur découvert* (1986). Characteristically, *Les Anciennes Odeurs* fits into an aspect of the plot of the later novel, whose central character, the schoolteacher Jean-Marc, is here in dialogue with his ex-lover Luc, an actor; the motif of their relationship, and another confrontation of the two characters, occurs in *Le Coeur découvert* but seen from a different angle. The play is a conversation, recreating a relationship in its positive and negative aspects and, in so doing, exploring the two incompatible models around which (as we have seen) contemporary gay lifestyle and its literary representation revolves: pleasure-based communalism and couple-based individualism. In the novel, where the focus is on alternative family units, Luc's promiscuity will be shown in a negative light. Here, it is simply a facet of difference. But what the play conveys is not the rift which the temperamental opposition of Jean-Marc and Luc might suggest, but a version of the theme touched on by Rochefort in *Printemps au parking*: the idea that there is a special level of communication between two members of the same sex who have experienced complete emotional and physical intimacy which gives them access to 'another way of being male'. Tremblay does not treat his characters as interesting or exceptional *because* they are homosexual. Homosexuality is neither a curse nor a blessing in this play: it is merely a fact. But at the same time it is a fact which creates an opportunity. Because Jean-Marc and Luc have undergone, man to man, the physical intimacy of passion, not just as sex but as *love*, they have also learnt the hard way something which is no less forbidden to 'normal' men in Western culture, whether in their commerce with other men or with the opposite sex: the intimacy of the word. They have acquired a special gift of verbal communication which affects the effectiveness of the emotions, particularly tenderness. The transvestites of the early plays challenge even the gay reader as symbols of oppression and revolt; the characters of *Les Anciennes Odeurs* move us by the achievement they represent in real human terms. And, characteristically, this achievement has an implicit social element. Class and age difference is no longer a fascination with the 'other' as in an earlier gay tradition; these barriers have also been transcended through the special gift of communication which same-sex intimate relations bestow on their participants.

Le Coeur découvert forms its own intertext with portraits of conventional heterosexual family units in Tremblay's *Chroniques*. It too privileges plurality of experience (not for nothing is its subtitle *roman d'amours*) and the special communication to which homosexual love has access, but its focus is contrastive rather than merely comparative. At the centre of the novel Jean-Marc's new relationship with a much younger man, Mathieu, who turns out to have been married and to have a four-year-old son, Sebastien, stands in explicit opposition to the relationship between Mathieu's ex-wife Louise and her new husband Gaston. Tremblay sets up, through this central opposition, a wider commentary on the inade-

quacy of conventional social structures, inviting comparison between the special understanding which informs the irregular social
unit constituted by Jean-Marc, Mathieu and Sebastien on the one
hand and Jean-Marc's lesbian friends on the other, and the destructive rivalries and tensions which characterize Louise's second marriage and the couple's relationship to Gaston's male-chauvinist
dominated family. There is nothing Utopian about the portrayal of
the gays, male or female: it pinpoints the habitual dangers of unfettered egotism and the ghetto mentality among homosexuals, who,
having refused to accept the external checks and balances of conventional social structures, are obliged to create their own internal
ones. Equally the heterosexual characters are not all negatively
drawn; Louise is a perceptive sympathetic figure, and Gaston is
presented as the victim of his homophobic upbringing and family
environment. But the novel does offer a potentially liberating model
of a family unit, and the values which it promotes through the study
of its central emotional relationships are clearly intended to offer its
gay readers a positive example of the potential inherent in gay love
in general.

The strength of Tremblay's work, as far as the question of
self-image is concerned, is that in one combined move it rejects all
sense of guilt and countercharges with a claim of superior sensibility. The thrust of its argument is twofold: first, by integrating the
experience of sexual oppression into a broader spectrum of class
and cultural oppression, it emphasizes that homosexuals are
victims and not transgressors, that their 'otherness' is an arbitrary
division and not an essence; second, it asserts the special qualities in
gay experience in general, and gay relationships in particular, from
which both the individual and the community can benefit. Tremblay's texts could not have been written by a metropolitan writer;
they are too firmly rooted in the circumstances of French Canada,
where gay sexuality in particular is caught between the US model of
ghetto promiscuity and the repressiveness of a singularly puritani-
cal indigenous brand of Roman Catholic morality.

It is interesting to contrast Tremblay's work with a very
different product of French-Canadian gay art, Jean Beaudin's grip-
ping and very moving film *Being at Home with Claude* (1992, from
the play by René-Daniel Dubois).[16] The theme, the interrogation of

Yves, a rent-boy who has murdered his middle-class 'straight' student lover, has ingredients of the traditional negative self-image: the otherness of class difference, motifs of sexual decadence and crime, the equation of love and death. But in Beaudin's treatment these elements are deliberately emptied of their usual symbolic value, leaving the viewer with a sense of the real value of the relationship itself, the emotional and physical oneness achieved by the two young men, for which the intense physicality of the opening images of the film is itself a metaphor. The sexual closeness of Yves and Claude has abolished class and intellectual differences *for them*. But that abolition cannot hold good outside Claude's flat, because society will not recognize it. Consequently, although it was Yves who killed Claude while the relationship was at its apogee – killed him, indeed, precisely because the relationship had nowhere to go but down – it is society which emerges as responsible for the murder, in that it was society's values which rendered the survival of such a relationship impossible. The film reflects the same indivisible link between social and sexual oppression as much of Tremblay's work does, but from the viewpoint of defeat. Between them, *Le Coeur découvert* and *Being at Home with Claude*, thus create an intertext which embodies the negative and positive poles of the same socially and culturally rebellious gay self-image in a distinctively French-Canadian form, demonstrating the potential of gayness, the need to reject a ghetto mentality and the extent to which that ghetto is imposed from outside by society.

If we look back at the way in which gay male self-perception and its representation develop in French literature over the twentieth century (at least until the advent of AIDS), we find certain basic patterns. There are three main phases: in the first, a discourse of sexual otherness as deviance and inadequacy is developed; in the second, there is an attempt to redefine that otherness in neutral terms as a simple *difference*; in the third, the redefined 'difference' is examined and developed in terms of its social, metaphysical and aesthetic implications. Underlying these phases is the persistence of recurrent motifs which have their roots in a negative discourse but which certain writers manage eventually to discard, neutralize or even absorb into a positive discourse. And cutting across both these patterns are fundamental binary oppositions – flesh and spirit, sex and love, straight and gay, same and other – which individual writers choose to highlight or, on the contrary, to synthesize. Probably the only tenet which all the writers I have considered hold in common is the essentialist view that homosexuality is an innate condition over which the individual has no control. But even here we can distinguish three distinct groups: those who see the innate nature of sexual orientation as predetermining the totality of an individual's character (e.g. Proust); those (e.g. Bory) who see it as creating a neutral 'fact' akin to, and no more significant than, the colour of one's hair; and those (like Camus and Hocquenghem) who see it as a 'fact' which can be exploited by the individual as the basis for a different approach to human relations.

The main problem of the literary representation of adult male gayness has been its dual subordination to a language of Romantic rebellion, outlawry and sickness, and to patriarchal principles of division and classification. It has only been through a refusal to accept the validity of such principles that writers have begun to transcend the limits imposed upon them by the inherited discourse. The arch-synthesizer in this respect is Michel Tremblay, who overrides such fundamental conventional divisions as truth and lie, art and life, tradition and experiment in his quest to portray the complexity of individual and social identities. At the same time the most effective transcendence of tradition has been achieved by those, like Tremblay, who absorb it rather than reject it. All this interplay of division and synthesis makes perfect sense if we consider the intrinsic paradox of homosexual desire. It is the pursuit of that which is the same (male) and yet other (another male); it reflects both what a male already is (sameness) and what he desires to be (otherness). Within its inherent duality it can accommodate almost unlimited elements of difference (class, age, looks, intellect, temperament) without ever completely cancelling the element of similarity, and vice versa. Consequently, the achievement of group unity (gay liberation) facilitates the explosion of diversity (e.g. lifestyle debates), which in turn generates a literary experimentalism which is nonetheless constrained by the terms of the tradition against which it reacts.

Notes

1.   Quoted in Daniel Garcia, *Jean-Louis Bory* (Paris: Flammarion, 1991), p. 210.

2.   Quoted in George Stambolian and Elaine Marks, *Homosexualities and French Literature: Cultural Contexts/Critical Texts* (Ithaca and London: Cornell University Press, 1979), p. 112. (The interview is reproduced in English translation. I suspect that 'wants' has been used to render *veut*, which would in fact mean *intends* in this context.)

3.   In May 1968 student unrest, stemming from dissatisfaction with the French University system, led to the closure of the Sorbonne, an act which in turn led to further unrest, strikes and riots. The trade unions seized on the situation as an excuse to call a general strike, and the students occupied the Sorbonne buildings. Although the immediate outcome of the 'events' was an overwhelming victory for the Gaullist party in the June parliamentary elections, the long-term political and social effects were profound, not least because the mobilization of radical forces outside the political system set a trend which the Gaullists could not reverse.

4.   In practice, even heterosexual men *have* suffered from a literary stereotyping that defined rules of 'manliness', which excluded the emotions and privileged mindless physicality, thus causing a crisis of confidence in men whose intelligence and sensitivity set them at odds with the stereotypes. It was not until the late 1960s that such stereotypes were seriously challenged.

5.   See Jonathan Dollimore, *Sexual Dissidence: Augustine to Wilde, Freud to Foucault* (Oxford: Clarendon Press, 1991), pp. 206–9, 211–12.

6.   'De l'amitié comme mode de vie', *Gai Pied* 25, April 1981. See also James Miller, *The Passion of Michel Foucault* (London: Harper Collins, 1993), pp. 258–9.

7.   Renaud Camus, *Notes achriennes* (Paris: POL, 1982), pp. 212–17, covering the sections headed 'L'Enclave', 'Triste histoire', 'Scandale', 'Corps constitués', 'Masque de chair' and 'S. M. VII'.

8.   The intention of those who initiated what came to be known as the *nouveau roman* in the 1960s was to find new literary techniques to replace those of a nineteenth-century mirror-realism which they thought inappropriate to twentieth-century perceptions of the nature of reality and of the problems of 'transcribing' the world into language. By the 1980s, however, writers were using these techniques for a multiplicity of purposes quite different from those for which they had originally been designed.

9. Attributed to Navarre by Gabrielle Rolin in her review of *Killer* in *Le Monde des livres*, 18 April 1975, pp. 19–20.

10. Tournier's *Le Roi des aulnes* (1970) has a strong pederastic under-current, and there is an implicit homoerotic element in *Vendredi ou les limbes* (1969), his reworking of the Robinson Crusoe story, but it is only in *Les Météores* that homosexuality becomes a central theme in his work.

11. For an account of these novels, see Jennifer Birkett, *The Sins of the Fathers: Decadence in France 1870–1914* (London:Quartet Books, 1986), pp. 163–8.

12. For a different intertextual use of the same texts, see below, ch. 6, pp. 168 and 170.

13. *Le Rapt de Ganymède* (Paris: Grasset, 1989), pp. 299–300.

14. Tremblay promotes a form of ongoing rebellion, where minorities – or at least groups traditionally excluded from power – can be-come progressive forces for change in their 'community' if they are prepared to try to leave their ghettoes without sacrificing their individuality. This holds good whether the disenfranchised group is gays or women or the working class *within* the province of Quebec, Quebec *within* Canada, or the Francophone author *within* French culture.

15. Some of Tremblay's thoughts on the writer and his art are to be found in two interviews which he gave on a visit to London in 1990, the first with Clare Bayley in *What's on in London* (14–21 February 1990), the second with David Oliver Crake in *Gay Times*, March 1990, pp. 48–51.

16. For factual details about the film, see the (not very perceptive) review in *Sight and Sound*, June 1993, p. 48. For a critical appreci-ation of it, see the briefer and more sensitive review in *Gay Times*, June 1993, p. 80. What I have described as 'the intense physicality of the opening images' the *Gay Times* reviewer defines more baldly as 'what must surely rate as the hottest gay fuck scene ever passed by the British film censor'.

Chapter five

AIDS Writing in France and the Gay Self-image

'The shock-wave of AIDS has brought monsters of a
species we thought extinct surging out of the depths of
our collective imagination.'

● *Alain-Emmanuel Dreuilhe*[1]

SINCE awareness of AIDS became general in the mid-
1980s, all gay male writers have ostensibly been faced with the
choice of silence or speech: choosing to face the issue or choosing to
avoid it. This choice is imposed on them precisely because of the
identification of AIDS with male homosexuals by the media and by
the set of concealed public assumptions which have derived from
that identification. AIDS can be contracted by heterosexuals; it can
be transmitted in infected blood, notably through the shared use of
needles by drug-takers. But in popular mythology, there is an assumption that infected sperm absorbed in anal sex is the sole
vehicle for transmitting the virus. Conforming to this pattern for its
own reasons, we shall see how AIDS writing in France never concerns itself primarily with heterosexual relationships, with drug-
taking or with the plight of haemophiliacs or others infected by
blood transfusions. Even where male/female relationships are
features, as in the novels of Cyril Collard, the AIDS theme itself still
derives from, and focuses on, the promiscuous gay sex which is
central to the experience of the novels' bisexual heroes. And

although Bernard in Dominique Fernandez' novel *La Gloire du paria* does contract AIDS as a result of a blood transfusion, it is still his identity as a gay man with AIDS on which the novel centres. It is in fact impossible to write about AIDS without writing, explicitly or implicitly, about gayness; as Lee Edelman puts it:

> As a historical phenomenon in the so-called Western democracies it [i.e. AIDS] has itself taken shape (been given shape) as that which writes or articulates another subject altogether: a subject whose content is suggested but not exhausted by reference to 'male' homosexuality.[2]

And the corollary of this is that it is impossible, in the late 1980s and 1990s to write about being gay without writing about AIDS.

If it is impossible, then why did I initially say that writers have a choice between silence and speech? The fact is that omission is itself a form of statement. If speech is direct representation of the issue, silence becomes indirect representation of it. Adam Mars-Jones, in the introduction to his collection of short stories on AIDS-related issues, *Monopolies of Loss*, presents the choice in more brutal terms when he says: 'Denial and apocalyptic brooding each has its attractions.' By 'denial' he means refusal to grant the disease a central role in gay experience. At one point, in looking for a potentially positive alternative to AIDS-centred literature, he proposes that the truly responsible course of action for the contemporary gay writer might be seen as the production of 'sexy nostalgic fiction set in the period before the epidemic, safeguarding, if only in fantasy, the endangered gains of gay liberation'. He presumably has in mind a work such as Alan Hollinghurst's *The Swimming Pool Library*. Such a form of silence is governed by the very topic it conspicuously avoids; it acknowledges that it is a major problem for the gay writer that in writing about AIDS he automatically contributes to a public mythology which equates homosexuality with disease and death. More precisely, it reinforces a public mythology which gives a moral basis to the procreational sex/recreational sex opposition by setting the equation heterosexuality = monogamy = procreation = life against the equation homosexuality = promiscuity = disease = death. Note that heterosexual sex, in this mythology, is *never* recreational, whilst homosexuality, by default, is never seen as even metaphorically procreational.

The importance of public mythology is underlined in Fernandez' *La Gloire du paria*. Bernard has gone to discuss his proposed play with Xavier, the representative of the socially sophisticated but non-intellectual section of the gay community in Paris. When Bernard announces that the subject of the play will be AIDS, Xavier exclaims:

> 'It's not the moment, with Le Pen taking one vote in ten and the Socialists falling apart, to go around saying to people: "You were right; if you're born deformed it is because there's a curse on you." That's the only effect your play will have. The less talk there is about AIDS, the better. Life is complicated enough for us already, without our washing our dirty linen in public.'

In fact, as we shall see, however quietist *non*-intellectual French gay circles may be, denial or silence is emphatically not a method of safeguarding the gains of gay liberation which French writers (notably Collard and Hocquenghem) who try to paint a positive picture of non-monogamous sexual behaviour consider appropriate.

There is, however, another form of silence raised by Mars-Jones which does occur in French AIDS writing. Mars-Jones found that his own problems in writing about AIDS were overwhelmingly attached to the *name* of the condition. By suppressing that – he wrote a story using the name 'Slim', a term which is used in parts of Africa for AIDS – he was suddenly able to write about the epidemic. James W. Jones comparably argues that the name AIDS evokes certain negative images which reduce the ability to transcend the limits which the images themselves impose. But Jones is thinking less of the author's problems than of the reader's. Precisely because the reader will automatically equate homosexuality with AIDS, he argues, the writer should not articulate that equation, since to do so is to return to the old identification of homosexuality with illness which the gay liberation movement had striven to eradicate. By describing the effects of the virus but denying it the symbolic power of its name, the author will marginalize it, retaining a focus on the individual or community instead, and drawing the reader into a sympathetic experience of that individual's (or community's) problems.

There are indeed French writers who avoid the term 'AIDS' in this way, but it is difficult to generalize about the effect of this 'silence' in the way in which Jones does for contemporary US fiction. The silence, in French texts, represents different things in different contexts. In Jean-Noel Pancrazi's *Les Quartiers d'hiver*, for example, the way in which the *habitués* of 'Le Vagabond' use the term *le mal mauve* (the mauve disease) instead of *le sida* (AIDS), symbolizes precisely their escapism, the way in which the gay community itself, or at least a section of it, cannot cope with the reality of what is happening to it. By denying the virus its name, they shut out its implications, just as they shut their eyes to the thinning of their ranks. Suppression of the name 'AIDS' in *Les Quartiers d'hiver* thus becomes part of the theme of absence, itself associated with a whole imagery of decline and sterility (of which the reference to winter in the title is a part).

By contrast, the suppression of the term in Cyril Collard's *Condamné amour* relates to the fact that the disease *itself* has a symbolic function within the novel. The 'divine virus' with which Sylvain is infected is, as Professor Meyer puts it to Carole and Bertrand, 'a sickness of modernity'. As such it represents a whole series of motifs of decline and disintegration – emotional, erotic, social and spiritual – which stand in opposition to the theme of the transcendent value of writing. The 'virus' is not just AIDS; it is also Sylvain's obsession with the image of Thomas, or his obsession with transforming experience into text. To use the term *le sida* would therefore be to risk focusing on only a small part of the symbolic value of the disease. Then again, the 'terrible sickness' from which Adam, the hero of Guy Hocquenghem's *Eve*, is already suffering at the start of the novel and which kills him on its last page, is also never named. But the reason for this equally symbolic anonymity is a very different one. Hocquenghem has no desire to play down the experience of the disease itself, as Pancrazi or Collard tend to: frequent scenes are devoted throughout the book to Adam's fever, his aphasia, and to his eventual decline and death in hospital. But the structure of the novel depends on the interplay of a series of myths, of which a rewritten Genesis myth is the overriding one. Hocquenghem therefore avoids the particular set of associations which the term 'AIDS' would bring with it, so as not to create an imbalance between it and the governing mythology of the narrative.

Perhaps more important than the absence of the name *le sida* in these texts are the words which the writers use *instead*. If silence is just another form of periphrasis, another way of indicating AIDS via indirection, so are the replacement metaphors used by Pancrazi, Collard and Hocquenghem. Such metaphors in fact create a bridge to texts in which writers address the problem of AIDS openly, such as Alain-Emmanuel Dreuilhe's *Corps à corps: journal du sida*, in that both groups use metaphors which fall into the same main categories: (1) a thoroughly phallocratic military vocabulary, as in Pancrazi's image of Parisian gays as 'defeated soldiers wandering in the shadow of the walls of a city which they had even forgotten that they had ever once wanted to conquer'; and (2) a medical vocabulary with discomforting associated or reflected meanings, e.g. *la peste* (plague), *le mal* (illness). The habitués of 'Le Vagabond' in *Les Quartiers d'hiver*, by using the phrase *le mal mauve* (the mauve disease), subconsciously accept a heterosexual classification of the condition: the connotations of *mauve* (e.g. the mauve decade) make the illness a specifically gay one, whilst under the innocent meaning of *mal* = illness lies the more sinister *reflected* meaning *mal* = evil. Thus, whilst, as I said earlier, suppression of the name *le sida* becomes part of the theme of evasion, the substitute term chosen indicates acceptance of guilt.

The problems of this sort of metaphorical language are outlined by Susan Sontag in *AIDS and Its Metaphors*, but Sontag is largely concerned with writing by non-gays. It is a mark of the difficulties facing gay writers on AIDS in any language that they are unable to break away from systems of metaphor borrowed from 'the enemy', as it were. Dreuilhe's *Corps à corps* is an extended cadenza on interrelated, ornamented military images, and even Guibert, the least susceptible of writers to these sorts of clichés, cannot escape from the natural militarism of the language of medicine: 'each reinjection of the AIDS virus ... *launches a fresh attack* on the already contaminated sick man', and 'the AIDS virus *attacks* first, weakening the *defences* of the immune system by stages' (my italics).

For a gay writer to choose silence on the topic of AIDS is, as we have seen, merely for him to approach the subject indirectly. What about direct approaches? Mars-Jones refers to 'apocalyptic brooding', but this is only one of a number of possible stances, based on a range of thematic and formal preoccupations. There are two obvious perspectives from which to view the functioning of AIDS texts. The first is thematic, ethical, political in the broad sense; the second is formal, under which heading I include not only such issues as structure and narrative voice but also strategies for inserting the text into the existing literary tradition. Taken together these two perspectives provide us with a third, one which can roughly be described as a reception perspective: the relationship with the *reader* which the text seems to establish through its particular combination of themes and forms. Let us look at the literature of AIDS from these angles.

Thematically, there are three main groups of concrete motifs which recur across a number of AIDS texts. The first is the experience of the syndrome and of attempts to treat it and the infections which it permits. In some French texts, notably the novels of Collard, the experience of the syndrome itself, as opposed to the fact of being marked by it, is relatively unimportant; thus in *Les Nuits fauves* the paragraphs devoted to the narrator's trips to the clinic, his sarcomas, his AZT treatment are rare and laconic, sufficing simply to give the medical condition a genuine physical presence in the novel. In other works there is more focus on the problems of diagnosis and treatment than on the experience of the individual: Chapter 9 of *La Gloire du paria*, for example, describes a visit to a clinic which is also a research unit, the main function of the scene being to satirize the way in which the medical establishment is more concerned with intellectual rivalry and international glory than with curing patients. But in a significant group of works, ranging from Dreuilhe's *Corps à corps* to the Guibert trilogy and his *Cytomegalovirus*, the relationship between the infected individual and the virus is the focus of the whole work. Mars-Jones, with a characteristically Anglo-Saxon reluctance to accept a blurring of the distinction between fiction and documentary, expresses doubt as to whether the novel as a genre is capable of containing a medical narrative of this kind: 'in any individual case of AIDS the virus has a narrative of its own, a story it wants to tell, which is in danger of taking over'. Less easily intimidated, French writers, whether in ostensibly non-fictional or fictional texts, approach the problem of the medical narrative in just this sort of way, precisely in order to explore the psychological and metaphorical implications of a 'take-over' by the virus.

The second main group of concrete motifs explores the response of others – society, parents, friends and lovers. *La Gloire du paria* gives considerable space to the issue of heterosexual responses to AIDS, defining them in terms of ignorance, prejudice and panic. These responses are both represented in the action of the novel – after a television feature on AIDS in New York, the local butcher will no longer let his son serve a known homosexual such as Marc – and are also made a subject of debate between Marc and Bernard. These debates are simply settings for two voices of the kind of reflective soliloquy which Dreuilhe conducts in *Corps à corps* on the social death which dying from an AIDS-related disease occasions, on the heterosexual feeling that gays have only 'got what they were asking for', or on the desire of the general public to remain ignorant.

However, this detached analysis of general attitudes is rare. For the most part, in dealing with the responses of others, French AIDS texts focus on the implications of AIDS for those close to its victims, portraying betrayal by a friend (Guibert's *A l'ami qui ne m'a pas sauvé la vie*), the response of families, whether positive (Fernandez' *La Gloire du paria*, Manière's *A ceux qui l'ont aimé*) or negative (Navarre's *Ce sont amis que vent emporte*), and the emotional torments of the lover who survives his beloved, whether briefly (*Ce sont amis que vent emporte*) or more permanently (*A ceux qui l'ont aimé*). The last-named is a particularly interesting case in that the narrator is an ex-lover. Manière makes the point that his devotion, both before and after his death, is thus an act of choice. Only in *Les Nuits fauves* is the question of the partner who is endangered without his or her knowledge (Laura) featured, but both *Les Nuits fauves* and Guibert's *Le Protocole compassionel* portray scenes of wilful risk: in the former, Laura and Samy, now knowing the narrator to be HIV positive, choose to have unprotected penetrative sex with him; and in the latter Djanluca specifies his reason for sodomizing Guibert (without a condom) on the terrace in Elba as the desire to dice with death. In fact, the status of the motif of 'the response of others' in various texts is so dependent on its relation to other motifs, and on such formal questions as narrative voice, that its thematic significance is less monolithic than might seem the case at first sight.

The third main group of concrete motifs concerns the re-examination of the victim's values and lifestyle and of how he came to contract AIDS. This is the thematic area in which the texts present the greatest unity, the only exception being *A ceux qui l'ont aimé*, which ignores the dead man's past. *La Gloire du paria* is a little different from the other texts in that, despite Bernard's fascination with back rooms, he leads a blameless monogamous existence, his death ironically the result of an infected blood transfusion. But even in this case Bernard and Marc, in their ritual suicide, voluntarily assume the kind of gay identity which society has automatically attributed to them: Bernard dies without knowing, and Marc without revealing, that the infection was an accident rather than the result of sexual contact. In other texts, the victims have at some point enjoyed multiple sexual relations, often anonymously promiscuous, of a sort which lie outside the norms of Judaeo-Christian heterosexual morality. In *A l'ami qui ne m'a pas sauvé la vie* Muzil, the Foucault character and the first of Guibert's friends to die of AIDS, is described as adoring violent orgies in San Francisco saunas, whilst in Chapter 19 Guibert lists some of the sexual adventures, stretching back over a period of eight years, in which he and his equally infected married lover Jules have indulged. In Pancrazi's *Les Quartiers d'hiver* the dead painter Joep regularly indulged in sado-masochistic orgies; in *Ce sont amis que vent emporte* Roch and David are infected through a threesome with Zachary; in Hocquenghem's *Eve* Adam continues an irregular sex life even though infected, conducting a threesome with his 'niece' Eve and the black Seth. And in *Les Nuits fauves* the narrator alternates sexual encounters with Laura, Samy or Jamel, with bouts of anonymous group sex in open-air Parisian cruising-spots.

Only in three texts – *La Gloire du paria*, *Corps à corps* and *Les Quartiers d'hiver* – have I found non-monogamous sex to be in any way held up for our disapproval. In the first two of these texts there is no consistent acceptance of society's values, although Dreuilhe's espousal of chastity can be seen as a negation of his sexual identity, as can Bernard's declaration: 'If my turn came to be infected, I should be led to examine my conscience and to ask myself in what way, by my lifestyle, I have contravened the order of the world.' It is the Joep sections of *Les Quartiers d'hiver*, with their identification of the physical with the evil and the spiritual with good, which offer the only open, systematic critique of a promiscuous gay lifestyle, and they do so in a moralizing tone: 'How could there co-exist in Joep such a fervent desire for the ideal and such a need to degrade himself?' But the very terms of this critique reveal its roots in a literary tradition which we met in Chapter 2, the Romantic image of the artist-outcast, and this tradition carries its own redemptive element, the Baudelairean vision of corrupt experience as a necessary stimulant to the artist's imagination. Other writers – Collard, Navarre, Guibert – defiantly refuse to make any identification between the accident of physical responsibility – promiscuity inevitably risks facilitating the spread of the virus – and moral blame.

Classifying the texts thematically tells us something about the balance of their preoccupations, but it is not a very interesting exercise in any other respect. However, with these three groups of concrete motifs, centred on the virus, on the attitudes of society in general and of those close to the victim in particular, and on the victim's lifestyle, particularly his sex life, we can associate a number of abstract motifs, familiar to us from earlier chapters, which link the texts in a potentially more interesting way, opening up onto formal issues which we have not yet considered. With the theme of the attitude of others we can associate the related motifs of *otherness*, the victim's own sense of difference, and of *solitude*; and with the themes of sexual lifestyle and of the virus itself we can associate the Romantic interrelation of love and death, Eros and Thanatos. Let us start with the awareness of difference.

As we have seen earlier, most gay literature is charged, positively or negatively, with a sense of difference, of being other. In *La*

Gloire du paria this otherness is seen at first as a matter of age and temperament. Bernard, in his forties, represents a generation of homosexuals forced to define themselves against the norms of a hostile society; his domesticated young partner, Marc, cocoons himself within the comfortable pseudo-heterosexual norms of a generation which feels a degree of social acceptance. AIDS is the catalyst which, by causing society to reject homosexuals again, gives back to Bernard his pariah status, a status with which Marc associates himself by the final act of suicide. In Collard, Hocquenghem, Guibert and Pancrazi, otherness is emphasized as a function of lifestyle rather than generation, and, in the latter two, awareness of otherness crystallizes in a sense of complete solitude as death approaches. Henri Marsan, in an article in *Le Figaro littéraire*, emphasizes the importance of this motif of solitude, and links it to the theme of the interrelation of love and death via sin, guilt and fear.[3] In AIDS texts, he claims, death is presented as a punishment for having lived alone, for rejecting society's requirement to procreate, and above all for raising pleasure to the status of a valid end in itself. The first stage of this punishment is 'a dizzying dive into solitude' as the AIDS victim, leper-like, becomes 'other' even to his fellow gays; the second stage is his total annihilation, since in death 'the AIDS victim leaves nothing behind him'. This highly moralistic reading fails completely to account for the way in which, in a majority of the texts, otherness, solitude and the Eros and Thanatos motif are redeemed through association with a set of motifs both concrete and abstract very familiar to us in earlier versions of the pariah myth and which override the motifs we have looked at so far: art and the artist in general, and the writer, writing and the writing of the work in hand in particular.

It is, of course, impossible to consider art and writing as themes separately from the question of the *form* of the texts themselves, the actual practice of writing which they embody, since all reference within a work to the act of literary creation produces a self-referential system, the work commenting on the theory and the theory commenting upon the work. So before we look at art and the artist as motifs, let us look swiftly at the second of the perspectives which I proposed earlier: the form of the texts and the authors' often self-conscious attempts to insert them into pre-existing literary traditions.

Like all modern gay authors, French writers on AIDS have to reconcile the desire to speak about the world as it is, both for the benefit of other homosexuals (solidarity, self-affirmation, reassurance) and to enlighten the 'straight' reader, with the need to avoid any sort of traditional realism that will reinforce heterosexual, patriarchal norms (a problem similar to that faced by women writers). They also have to face a further dilemma. Since the 1960s most French intellectuals, and consequently to a significant extent French creative writers, have been conscious of the problem of defining a relationship between the real world and a linguistic representation of it, particularly in fiction. Renaud Camus, in *Elégies pour quelques-uns* – a text whose reflections on the theme of absence are to some extent inspired precisely by the AIDS crisis – sums up the point perfectly when he defines books as the instruments of the double and reciprocal absence of both author and reader.[4] This poses major problems for AIDS fiction, since much of it is attempting to preserve either the writer or his beloved in literature, to overcome a threatened or actual absence in the real world by creating a permanence in language. The writers are trying, in other words, to find ways of creating a presence from two absences. How do they go about this? Mars-Jones, from the perspective of the English novel, reflects perplexedly:

> In any novel about AIDS there are likely to be rites of passage, hard to avoid but hard to reshape, retroviral equivalents of the Stations of the Cross: first knowledge of the epidemic, first friend sick, first death, first symptom. ... How do you tell a fresh story when the structure is set?

French writers seem to find this structure not only easy to reshape but easy to avoid altogether; the texts are notable for their formal diversity. The difficulty for the critic is that points of apparent formal similarity are frequently misleading. Pancrazi and Fernandez, for example, eschew traditional narrative to the extent that neither uses plot to shape his novel. But this plotlessness is used to entirely different effect in the two novels concerned. *Les Quartiers d'hiver* takes its focus from *place*, the bar 'Le Vagabond', and from a series of character sketches of the bar's *habitués*. But that suggests a sense of the definite present which does not quite exist in the book. The text is framed as a first-person narrative, but the narrator is elusive. Unlike the characters whom he summons up, he has no physical identity himself; and within his narration the text shifts to the pages of the already-dead Joep's notebooks. At the same time the temporal sequence of the novel is fragmented because it records people and events filtered through memory. In other words, the 'present' of narration disguises a constant 'absent' of the narrated. What *is* constantly present, on the other hand, is a system of recurrent metaphors, particularly of darkness, winter and decline. For example:

> The winter night had come inside. There was snow swirling in the mirrors of the *Vagabond*, which became fogged around the silhouettes of customers who, in the lustreless icy depths of the glass, were like prisoners asleep on their feet in a velvet hell. Christian drew me back gently to his chest; there were too many trees felled around us without our getting wind of what was happening. God was only a cheating lumberjack who, profiting from the fact that the earth became blind in winter, sneaked up with muffled tread and smothered the children who still loved one another in the secret of the snowy forests.

Rather than a story about a specific death or deaths, the text thus becomes a poetic reflection on, and dramatization of, the general experience of decline, loss and absence.

The structure of *La Gloire du paria* works on an entirely different principle. Its omniscient narration is divided into chapters which are first and foremost expositions of themes, almost miniessays; character, setting and action are subordinated not to *metaphor* this time, but to the exposition of a series of ideas, largely through a running dialogue between Bernard and Marc. Thus, in Chapter 1 Bernard presents the concept of the pariah, the man who can only define his identity through his rejection of and by society; in Chapter 2 Marc counters with the argument, using Genet as his example, that it is no longer possible for a homosexual to define himself in terms of social transgression; Chapter 3 then looks at the generation gap between the two lovers and relates it to the differences in values which the opening chapters have revealed. Fernandez uses this structure to play off against one another a series of opposing terms – security versus uncertainty, acceptance versus rejection, contentment versus suffering – in such a way that the apparently negative terms are represented as necessary to any form of positive experience. As Bernard puts it in his interior monologue in Chapter 7: 'But suffering is the guarantee of the authenticity of real emotion; the modern world, by turning its back on pain, has deprived itself of the means of experiencing the passions in all their profundity and beauty.' Accordingly, AIDS becomes the perfect emblem of suffering, as Fernandez re-expresses the equation homosexuality = death in the neo-Romantic form: death = the justification for, and apotheosis of, love.

Plotlessness of varying sorts is in fact frequent in French AIDS fiction, a fact which can be made to fit with the removal of the possibility of development from the characters' lives by the imposition of an arbitrary and untimely ending, in physical decline and death. But plotlessness is not universal. Hocquenghem's *Eve*, for example, has a perceptible story-line, as do the Collard novels, although the status of plot in *Eve* is affected by the mythological element and in Collard's *Condamné amour* by the impossibility of determining whether and where the action shifts between the real and the fantastic. What is more, where conventional plot is absent, what replaces it varies considerably, and the variation is not explicable merely in terms of the presence or absence of a given theme or themes. The form of *La Gloire du paria* (which is in fact relatively conventional in most respects) serves simply to emphasize the intellectual arguments. *Ce sont amis que vent emporte*, a novel whose thematic focus is also the reversal of the negative implications of the love = death equation, is quite different in form. Clearly, then, listing the formal differences between novels with similar themes is unlikely to yield much of interest. But there *are* groupings of features which are worth noting, because they seem to have direct relevance to the issues of gay identity and reader-reception, the issues toward which I am working.

The greatest formal similarity between the French AIDS narratives I have read is that almost all of them are couched in the first-person singular as the primary or sole narrative voice. Of the two texts which avoid first-person narration, *Condamné amour* and *La Gloire du paria*, the latter uses a great deal of dialogue and interior monologue to give its characters some equivalent direct access to the reader. However, the fact that first-person narration predominates is less significant than it sounds, because it hides important differences. In *Eve* and *Les Nuits fauves* the 'I' is not speaking from an identifiable 'present of writing' of the sort used by the first-person voice in an autobiography; in all the other texts the 'I' does exactly that, such that there is no immediate difference between the narrative voice of non-fiction texts such as Dreuilhe's *Corps à corps* or Jean-Paul Aron's *Mon sida* and that of the Guibert, Navarre or Manière texts. This, however, is another oversimplification. In *Eve* the text shifts constantly between omniscient third-person narration and the voice of Adam. The novel deals with a number of different time-layers, but there is no definite link between any specific time-layer and either form of storytelling. In *Les Nuits fauves* the first-person narration is constant, but the first third of the novel is told in the past historic (the traditional tense of *written* past narration), the rest in a dramatic present. In both novels what counts is the shift itself, because the shift relates to a thematic change. Adam's first-person narration concentrates on his relationship with Eve and on his experience of illness. He dies, symbolically, in the third person at the very moment that his (healthy) incestuously conceived replacement is born. In *Les Nuits fauves* the narrator moves into a present sequence as his relationship with Laura develops, and simultaneously he develops full-blown AIDS, in the form of Karposi sarcomas. In these two novels, then, the first-person voice is part of a novelistic strategy for highlighting certain themes.

If we take the group of texts with a consistently autobiographical voice, we find that they too fall into different groups. All these texts use a reflective first person, and incorporate diary entries and letters to give different perspectives. But in *Les Quartiers d'hiver* the shadowy narrator is hardly more than a voyeur-figure, even if his biographical and moral reflections set the tone for the material for which they provide a framework. In *Ce sont amis que vent emporte* and *A ceux qui l'ont aimé* the narrator reflects on the illness and death of his lover. In the Guibert trilogy the narrator records the history of his own movement towards death. These differences of relationship between narrator and narrated are marked by a difference in the relationship between fiction and reality. *Les Quartiers d'hiver* only gives a sense of the 'present tense of writing', of the sort which characterizes autobiography, in its last three pages, as the narrator prepares to leave the dying world of 'Le Vagabond' and the Paris of which it is the microcosm; prior to that the novel uses the past historic, the tense of traditional storytelling.

The two novels which are 'recounted' from the perspective of a lover, *Ce sont amis que vent emporte* and *A ceux qui l'ont aimé*, use *fiction* more self-consciously. The eleventh chapter of *Ce sont amis*, immediately after the account of how the lovers were infected by Zachary, is entitled 'Fiction de David' and shifts into the third person. Equally, the final chapter, recounting Roch's death, resorts to the eighteenth-century convention of guaranteeing the 'true' status of the preceding narrative through the pen of a third character, the anonymous Doctor K. Thus the ambiguity between *real* and *fictional*, which I noted earlier as important to the plot of *Condamné amour*, is here resolved into a formal opposition: the truth as voiced by Roch, the projection of David's truth onto him by Roch, and the rather awkward appeal to the traditions of eighteenth-century realism to guarantee the *plausibility* of the narrative as a whole. *A ceux qui l'ont aimé* confronts the issue even more directly. It consists of a first-person autobiographical-style narrative, which itself announces in its first section that its narrator has had an idea for a short story, and a third-person narrative, entitled '*L'intercesseur*', a short story which is offered as an answer to the central problem of the text – how someone with no religious belief is to sustain a sense of his lost lover's presence. This short story is prefaced by a statement equating the truth-value of *both* sections of the book:

> You will recognise that this is the short story announced in the first chapter of the preceding narrative. Just as the authenticity of the latter was proportionate to its scrupulous conformity to lived experience, so the truthfulness of the former derives from its invention.

In the Guibert trilogy this self-conscious fiction separates out into the theme of writing, the theme of photographing or filming and the theme of the *faux*, the fake: Bill's false friendship, the false claims made for drugs (particularly in *Le Protocole compassionel*), art forgeries (in *L'Homme au chapeau rouge*). There is, in other words, an extended meditation on the fake which explicitly includes reflections on writing: 'It's when what I write takes the form of a diary entry that I have the clearest impression of fiction' (*Le Protocole*), thus encouraging the reader to question the relative nature of truth and fiction.

We can relate the use of fiction within fiction to two further aspects of the texts. The first is the insertion of the text into the existing literary tradition, and the attempt to validate its values in some way by an appeal to acknowledged authority. The second is the theme of writing itself, particularly in its *mise-en-abîme* form (reference within the text to its own writing). By 'insertion into the existing literary traditions', I mean reference, overt or covert, to writers and writings, designed to set up comparisons or contrasts which will affect the way the reader interprets and evaluates the text in hand. The simplest examples of overt reference are to Genet in *La Gloire du paria* and *Condamné amour*, to Gottfried Benn in *Condamné amour* and Thomas Bernhard in *A l'ami qui ne m'a pas sauvé la vie*: a tradition of rebellion, of alternative authority, is appealed to in both the person and the writings of the author invoked. The insertion becomes more significant in the case of *Eve*, where Hocquenghem, after the pattern of Zola in *La Faute de l'abbé Mouret*, rewrites the Genesis myth of creation, but does it in such a way as to challenge not only conventional Christian notions of morality and the purpose of existence, but also the confused patriarchal rewrite of morality represented by Zola. In Zola, paradise, the walled estate of *Le Paradou*, shuts out reality and its foulmouthed substitute archangel, but only for a time. In Hocquenghem, paradise is the otherness of the Caribbean (the deliberately paradoxical choice of the Virgin Islands) and of tropical South America, and when evil breaks in, in the shape of the drug smuggler Boy, Eve eradicates it by killing him. In Zola woman gives life back to man, but leads him to destruction through sexual initiation; in Hocquenghem Eve, Adam's *in vitro* twin, is the channel for his (pro)creative survival through heterosexual initiation.

But the subtlest form of insertion is also the most widespread and thoroughgoing. There are two basic Romantic myths which involve untimely death: the myth of the artist wronged by society, of which Chatterton is the archetype; and the myth of the beautiful young lover marked for death in retribution for moral transgression, of which the archetype is Dumas *fils'* Marguerite in *La Dame aux camélias* (the pattern for Verdi's Violetta in *La Traviata*). Much French AIDS fiction consciously asserts its neo-Romantic status. If Bernard, in *La Gloire du paria*, gains the reader's acquiescence when he observes: 'A Neo-Romantic. That's what I am! ... And not even *Neo*-Romantic, just Romantic pure and simple. A belated Romantic!', it is not because of his qualities as an author, of which we know little, but because AIDS will give back to him the outlaw status which will allow him to play out the role of Romantic hero. The autobiographical narrators of Guibert and Collard's texts fit the dual model of Chatterton and Marguerite/Violetta perfectly: young, poetically handsome, talented, they challenge the sexual norms of society by overt expression of homosexual eroticism and by refusal to conform with the norms of formal or generic order. *AIDS* is the agent of society's revenge, a punishment brought on the hero by the very lifestyle which constitutes his rebellion. But his transposition into a literary archetype will protect him: as text, he survives.

The technique of anchoring a work in a pre-existing literary tradition is common enough in homosexual writing, as we saw in Chapter 2, but there are offbeat features about the way in which AIDS writers have used the technique which are worth noting. The standard function of a reference to another text is, as with T. S. Eliot's 'objective correlative', to bring a whole literary context, encapsulated in a brief context, to bear upon an aspect of a new text. In just such a way, in *Ce sont amis que vent emporte*, a quotation from the libretto of *Carmen* suggests something about David and Roch's relationship, as do Roch's applications to his lover of the Rimbaud phrase 'le dormeur du val'. Similarly, when Guibert transposes the details of Foucault's sex life and his death from AIDS to a character named Muzil, he plays ironically on Foucault's *public* image as a 'Mann ohne sexuelle Eigenschaften' (a man without sexual qualities).[5] The reference can be quite clear, even when no open parallel is made in the text. Guibert, for example, more than once associates the arrival of death/or the passage between life and death, with mirrors, an image fundamental to Cocteau's *Orphée*, and therefore particularly relevant to the death of an artist from sexual causes: 'But each of us was already in the other world as far as the other was concerned: separated by an invisible mirror forming the passage from life to death and – who knows? – from death to life.' But in the earliest examples which I examined above the reader is being asked as much to consider a character in the light of an author, that is to match text against biographical reality. Hocquenghem is rewriting Genesis as part of redefining the gay author, generically, as the creator *par excellence* in a godless universe; in that case he matches *author* with author (taking God, for the sake of argument, to be the author of the book of Genesis). Guibert and Collard go further: they present the author as *text*.

This brings us neatly back to the theme of writing. The end of *La Gloire du paria* also, we are told, represents the climax to the play Bernard is writing (about AIDS); *Condamné amour* is in part both Sylvain's novel and Carol's falsification of it; *Ce sont amis que vent emporte*, *A ceux qui l'ont aimé* and *A l'ami qui ne m'a pas sauvé la vie* are all obsessed with the motif of their own creation. At one level writing and the writer are only a thematic hyponym of the set in which 'art and the artist' is the superordinate, with an extensive set of co-hyponyms – *Ce sont amis que vent emporte* offers us 'sculpture and the sculptor' and 'dance and the dancer', for example – of which the most frequent and significant is 'film and the director/cameraman'. The artistic identity of the two lovers in Navarre's novel is a central issue. In particular, the transience of dance as a performance art, and the problem of transforming performance (the living quality of a process) into words/text (the dead quality of a state or condition) is a pervasive motif. Roch's memories of David are filled with actions of dance and with images drawn from dancing. There is also stress on the idea of dance as language, as communication. The artist *is* his art, therefore David *is* dance, Roch *is* sculpture. In *Les Nuits fauves* the hero, a film-maker, is also his art in the sense that he experiences the world cinematically, in terms of fragmentation, distance, the eye that arranges light, shapes, perspectives into temporary meanings, the emblem of the theme of *regard* (looking).

But whereas 'dance and the dancer' has to remain a theme, and 'film and the director/cameraman' can only take on any other role in the texts metaphorically, through cinematic techniques of description and narration, 'writing and the writer' are, through *mise-en-abîme*, concurrently both the subject and the object of the texts. Thus in *Ce sont amis que vent emporte* the writing of the text tries to *be* that which it is transposing, particularly when what is being transposed is dancing or dancer; the actions of reality and the act of writing become metaphorically interchangeable. As Roch puts it: 'Here, nothing develops, everything is enveloped in the sheets of the pages, we intertwine.' In the Guibert trilogy, and more specifically in the first volume, *A l'ami qui ne m'a pas sauvé la vie*, much of the technique of the novels is designed to emphasize the primacy of writing. The temporal fragmentation of the narrative, for example, is designed as Emily Apter points out, to 'take us out of fixed time into that of the writing cure'. In both *A l'ami qui ne m'a pas sauvé la vie* and *Le Protocole compassionnel*, the body of the writer becomes identified with the body of the text. And as the body of the writer is, from the first page of the first novel, identified with AIDS, the writing of the text is a dual writing of the writer and of that which is destroying him. Guibert's perception of the future of his condition and of his book are parallel. Thus in Chapter 2 he juxtaposes his uncertainties as to the outcome of both:

> I don't know where I am when it comes to the question of being condemned or whether there'll be a remission. I don't know whether the prospect of salvation is a trick held out to trap me, to keep me quiet, or whether it's a real bit of science fiction with me as one of the heroes, I don't know whether it's absurdly human to believe in this act of grace and this miracle. I can glimpse the architecture of this new book which I've had in me all these last weeks but I don't know how it's going to develop, I can imagine various ends for it which for the moment all derive from premonition or wishful thinking, but the totality of what will happen in reality is concealed from me.

The fate of the body and of the text are inextricably intertwined, and the only response to this condition which Guibert can
encompass is to accept a neo-Cartesian equation, 'I write, therefore
I am', which will outflank the AIDS virus within himself. But paradoxically, therefore, the completion of the book which 'preserves'
him is itself a sort of death. As Roch notes in *Ce sont amis que vent
emporte*, writing is by definition a process, an unfinished state. By
constructing a monument to himself in *A l'ami qui ne m'a pas sauvé
la vie* Guibert risks being entombed: 'The *mise-en-abîme* of my
book encloses me within it.' The point turns up in a developed form
at the end of *L'Homme au chapeau rouge*, where Guibert laments
that he is unable to rewrite fifty pages lost in Africa when a suitcase
went astray, because 'once things are written they are as if obliter-
ated'. Writing is an act of presence; the written is a state of absence.
Interestingly in *Le Protocole*, although the act of writing remains a
subject, and the techniques of the novel sustain the reader's awareness of that act, the focus of the theme of art is transferred to film,
and in *L'Homme au chapeau rouge* to painting. In the pictorial arts
the 'person' is present in a more literal way than in writing, and in
the performing arts more literally still – although even on film there
is still a presence/absence paradox.

So far I have dealt with the theme of art as preservation, the
preservation of the self, or the beloved, as text. Perhaps slightly
simplistically but on a parallel plain, *Les Quartiers d'hiver* and *A
ceux qui l'ont aimé* can also present art as redemption, the reason
for, or justification of, a life. The technique of writing in all these
cases is part of an act of preservation and/or redemption. But *mise-
en-abîme* is as much a function of mirrors as of writing, and mirrors
relate to motifs of reflection, the reflection of the self in the other,
the Narcissus myth, which are constants in homosexual literature.
At the same time art is itself a hyponym within a set of themes of
which the superordinate is the *fake*. Now, connections can readily
be made between pictures, films and photographs, mimesis, truth
and fiction. We are in fact dealing, particularly in the cases of
Guibert and Navarre, with a network of motifs which relate to two
problematic sets of basic oppositions, 'false and true' and 'self and
other', oppositions which gay AIDS writers are forced to confront

and to rewrite in their attempts to recreate themselves and their lovers through art.

I say 'rewrite' because in gay terms these oppositions need synthesizing. I have already raised *otherness* and *the other* thematically as respectively the sense of difference from heterosexual society experienced by the homosexual and the response to AIDS sufferers of those around them. Even at this level there is a direct interrelation between the *regard* (looking) of others and self-perception. As Guibert observes in *Le Protocole*, on the one hand the way others look at him makes him feel other than he sees himself, and perhaps this imposed feeling is 'reality'; on the other hand since the publication of *A l'ami qui ne m'a pas sauvé la vie* itself changed the way in which others 'see' AIDS sufferers, their perceptions too are only interpretations. But otherness in a different sense is also a central theme in same-sex love itself. The gay man desires what is himself (male) and yet other (another male), and this difference is itself a source of fascination. Hence the way in which difference is often symbolically focused in being literally *foreign*. Thus Roch's lover David in *Ce sont amis que vent emporte* 'was born in Alexandria, of a Baltic father and a Jewish mother'; Edouardo and Joep in *Les Quartiers d'hiver* are Portuguese and Dutch respectively; Sylvain in *Condamné amour* is obsessed with a boy who is half-Berber; the narrator in *Les Nuits fauves* favours North African boys. The beloved is a mirror, but a mirror which preserves difference. So Roch describes Zachary, the American negro from whom he and David contract AIDS, as 'the black mirror, the night of our lives'.[6] This paradoxical identification of sameness and difference is neatly metaphorized in Hocquenghem's *Eve*, where Eve, physically a younger mirror image of Adam (and as it emerges the product of an *in vitro* cloned embryo, only the sex of which differs genetically from him) represents the projection of his feminine dimension, and the two of them have sex with Seth the South American negro, who represents difference but, through his maleness, sameness (for Adam, at least).

The beloved, then, is the metaphorical mirror, and his *regard* is a necessary confirmation of the self of the AIDS-sick lover. The 'real' mirror on the other hand becomes an increasing problem for the AIDS sufferer as it marks the process of physical decline. At the beginning of *A l'ami qui ne m'a pas sauvé la vie* Guibert records how the mirror first warned him of the alien presence within him: 'I felt death approaching in the mirror, in my gaze in the mirror, well before it really took up a place there,' and wonders whether he was already projecting that death into the eyes of others through his own. By the end of the book he sees that his strategy for dealing with the mirror ought to be to treat his reflection as *other*, to see his image as the separate reflection of his dead self:

> I had just discovered something: I had had to get used to the image of this skeletal face that the mirror offered me each time as if it were no longer mine but already belonged to my corpse, and – zenith or nadir of narcissism – I had had to manage to love it.

In loving the otherness of his decaying body, the AIDS sufferer would come to terms with, and in that sense conquer, the imposition of self-estrangement which the alien element of the virus within him has attempted to impose, in the same way that a gay man must learn to interpret in positive terms and to love the negative image of himself, and the consequent sense of guilt or inadequacy, which society attempts to impose on him.

Photographs and films are at one level the preserved form of the eye of the mirror. But they are also images of art. The desire to love the otherness of his body which Guibert experiences at the end of *A l'ami qui ne m'a pas sauvé la vie* is transformed into an obsession with recording it, and in particular with videoing his own medical examinations, in *Le Protocole compassionnel*. Within the written text Guibert has already identified, in Emily Apter's words 'the subversive homologies between sexual violation, nosological voyeurism, and the medical rape of the subject as crucial constituents of *sida* narrative, integers of *raison d'être*'.[7] Film offers a more direct image of these homologies as an eternally repeatable process, an unfolding series of metaphors, which is at the same time, like a mirror image, identifiable with the subject in 'real life'. It comes one degree closer than writing to the preservation of the physical self. Thus with appropriate symbolism at the end of *Le Protocole*, the finishing of Guibert's book coincides with the making of his first film. But even mirror images are no more the 'real' self than the beloved is the 'real' mirror of the lover. They preserve a limited truth through an illusion. As Guibert observes in *Le Protocole*: 'You get used to your own mirror, and when you find yourself in an unknown mirror in a hotel, you see something else.' The problem is clearly greater for photographs and films, greater still for paintings. What in this context *is* truth? When is art merely artifice, when and how does it transcend that condition?

It is a meditation on the *fake* in art and life which provides the central matter of the third novel in Guibert's trilogy, *L'Homme au chapeau rouge*. The text has four main strands, all connected with the true/false opposition and all characterized by mystery/ uncertainty. Already in *Le Protocole* Guibert records how AIDS itself and AIDS research is bedevilled by suppressions and falsifica- tions in drug-testing processes and results, a point which he juxta- poses, unmediated, with the problem of truth in writing. In *L'Homme au chapeau rouge* the themes of fake paintings, of the search for the truth about the disappearance of Vigo, an art dealer, and of false medical diagnosis are intertwined with examples of Guibert himself lying or catching his friends out in lies. The book becomes a reflection on the relationship between reality and fiction, and on both the necessity and the near-impossibility for the AIDS- struck artist of conquering life in art. Art, like the mirror and the beloved, must be both sameness and difference, both other and the thing it reflects.

Why is it so important to the writers to solve this particular problem? The answer lies, I think, not just in the question of preser- vation, redemption and the pursuit of meaning, but in the issue of procreational and recreational sexuality. Hocquenghem's Adam symbolizes the issue perfectly; by combining his masculine and feminine halves through a sexual act, he is the author of a second Adam who is the product of his *re*-creation (it is in the moment of death that his soul transfers to it): it is *the book itself*. The simplistic public mythology which equates heterosexuality with procreation and life is countered by an equation of homosexuality with rec- reation = death and procreation = art, *at the same time*.

What, then, is the precise connection between the two halves of the title of this chapter? In what way does AIDS writing as such relate to a problem of gay *self*-image? French literature written by homosexuals presents a duality of negative and positive images throughout the first half of the century and beyond, with the emphasis heavily tilted toward the negative, as we saw in Chapters 2 and 3. But a just-pre-AIDS novel such as Dominique Fernandez's *L'Etoile rose* (1978) gives the impression that for the generation coming to maturity, post-May 1968, the duality had been resolved: the idea of homosexuality as sin or sickness, the question of responsibility for one's sexual identity, even the nature-versus-nurture debate were no longer relevant issues. By the end of the 1970s, as the opening chapters of *La Gloire du paria* confirm, French (or at least Parisian) society could be interpreted as accepting of, if not welcoming towards, homosexuals. AIDS, by fostering the old equation homosexuality = illness, not only brought back to the surface all the old prejudices of society at large, it also forced gays to look at themselves and their lifestyle afresh. Hence the importance of how the individual sees and is seen in AIDS texts, both literally – AIDS challenges the 1980s gay obsession with physical beauty as the main defining feature of an individual's worth – and metaphorically.

Both the resulting reassessments and the ways in which they relate to a writer's stance towards the experience of being HIV positive are unexpectedly ambiguous. There is, for example, no clear equivalence between a positive attitude to gayness and a determination to fight the AIDS virus within oneself. There is as strong a sense of guilt at being gay in Dreuilhe's *Corps à corps*, despite its refusal to accept the death sentence and its insistence on the pleasure and meaning to be found in writing, as there is in Pancrazi's portrait of a refusal to face facts in *Les Quartiers d'hiver*. Indeed, even an overtly defiant text such as *Les Nuits fauves*, with its ubiquitous explicit homoeroticism, panders by its neo-Romantic resuscitation of the *Dame au camélias* motif, to the notion that a particular gay lifestyle *is* morally reprehensible and can only be redeemed in death, a motif which, given the complex relationship of novel to film and of writer to the actor of the central role, has to be seen as both part of self-image and as a concession to the views of the potential average reader/viewer. Even the literature of salvation through art creates the same problem as earlier versions of the same theme in Cocteau, Genet *et al.*, namely that this is a solution not available to the *reader*, and which therefore has no effect on *his self-image*. Possibly the most coherent assertions are in the novels which celebrate couples, *La Gloire du paria* and *Ce sont amis que vent emporte*. In particular the latter celebrates an emotionally intense but physically open-ended, distinctively gay relationship, which it presents as ironically owing its preservation in writing to the very condition which destroys it in 'reality': 'This *Fin-de-siècle* plague is our honour, our victory and the seal upon us.' But many gay readers will see these novels, even *Ce sont amis que vent emporte*, as in some sense selling out precisely because to locate the validity of gay experience in the couple could be said to pander to heterosexual stereotypes of how society should be structured.

This brings us to the crux of the problem which I think the AIDS writers face, and to which there is no solution. The ambiguities of image offered by the text are complicated by a key imponderable: the reader. Navarre, in observing that writing is reality, the written merely being the reproduction of the real, comments that each reader 'writes' a text in his act of reading, and thus preserves writing as an *act* and not an object. But does it not make a fundamental difference whether the reader is male or female, gay or straight, HIV positive or HIV negative? Joseph Cady has tried to argue that what counts is whether the reader is or is not thrust into 'a direct imaginative confrontation with the special horrors of AIDS' in a given text. He contrasts what he calls immersive AIDS literature, in which the writer does not mediate in any way between reader and medical condition, with counter-immersive literature, which

> focuses on characters or speakers who are in various degrees of denial about AIDS themselves, and it customarily treats its readers the way its characters handle their disturbing contacts with AIDS, protecting them from too jarring a confrontation with the subject through a variety of distancing devices.[8]

This seems a dangerously simplistic approach. As we have seen, there are very complex relationships between theme and form in all the texts, and to reduce them to an immersion/counter-immersion opposition on a largely thematic basis seems arbitrary. It could be argued in reverse that to confront many readers with an unmediated account of the 'special horrors of AIDS' is inevitably to risk alienation through revulsion, or worse still that blunting of sensibilities which exposure to Vietnam atrocities had on many television viewers and film-goers. On the other hand no one should argue, surely, that AIDS writing is for a ghetto readership, and the success of Guibert's novels and of Collard's *Les Nuits fauves* runs counter to any such suggestion. Perhaps the most significant achievement of AIDS writing in France has been to reopen the debate about the relationship between writer, life, text and reader, in the specific context of sexual identity and alternative lifestyle. The problem of gay self-image has accordingly been reopened as part of the re-assessment of fundamental *aesthetic* issues, which have taken on new and unexpected *ethical* connotations.

Notes

1. *Corps à corps: journal du sida* (Paris: Gallimard, 1987), p. 11.
2. Lee Edelman, 'The mirror and the tank: "AIDS", subjectivity, and the rhetoric of activism', in Timothy F. Murphy and Suzanne Poirier (eds.), *Writing AIDS: Gay Literature, Language and Analysis* (New York: Columbia University Press, 1993), p. 10.
3. Henri Marsan, 'Sida: l'amour fatal', *Le Figaro littéraire*, July/August 1992, pp. 56–9.
4. See Renaud Camus, *Elégies pour quelques-uns* (Paris: POL, 1988), sect. VII ('Prosopopée de l'absence') pp. 69–85. Camus is referring to the fact that, although a book presupposes both a writer and a reader, neither of them are *literally* present in it; it is merely a collection of words.
5. In choosing the name Muzil, Guibert is making a reference to the German writer Robert Musil, best known for his novel *Der Mann ohne Eigenschaften* (The man without qualities).
6. Note the traditional equation of darkness = negativity, which makes Zachary's colour an issue in this image. This is in complete contrast to the simple equivalence established between white Adam and black Seth in Hocquenghem's *Eve*.

7.   Emily Apter, 'Fantom images: Herve Guibert and the writing of "sida", in France', in Murphy and Poirier, *Writing AIDS*, p. 84.
8.   Joseph Cady, 'Immersive and counterimmersive writing about AIDS: the achievement of Paul Monette's *Love Alone*', in Murphy and Poirier, *Writing AIDS*, p. 244.

Chapter six

Pederasty and the Cult of Youth

'Perverting the young! As if initiation in sexual pleasure was in itself an act of perversion! In general it is quite the opposite!'

● *André Gide*[1]

IN British English the word 'pederast' is a very emotive one, denoting a man who has sexual desires for, and probably relations with, a pre-pubescent or pubescent child of either sex. Although technically it should cover anyone who has a sexual interest in minors of any age, it is not much used in cases where the object of interest is a boy as old as sixteen. But in French the word *pédéraste*, while capable of a similar meaning (as in Fernandez' definition: 'A *pédéraste* is an adult male who has a taste for pre-pubescent boys'[2]) is also, especially in the shortened form *pédé*, the common and generally insulting word for a male homosexual. Language never being merely a question of labels, this reflects a significant confusion of categorization within French society and marks an area of difference of perception between French and Anglo-Saxon culture. Even in Britain heterosexuals frequently identify homosexuality with 'interference with children'; in France the identification of homosexuality and pederasty is stronger still because rooted in the language. Hence the emphasis on the protection of minors in such anti-homosexual discriminatory legislation as used to exist, and the harping on the same theme in the parliamentary speeches of right-wing opponents of gay rights in the 1970s and 1980s.

In practice French perceptions of bands of age-preference and their significance can be very different from the British equivalents. As we saw above, Fernandez firmly distinguishes pederasty as an interest in the very young, and assesses the number of homosexuals who have such tastes as about 4 per cent. Roger Peyrefitte suggests in his writings that his own tastes are for boys between twelve and seventeen; Montherlant's homophilic adolescent heroes age from thirteen to sixteen, at which point society is seen as 'reclaiming' them; Gide, who speaks with approval of thirteen to twenty-two years as the age for male 'amorous friendship', began his own relationship with Marc Allegret when the latter was fifteen; and there are a number of writers (e.g. Eekhoud) who focus on adolescent and young adult males between about sixteen and twenty-four. At the same time there are writers like Genet who write about adolescent sexuality (e.g. in *Miracle de la rose*) in exactly the same terms as they write about adult sexuality, in such a way that age is not a marker of difference of any kind. This leads to a much greater sense of sexuality as a spectrum of related interests than is the case in Anglo-Saxon culture. Accordingly, Gide and Peyrefitte make it plain that they see themselves as homosexuals, of the subspecies 'pederast', a term which they use without any negative connotations. Equally, Jouhandeau, while explicitly stating, 'I am as little of a pederast as is possible', goes on in terms which make it plain that he does not see any real difference in *kind* between his own sexual tastes and those who are attracted to adolescents:

> Many *who share my sexual preferences* are surprised that these are directed exclusively towards fully formed adult males whereas what *they* value is above all that moment of hesitation, of crystallization in nature, the borderline between adolescence and adulthood.[3]

Given that the clear Anglo-Saxon division between pederasty and inter-adult male (or female) homosexuality is not generally acknowledged in France, it is perhaps not surprising to find, especially in the relatively liberated 1970s and 1980s, writers who would not see themselves as pederasts in Anglo-Saxon terms, such as Bory and Hocquenghem, who take care not to condemn pederasty out of hand. Even Fernandez, while acknowledging that the pederasty can be a form of physical or moral violence, also claims that it can be the basis of a beautiful, wholesome relationship which will help the boy concerned to develop more rapidly than he would within his family circle. The French simply do not seem to find age *alone* a good criterion for defining the nature of a relationship, or, consequently, the allegiances of a text. Adolescent sex is not, in a French text, automatically a pederastic theme. For example, the fact that one of the central figures in Copi's *La Guerre des pédés* is fourteen years old does not make the novel pederastic – even given that Copi uses the motif of adolescent androgyny – because the character in question, a Brazilian hermaphrodite, is used as a comic representative of the myth of gigantic male endowment and its effects in sexual possession. The novel uses its embryonic motifs of adolescence or androgyny in such a way as to satirize myths of masculinity, and not to construct any sort of commentary on adolescent sexuality. As we shall see, within French literature what can loosely be regarded as 'pederastic' texts (identified on the pragmatic basis that they are focused on relationships with, or between, minors in a context where the fact of age is made to seem significant) group themselves around certain themes and modes of presentation. But such texts also share themes and patterns with other texts which do not concern themselves with the same age group. Pederastic literature thus frequently shades off into the wider literature of male gayness both thematically and formally.

The initial late nineteenth-century model for pederastic literature, as I suggested in Chapter 1, was 'Greek love', in the form of the development of an emotional and physical relationship between mentor and pupil. The topic, defended openly by such English and German advocates as John Addington Symonds and von Schweitzer, was little expounded in France, where it principally appears in a lesbian form, notably in the little sketch of Sappho and her pupils used in the prelude to Louÿs's *Chansons de Bilitis*. But the period 1890–1914 was also one in which adolescence, as opposed to childhood, became a literary subject in its own right, and with it adolescent sexuality. A separate tradition of pederastic literature therefore begins to develop with its roots in the other aspects of *Chansons de Bilitis*, the passionate mutual emotional and physical attachment of two adolescents. This theme easily coalesces with that of school life to be found in turn-of-the-century mainstream heterosexual writing (Alain-Fournier's *Le Grand Meaulnes*, Valery Larbaud's *Fermina Marquez*), emerging in the lesbian school scenes of Colette's 'Claudine' books and a long succession of accounts of adolescent male sexuality in school from Achille Essebac's *Dédé* onward. At the same time the school settings automatically gave an opportunity to incorporate the mentor–pupil model alongside studies in inter-adolescent relationships. These two converging traditions do not cover the full range of the subject, however, because adolescents were also taken as the focus for the study of other homosexual motifs, notably prostitution (Carco's *Jésus-la-caille*). This formed part of the theme of the adolescent as sex-object whose less reputable side was anonymous pornography of the sort represented by, for example, *Pédérastie passive, ou mémoires d'un enculé* (1911), a description of boarding-school orgies which prepare the central character for an enjoyable life (in his twenties) as the toyboy of a rich admirer.[4]

All this seems to create a neat classification, but like most neat classifications it hides more than it conceals. For, pederastic texts contain networks of motifs which raise the same sorts of problems of self-image and reader-persuasion as other male homosexual texts, and which exist in a mutually reflexive relationship with wider issues of desire, identity and power. Let us begin by looking at some of the thematic issues predominating in the work of authors who were themselves pederasts to see how these themes construct comparative and contrastive relationships between texts.

The theory of the value of the mentor/pupil relationship is set out for the first time in the fourth dialogue of Gide's *Corydon*, the defence of pederasty whose final published version appeared in 1924.[5] The main arguments of this dialogue are moral. Gide is obsessed with the idea of female purity and argues for diverting young male sexual instinct, which tends toward the pursuit of pleasure, away from women, who should be kept chaste for marriage and motherhood. At the same time Gide argues that the function of pederasty is not merely to satisfy physical desire but to raise the beloved intellectually and morally. He cites all the standard examples of how pederastic relationships in history have been morally fortifying (the Spartans, the Theban Band), and this then leads to the final idealization of the role of the older friend: 'Let this lover jealously protect the boy, watch over him and, being himself exalted and purified by this love, let him guide him towards those radiant peaks which can never be reached without love.' The argument is even put forward that if boys experience this sort of educative relationship between the ages of thirteen and twenty-two, they will be better prepared to become good husbands in heterosexual marriages thereafter.

There are a number of things to note about these ideas. For the moment let us confine ourselves to three issues which will arise in later pederastic texts. First, the arguments imply an attitude to women which is fundamentally misogynist – it places a 'duty' to perform symbolic maternal and spiritual functions for the benefit of men above their right to fulfil their own natures. Secondly, the arguments do not offer any solidarity with adult homosexuality but consciously distance themselves from it by proposing pederasty as a preparation for heterosexuality. Thirdly, there is no mention of the effect of the inevitably short-term nature of such relationships on either the beloved or the lover, who has, as each boy passes to maturity, to start the cycle again.

The first two points are born out in Gide's other works. Female characters in Gide are either destructive (Alyssa, Mme Sophroniska) or ineffectual (Juliette, Marceline, the pastor's wife). He can only visualize them as Penelope or Helen, the 'patient wife and mother' (Pauline) or the 'whore' (Carola).[6] As for hostility to other forms of homosexuality: despite a note to the preface of the 1924 edition of *Corydon* acknowledging that it is a great defect of the book not to deal with 'inversion', 'effeminacy' or 'sodomy' (the choice of terms already reveals hidden prejudices), Gide clearly entertained classically heterosexual views on all forms of homosexuality except his own. In particular a passage of undated notes published with his *Journal* entries for 1918 contains the standard wrong-headed distinction between active and passive partners, and castigates the passive partners as being 'intellectually and morally warped'. What is important in this rejection is not so much its lack of solidarity but the determination which it reveals to reject anything potentially 'feminine' in the male. Gide is a victim of total 'straight' stereotyping.

The third point, the problem of transience, he ostensibly addresses in *Les Faux-monnayeurs* in his treatment of Edouard's relationship with his nephew Olivier. But this example is very problematic. In the first place Edouard is a very flawed character to act as mentor, even if he is presented as the positive counterpart to the pseudo-mentor Passavant, who exploits his relationships with young men for his own ends. In the second place the eulogy of pederasty is placed in the mouth of Olivier's mother, which must make it the least plausible statement on the subject ever included in a work of fiction. In the third place the novel gives no space for the development of the relationship such that the reader could judge its potential value. And fourthly, though the theme of transience is suggested by the way in which Edouard's roving eye alights on young Caloub when he has barely begun his relationship with Olivier, there is no exploration of what this might mean to any of those involved, particularly the emotionally unstable Olivier. So *Les Faux-monnayeurs* leaves us with only a very sketchy model of the sort of relationship which his theory suggests is central to the justification of pederasty.

These three points – misogyny, suppression of the feminine within the male and the question of how to come to terms with transient relationships – also occur in a number of texts by later writers. The motif of the mentor/pupil relationship itself is handled in two different ways which can roughly be seen as *positive* and *problematic* respectively. By positive I simply mean that the effect of the older friend on the younger is presented as in itself a good thing. The sustainability of the relationship within a social context is a different matter; this is only possible when the author places the relationship *outside* France, in the welcoming 'otherness' of Italy, Spain or North Africa. (This otherness seems to have less to do with the Decadent technique of 'sanitizing' homosexuality by projecting it across time or space than with the purely pragmatic issue of the greater ease with which Mediterranean cultures accepted and permitted pederastic practices.) Thus Adelsward-Fersen, in Peyrefitte's *biographie romancée L'Exilé de Capri*, picks up the beautiful fifteen-year-old Neapolitan Nino and carries him off to Capri where he proceeds to educate him and to introduce him to culture as well as into his bed. When, as in Tony Duvert's *Quand mourut Jonathan*, the mentor is subject to the prejudices of contemporary France, he will be defeated. But already in the two texts I have named we can see divergences on the other points raised by the fourth dialogue of *Corydon*. Fersen's violent hostility to Nino's heterosexual escapades, like Jonathan's pleasure in the illustrations he produces for an edition of Sade's *Justine*, are both misogynistic. But Peyrefitte balances this by bringing out the androgynous quality of adolescent beauty and making it an emblem of a broader marriage of masculine and feminine in Italian culture as a whole, whereas there is no compensating presentation of the feminine in Duvert's book. Even in texts which present the mentor/pupil role positively, there is clearly no simple equation between pederasty and rejection or acceptance of the feminine *within* the male.

If we look at what I have called 'problematic' mentor–pupil relationships, the pattern becomes more complex still. The obvious examples are Père de Trennes in Peyrefitte's *Les Amitiés particulières*, the Abbé de Pradts in Montherlant's *La Ville dont le prince est un enfant* and *Les Garçons* (which for these purposes I shall treat as a single text[7]) and Xavier de Balcourt in the first part of Martin du Gard's *Maumort*. Xavier is the simplest case: he is a young man, tutoring two adolescents, one of whom (Guy) is sexually precocious and highly physically provocative. Xavier becomes very emotionally involved and physically aroused, but nothing happens. The text therefore appears to offer us a mentorship inhibited by the social or psychological factors which prevent the mentor from coming to terms with his sexuality. There are, however, two disturbing features about this text. First, it raises the issue of the boy-as-erotic-object, to which we shall return shortly. Second, because Guy dies of tuberculosis, the whole episode becomes retrospectively inserted into the *Dame aux camélias* tradition,[8] the relevance of the Eros/Thanatos model being reinforced by the suicide of Xavier himself later in the novel (see Chapter 2 above). The potential sexual irregularity is exorcized by ritual deaths.

The other 'problematic' texts are problematic for conventional moral reasons. Not because they involve priests with peder-astic tendencies, but because in the pursuit of their desire to help the boys concerned both de Trennes and de Pradts do considerable wrong to others. The complicating point here is the presence of a secondary motif, a variation on the adult mentor/adolescent pupil pattern. Both Peyrefitte and Montherlant introduce a pederastic relationship on the mentor/pupil pattern between an older and a younger boy. The priests, motivated by jealousy, attempt to use the power of their position to defeat their rivals. But since to use a patriarchal weapon (hierarchy) in pursuit of an anti-patriarchal end (pederasty, the negation of the family power structure) is a contra-diction in terms, they duly defeat their own ends.

As far as the issue of the feminine in these texts is concerned, feminine influence itself tends to be at best absent, more often negative (notably in the case of Alban's mother in the Montherlant texts), but in all of them the inherent androgyny of the adolescent body is made a source of pleasure both for the characters and (potentially) for the reader. In this respect they are linked to a text like *L'Exilé de Capri*. In *Maumort*, for example, femininity is pre-sented as a positive quality in the descriptions of Guy's body, where Martin du Gard makes great play with the contrast between the virility of the boy's large cock and abundant black pubic hair and the grace and delicacy of the rest of his body. The feminine is accepted when it is *male* femininity, as it were. However, *Les Ami-tiés particulières* raises the same problem as *Maumort*: Peyrefitte places the Georges/Alexandre relationship under the sign of death – Alexandre commits suicide when Père de Trennes allows him to think that Georges no longer loves him. The text is thus inserted into the love = death tradition. In *Les Garçons* literal death (as opposed to the metaphorical death which social interdict imposes) only comes with the Great War, which becomes in turn a symbol for the destructive power of society; there is therefore a closer parallel with *Quand mourut Jonathan*, where Serge's implied suicide at the end is a direct result of society's failure to allow him access to the one person who really understands him.

By one means or another society imposes a code of hetero-sexual machismo which counteracts the beneficial effects of peder-asty. The issue of the transience of relationships, never really allowed any space in any of the four texts, is subordinated to this death motif. Admittedly Montherlant's insistence on the passage towards masculinity, symbolized for example by the way in which the gender of La Fauvette becomes unstable between *elle* and *il*, gradually giving way to the masculine Le Fauvetton, underlines the inevitability of change in any relationship involving an adolescent. But in general it is death, literal and/or in the metaphorical form of social interdict, which intervenes to end all relationships. The difference is that in the case of *Maumort* and *Les Amitiés particulières* the literary associations of the love/death motif create a sense that pederasty is *ill-starred* in some inherent way, whereas for Montherlant and Duvert the symbolic associations of death are modified by the fact that outside agencies are solely responsible.

If we move to a second recurrent aspect of pederastic literature, adolescent male sensuality, we find that, here too, what might seem to be a fixed textual presence has in fact a shifting value in different texts. What is more, there is often a fundamental tension between the motif of sensuality and the moralizing pretensions of the mentor/pupil model. The roots of this tension go back to Gide's *Corydon*, the text from which we started. *Corydon* is usually thought of as a moralizing text because that is the tone on which it ends. But the fourth dialogue was only added to the *final* version of the work. The first version, printed in a handful of copies in 1911, contained only the first two dialogues and less than half of the third. Until the second private edition (1920), then, *Corydon*, apart from attacking society for the blighting effect on homosexuals of attitudes born of ignorance and hypocrisy, concentrated on two issues: naturalness and pleasure. It pursues these through a series of propositions: (1) man is not responsible for his own sexual nature; (2) there is a *normal* form of homosexuality (i.e. pederasty); (3) there is no simple equation between sexual orientation and such character traits as immorality and irresponsibility; (4) for both sexes the sexual instinct is naturally indeterminate, with the pursuit of pleasure as the only goal; (5) homosexuality is a necessary by-product of the overproduction of males in most species; (6) the natural beauty of the male body surpasses that of the female body.

When he resumes the third dialogue in the 1920 version,

Gide simply extends two previously enunciated motifs – male beauty and the natural neutrality of desire – arguing for the superiority of the former from the preference of High Art for the male nude and from the prevalence of homosexuality in societies undergoing artistic renaissance; and in the second case insisting that, unfalsified by social constraint, the adolescent male seeks his pleasure in any outlet. If we consider the text in its 1911 version, stopping after the argument that the young naked male body is by nature more beautiful than the female body, we find ourselves with a work whose *moral* import is minimal: it is exclusively designed to argue for the naturalness of pederasty and for the superiority of the adolescent male as an object of desire. The corollary of this is that the focus is on the pederast, the desirer, the boy being merely a natural cause of, and worthy object for, that desire. When Gide completes the third dialogue, he does so in a way which emphasizes the pleasure principle but legitimizes it to some extent by an argument for the equal pleasure of the younger partner. The fact is that the moral arguments of the fourth dialogue, though not necessarily incompatible with the defence of pleasure, are completely detached from it. Gide conceived the work as a treatise about a certain sort of pleasure.

If we look at Gide's other writings we shall find the same dichotomy. Now, in practical terms this is a more serious problem than it sounds. *Corydon* does not offer any bridge between the boy-as-erotic-object (adolescent beauty as a legitimate object for desire) and the boy-as-spiritual-subject (the adolescent mind as a free space for spiritual and cultural development). The implication is simply that the former is the initial source of attraction and reward for the pederast, who in turn cultivates the latter. This suggests that in his non-polemical works Gide will interest himself in the exploration of such relationships, of which, as we saw, the Edouard/Olivier relationship in *Les Faux-monnayeurs* is an example. Unfortunately, it is the *only* such example. In all Gide's other works, pederasty is represented exclusively in its physical dimension. In *L'Immoraliste*, for example, Michel's implied relationship with the Arab boys is purely sensual, as is Lafacadio's liaison with his 'uncles' in *Les Caves du Vatican*. To make matters more complex still, in his autobiography, *Si le grain ne meurt*, published two years after

Corydon and the same year as *Les Faux-monnayeurs*, Gide seems to propose a counter-argument which clearly separates the spiritual from the physical: a spiritual relationship is what he seeks within marriage with his cousin Madeleine (Emmanuelle, in the book) and physical fulfilment is what he finds with young Ali in the dunes. In fact, the development of the mentor/pupil model in the fourth dialogue seems to have been a reflection of his own mentor/pupil relationship with Marc Allegret. But the pederastic dimension of that relationship is not presented anywhere in his work, except implicitly in a fleeting scene which evokes the joy of perfect togetherness in the 'Meetings' section of the *Nouvelles Nourritures terrestres*. Elsewhere, what Gide records is his sensual pleasure in the bodies of adolescent males, particularly North African boys, from Ali and Mohammed whom he encounters on his Algerian trips of 1893 and 1894, to the Egyptian boys with whom he amuses himself in the pages of the *Carnets d'Egypte* (1939). Such encounters inevitably recall the use of the boy-as-exotic-object in Jean Lorrain's 'Bathylle', distancing the reader comfortably from any moral issues by reducing the boys concerned to the rank of legitimately exploitable colonial possessions.

To complicate matters further, however, the status of the sensual pleasure is by no means always presented in terms as morally neutral as the arguments of *Corydon* might suggest. Despite assertions that sex released him from an inner hell, Gide colours his accounts of it with counteracting details, which link pleasure with darkness or horror. This is particularly true when the text introduces sex in a form other than the mutual masturbation favoured by Gide himself. Daniel B. sodomizing Mahommed, for example, 'seems gigantic, and as he lent over the little body which he was covering, he looked like an immense vampire feeding on a corpse'.[9] The moral unease which gives itself away in aesthetic detail of this sort is sometimes more explicit. For example, in *Et nunc manet in te* he presents the desire which made him photograph young Italian boys in the nude as *demonic*: 'I wasn't responsible for my actions. A demon took me over. It never possessed me more imperiously than on our return to Algeria, in the course of this same voyage.' His work therefore leaves us with conflicting strands of pederastic discourse: a positive, moralizing mentor/pupil motif, and an unstable discourse of desire and sexual pleasure which sometimes becomes negatively charged by metaphors of darkness and demonic possession.

After Gide, and doubtless in imitation of him, adolescent sensuality appears both as an aspect of various types of mentor/pupil relationship, particularly that between an older and a younger boy, and as an erotic theme in its own right. The Gidean moral unease, which can be interpreted as a genuine authorial unease or as a concession to the *reader*'s potential unease, also has a fluctuating presence in the texts. And, even more so than is the case in the presentation of adult male sexuality, a technique of 'neutralizing' eroticism through lyrical presentation is developed, designed to make it more easily assimilable by the non-pederastic reader. Apart from Gide, none of the main texts prior to the 1960s acknowledges sex acts between adult males and boys under seventeen. In Peyrefitte's *Les Amitiés particulières* even sexual acts between boys are excluded; the emphasis is entirely emotional (hence the ever-present symbol of the hothouse), physical contact is confined to passionate kissing, genital sex is equated with impurity. The notion that Alexandre might desire Georges is enough to set the latter off on a Baudelairean paradox: 'Was he one of those angels who are demons?', whilst, reassured by Georges that he has no physical intentions towards him, Alexandre says: 'I kept asking myself what you wanted of me. I was afraid it might be something wrong' (the French word used is the ambiguous 'mal' with its connotations of evil). In Montherlant's *Les Garçons*, where Alban and Serge do have sex, the value of the immense sense of pleasurable fulfilment which they derive from the act is modified for the *reader* by the symbolism of its context – the darkness of the changing room, the fact that Alban damages his hand in the process, the image of Serge's belt curling like a snake on the floor.[10] These two novels even take over the classical heterosexual symbolism of the nineteenth-century novel, where blond = purity and goodness, dark = desire and destructiveness. The angelic Alexandre is blond, Georges dyes a lock of his hair blond as Alexandre exerts a good influence on him, the demonic Serge is dark.

But these motifs come to mean different things within the value system of each separate work. Both novels present the love affairs of their boy-heroes as incompatible with the 'real' world,

both in its microcosm (school) and its macrocosm, an incompati-
bility which, given that this real world stands for incomprehension,
rejection and persecution, is an assertion of the positive value of
pederasty. But *Les Amitiés particulières* does so without troubling
the Romantic conventions of the misunderstood outcast and ill-
starred love on which it is built. Montherlant counters these with a
Baudelairean paradox, in which the energy of his heroes depends
on their desire, dark side and all; hence what the novel lacks in
genital acts, it makes up for in oral passion. Alban and Serge kissing
achieve a suspension of time and a transporting of themselves outside reality akin to the moment of drug-induced poetic inspiration
in Baudelaire's prose poem 'La Chambre double': 'They stayed
mouth to mouth, a long, long time: a long embrace, which created a
void around itself, motionless at the summit of complete oblivion.'
These elements are, as we shall see, part of the insertion of the
whole text into a Baudelairean universe in which beauty = evil and
childhood = perversity, but the two together = energy. The status
of sensuality is accordingly quite different from that in *Les Amitiés
particulières*, and its ambiguities seem much more conscious than
the hesitations embodied in *Si le grain ne meurt*.

Martin du Gard's *Maumort* moves us a stage closer to the
uninhibited hedonism of Gidean pederastic practice. Its chapters on
Guy and on the sixteen-year-old Maumort's experiences in school
are judiciously coloured (for period 'realism') by prejudices which
the narrator himself attempts to shrug off. Describing Guy's fascination with his own naked body or his obsession with sex in
general and masturbation in particular, Martin du Gard loads the
text with moralizing vocabulary: disorders, depravity, shameless-
ness, impurity. But some of these words are in inverted commas
even within the text; they show the narrator's unease at borrowing
from the world of cliché in which he necessarily lives. The narrator
is always careful to insist that, for him, purity is not a fetish and the
'troubles of the flesh' are a virtue. The same pattern recurs in the
school episodes. Having described Raoul de Luzac, who initiates
him into the pleasures of beneath-the-desk mutual masturbation, as
'close to being a monster of perversity', Maumort backs off: 'Badly
put; there was nothing monstrous about him and when all's said
and done not much that was perverse. He was naked uninhibited

instinct, as randy as a young animal on heat.' It is a return to the insistence in *Corydon* on the naturalness of adolescent desire, its pursuit of pleasure without inhibitions about where that pleasure may be found. Martin du Gard is in fact using a similar argument to Montherlant's, without the underlay of Baudelairean metaphor. Adolescent sensuality is necessary to a release of the adult sexual self, which in turn is needed for the development of the energy vital to the inspiration of the rest of the self: 'An individual derives the major part of his inner strength and riches from the full development of his sensuality.' Maumort is accordingly quite explicit in his paradoxes: Guy's 'impure and healthy breath' breathed fire into him, that is to say what was conventionally regarded at the period as undesirable was in fact necessary for the awakening of his own dormant potential.

In the context of inter-adolescent sex acts the defence of the value of initiation poses no problems for the writer and few for the reader. But more recent pederastic texts have returned to the representation of sex between adolescents and adults. This brings us back to the problem of the gap in the moral argument of *Corydon* – the failure to relate the idea of sexual pleasure to that of spiritual guidance. This gap is either ignored by later writers, as in Peyrefitte's autobiographical reminiscences, or filled by a different sort of moral argument, as in *Roy*, or rendered irrelevant by a radical calling into question of the categorization of pederasty as a separate sexual condition or set of acts, as in the work of Tony Duvert. To compare Peyrefitte and Duvert's approaches to the issue is instructive because it highlights the difference between the eroticization of the adolescent as *object* of desire and the eroticization of the adolescent as *subject* of desire, a distinction which relates not just to sexual practices but to the political (in the broadest sense) values which underlie the works of the two writers.

What I have to say about Peyrefitte's texts has nothing to do with the value of his tireless campaigning on behalf of homosexual rights in general and the interests of pederasts in particular.[11] Peyrefitte was probably the first significant French writer after Gide to be completely 'out', and his novel *Notre amour* (based on his relationship with Alain-Philippe Malagnac, whom he met on the set of the 1964 film of *Les Amitiés particulières*) was the first overtly autobiographical defence of pederasty in the post-war period. This does not alter the fact that Peyrefitte's account of pederasty reproduces the power structures of that very same heterosexual society which it decries. In the first place, the autobiographical sketch in the sixteenth chapter of *Propos secrets* places the writer's childhood 'years of purity, in which desires for impurity clarified themselves like wine' under the seal of the Baudelairean 'green paradise of childhood loves/innocent paradise full of furtive pleasures', thus associating adolescent sensuality itself with moral ambiguity. Secondly, the same text then focuses entirely on the pleasure of the *narrator*, firstly in masturbation, then in sodomy with both sexes. From the fourteen-year-old whom the eighteen-year-old Peyrefitte has, doggy-fashion, on a bed in the Grand Hotel at Foix, the narrative is one of the possession of adolescent sex objects. Whilst imagery confirms the 'naturalness' of the active partner in images such as 'while the geyser of my eighteen years was gushing', and 'a torrent of pleasure swept me along', the boys concerned are reduced to the anonymity of types: little Greek street vendors, a schoolboy, a page boy, a charming little fourteen-year-old Jew. More to the point, they are *bought*. The nearest thing to a consideration of any of them as *partners* in his acts is when he observes of one of them that he adored sodomy. But even in this case the boy is promptly reduced to his proper role as a prop on a stage set: Peyrefitte would have him leaning over the window-sill, so that he could look at the illuminated Parthenon as they coupled. Admittedly, the presentation of these adventures is coloured by a vocabulary of moral disapproval, but this is a literary sleight of hand, and revealed as such when at the close of the chapter the author overtly cancels the weight of the moralizing language with a quotation: 'Libertine behaviour is like war: a fine thing when you come back from it.' Peyrefitte simply replaces the conventional patriarchal power structure with one in which the adult pederast assumes the power role.

The pretence of a moral posture coupled with an exploitative approach to adolescent sexuality is at the very core of his novel *Roy*. Ostensibly the novel attacks the moral bankruptcy of contemporary US society. The fourteen-year-old eponymous hero takes the principle inculcated in him by his family that any act is legitimate if it makes you money, and uses it to justify launching into a very lucrative career of up-market prostitution. This course of action which, while he derives financial profit and a good deal of physical pleasure from it, eventually exposes him to blackmail and turns him into a (quite unpunished) murderer. At the same time he undergoes a very searching initiation into a vast variety of sexual experiences with boys (and once or twice with girls) of fourteen to twenty, an initiation which we are given to understand will not necessarily prevent him from being a good father and husband in later life.

The ostensible moral of the novel is that in an exclusively materialistic society, pleasure (promiscuous sex between peers) is morally neutral whereas profit (prostitution) corrupts. But this message is countered by the rest of the book in two ways. First, great play is made with the fact that Roy's supreme pleasure derives from sexual encounters with adults. For example, as the liberally endowed Los Angeles police chief[12] penetrates him fully for the first time:

> He kept touching the hair on those arms, that chest, that crutch pressing against his buttocks, and contrasting it with Bob's body hair, which was nothing to speak of. He realised that he would always prefer a man to a boy, because he liked a man's powerfulness.

The motif of willing sexual submission to power, at its most raw in the scene where Roy gets sexual pleasure from corporal punishment, implies an acceptance of the validity of exactly those hierarchical principles which characterize heterosexual society and which a pederast is in theory seeking to overthrow. At the same time the pornographic function of the text itself, with its repeated lavishly detailed accounts of Roy's escapades, is a submission of the adolescent hero to the controlling power of the adult *reader*. In the same way that Adelsward-Fersen sees Nino as an art object, Peyrefitte sees Roy as a sex object. Roy's body is there to be doubly 'enjoyed', chapter after chapter, in graphic detail, orally and anally, not just by those who possess him literally – the police chief, the consul, the pop star, the Saudi princeling, Jim or Bob or Otis or

Ramsay – but by those who possess him metaphorically as they read.

Duvert's texts are ostensibly as shocking from a conventional viewpoint as *Roy* or parts of the *Propos secrets*, but their moral basis is not in the least ambiguous. In Duvert's fiction, positive characters accept their own sexuality, whatever it is, and enjoy it. Negative characters, particularly representatives of 'families', distort their own sexuality and that of others. Duvert revels in sexuality itself and turns sexual freedom into a prerequisite for, and symbol of, social liberation. In his view the whole system of permitted and forbidden pleasures is symptomatic of the repressive socio-economic order of a profit-and-loss orientated society, and his first essay, *Le Bon Sexe illustré*, is an attack on both the social and sexual principles involved in such repression. His second polemical essay, *L'Enfant au masculin*, which deals more specifically with homosexuality, is a logical extension of the arguments of the first, attacking what he calls 'heterocracy' and the way in which (as he sees it) parents impose heterosexual behaviour patterns on children as a norm.

The two works taken together are a modern *Corydon*. Duvert takes Gide's argument for the naturalness of pederasty and extends it into an argument for the right of every adolescent to explore, enjoy and develop their own sexuality with whatever partners they may choose. This sexual liberation is much more thoroughgoing than that proposed by Gide. Whereas the latter denies sexual pleasure to women, Duvert preaches freedom of sexual expression to both sexes, at all ages, in whatever combinations. And far from insisting on the difference between pederasty and other forms of homosexuality, Duvert presents them as a spectrum. At the same time the role of the mentor is more closely defined as an *initiator* in rebellion: as a partner in sexual freedom, the pederast opens the adolescent mind to new categories of experience and thought. Adolescent sensuality is thus not subordinate to conventional morality or emotional ties, but neither is it seen as something to be exploited by interested adults for their own ends. Its release is a prerequisite for learning how to be free from the constraining categories of contemporary social values.

One practical consequence of this is that descriptions of sex acts in Duvert's fiction have a very different status from those in *Roy*. There is no fixing of roles according to age – the narrator of *Journal d'un innocent* is as likely to be penetrated by his young partners as to penetrate them – and their tendency to construct a hierarchy among themselves based on machismo is a subject for critique, a set of pretensions to be dismantled within the privacy of the bedroom. What we often have in Duvert, for example in *Le Voyageur*, is what we also find in Hervé Guibert's *Fou de Vincent*: an insistence on the details of the sexual act itself coupled with a fragmentation of the text which focuses the reader *away* from the participants as individuals, such that the text becomes a general reflection of, and on, pleasure (or in the case of *Fou de Vincent* obsession) rather than an invitation to specific possession. A reader might be excited by the descriptions of the acts, but, unlike *Roy*, the form of the text prevents him from voyeuristically possessing the actors. Furthermore, *Journal d'un innocent* actually defuses its own tendency to pornography through the short essay on the subject which it contains. This argues for the powerlessness of written pornography as against the power given to the *model* in pornographic photographs, who exercises control over the spectator without having to submit to him. The problem of how to combine the pleasure principle with the educational function of the mentor, which Gide never solved in theory or in practice, is thus resolved in Duvert by making sexual self-expression the basis of the learning process for the child or adolescent, and the principal bridge between individuals regardless of age, without limiting the validity of sexuality to one-to-one relationships.

So far I have identified two converging traditions – the mentor/pupil model and the portrait of adolescent sensuality – and have looked at some of the problems raised by attempts to treat them either together or separately. I spoke of the shifting value of these two elements in different texts, and it will already be clear that part of the reason for such shifts in values depends on what network of other motifs, for example the love/death equation, are used to colour the reader's response to the central themes. Obviously, such motifs can be drawn from a wide variety of sources and will not necessarily occur in all texts. But there are three motifs which are fairly constant in the group of texts at which I have been looking, and all three connect back to some aspect of *Corydon*: the first is hostility to society; the second is the association of nature and the natural with beauty or sexuality; and the third, which to some extent subsumes the second, is the use of art in general and literature in particular as a reference point.

Almost all pederastic writers present the family as a negative force on the development of the individual. It is easy to find a cynical explanation for this: families are clearly likely to come between an adult and the adolescent object of his desire. The arguments, nonetheless, must be rather more complex than that, since in practice hostility to the family as a constricting unit is also found in much heterosexual literature focused on adolescence. Throughout the twentieth century youth has been seen as a force for, and symbol of, change; as yet free from the dead hand of convention, adolescents retain full powers of energy and imagination which society automatically attempts to repress by moulding them in its own image. Without youth there is no rebellion; without rebellion there is no social or cultural evolution. Now, as early as the 1830s, Balzac perceived that the basic unit of social control was the family, the microcosm of society. As the nineteenth century progressed, a second competing microcosm emerged, boarding school. Both these structures by definition seek to inculcate a particular set of existing social values in the young, designed (usually) to make them conformist.

For Gide, who believes that human fulfilment depends on being open to the possibilities of new experience at all times, any agency which attempts to 'fix' an individual's personality is harmful. The family, in Gide's writings, is therefore on a par with the established Church or any other social structure which lays down rigid guidelines for values and conduct. In Gidean fiction families always distort: the Profitendieu, Molinier and Azaïs-Vedel families in *Les Faux-monnayeurs* are obvious examples of this distorting process, or, to use the metaphor inherent in the book's title, counterfeiting. Only illegitimacy, by extracting the adolescent from the standard patriarchal hierarchy, gives him some hope of freedom – hence the relative liberty of Lafacadio in *Les Caves du Vatican* and Bernard in *Les Faux-monnayeurs* – unless, like Olivier Molinier, he finds a pederastic mentor.

Gide's famous cry, 'Families, I hate you!' (as familiar to the French as Larkin's equivalent, 'They fuck you up, your mum and dad', is to the English) echoes in the work of Peyrefitte, Montherlant and Duvert, but the use which these writers make of the motif varies significantly. The closest to the Gidean position is Duvert, who like Gide denies that identity is a fixed quantity, and therefore presents his characters as in a state of permanent potential development, on which adults in general, and families in particular, exert a stifling or malforming influence. Thus, in *L'Ile Atlantique* families represent obsession with things material: in the case of the Seignelet family obsession with food, for example. The children of such families are treated as material objects, to be organized, emotionally manipulated, even brutalized, as in the case of Julien Roquin. These negative forces themselves determine the nature and extent of the adolescent rebellion which they unintentionally nurture. Despite a touching desire to achieve some sort of togetherness, the band of youngsters, in theft, in mutual sexual exploitation, in murder even, replicate the patterns of behaviour which their elders have taught them. Only Julien, at the bottom of the pile, realizes what is happening: 'Each of them had fled from a sick environment, a family: they were a group of mutilated creatures, stammering, limping, there would never be any communication between them, no new gesture would be created. It was too late.'

The fundamental difference between Duvert and Gide, as I indicated above, is that for the former it is through freedom to explore their sexuality that the young can hope to escape from the deforming values of society, whereas in Gide's case the status of adolescent sexuality *for the adolescent* seems much more peripheral. For Gide the adult mentor retains something of a patriarchal status – hence the way in which Pauline hands her son Olivier over into Edouard's care – but without the notion of power/possession. In Duvert, even in *Quand mourut Jonathan*, the true pederast renounces the conventional marks of adult status altogether.

Peyrefitte and Montherlant are quite different. Their texts are not concerned with the abolition of possession but with a change in the identity of the possessor. As Montherlant puts it quite openly in one of his essays: 'What is it I want then? The possession of those who please me, possession in peace and in poetry.' Their attacks on the family itself are similar in terms to those of Gide and Duvert. De Pradts, in *Les Garçons*, for example, constructs an elaborate defence of the need to protect Serge from the atmosphere of his family, while mentally generalizing this into the proposition, 'Where parents are, everything is poisoned'. The principal evidence of the process of distortion is provided by the motif of lying, the deceit which becomes second nature with adolescents to protect themselves from adult interference, but which love, as Serge tells Alban in *La Ville dont le prince est un enfant*, should obviate. The problematic status of adult pederasts in these texts lies precisely in the degree to which they replicate the status and negative patterns of the family; both de Trennes and de Pradts suppress and distort truths in pursuit of their own goals, and the very sublimation of their own sexual desire is itself the ultimate form of lying. In *Roy*, in particular, both Jack (the chief of police) and Luke (the black-mailer) force Roy not only to lie but to manipulate others, to steal, even to kill. This would suggest that these are conventionally mora-lizing texts, rejecting both the destructive influence of families and the dangers of adult pederastic interference, but this is not the case. Montherlant manages to suggest that any force which contributes, as de Pradts does, to the release of adolescent energies is justified, and that de Pradts himself is a victim of society in its microcosmic forms of school and Church. Peyrefitte goes further. Whilst the author does purport to castigate those adults who attempt to use social power of one sort or another to manipulate Roy, adult sexual exploitation of him within the text goes uncommented on; it is counterbalanced by the evident pleasure and financial advantage which the boy derives from his encounters. What is more, through his recurrent use of pornographic interludes Peyrefitte makes the *reader* the unhindered and unpunished exploiter of the boy's ado-lescent body.

The implication of the fiction of both writers, which is con-firmed by what they have to say about desire and possession in their non-fiction works, is not that hierarchies should be abolished but that power should be transferable. What Montherlant in particular wants is to enrol adolescent males in a cult of conventional mascu-linity which has the same overtones of repressed homoeroticism as much 1930s fiction of adult masculinity (Hemingway, André Malraux), and which has values in common with the *fascist* cult of youth as expressed in the ostensibly heterosexual writings (e.g. *Les Sept Couleurs*) of the homosexual writer Robert Brasillach, and with the modern cult of gay macho.

The point I have just raised about Montherlant brings us to the question of another recurrent motif, the masculine/feminine dichotomy, which is an aspect of an interrelated set of motifs of nature, beauty and art. If there are two points on which all our writers are united, it is that pederastic and inter-adolescent desire are natural, and that such desire is in part created by the inherent beauty of the adolescent male body. With the exception of Duvert, who rejects the categorization into masculine and feminine as a form of disguised intellectual control, a way of defining the acceptable, they even agree on the role of the feminine in both male desire and male beauty. But they differ on two significant points: whether it is desirable to eradicate this feminine element, and whether the young are naturally corrupt.

The argument from nature is of course central to *Corydon* and to Duvert's essays. Its most common form of literary reflection is the lavish application of motifs and images of nature to the adolescent characters, a technique which both underlines the naturalness of their acts and counteracts any tendency to reduce them to the status of objects by linking them to the inherent processes of growth and development in, for example, plant life. In Gide the connections tend to remain contextual: his 'ecstasy' with a young boat-boy on Lake Como is enveloped in the moonlight, the misty enchantment of the lake and the humid perfumes of the lakeside. The association is more direct in later writers. *Les Amitiés particulières* is full of flower images, linking the natural with the feminine: Georges and Alexandre meet regularly in the hothouse, they are associated with orange blossom and lavender, and the smell of lilacs through an open window when he is working reminds Georges of Alexandre; in *Les Garçons* boys are likened to flowers, birds, the sea; in *Maumort* Guy is compared to a wounded bird, and his sexual parts are graphically evoked in nature images: 'a heavy, living cluster swollen with youth ... tender fruits of flesh, silky and diaphanous like the petals of a three-lobed flower.'

The interesting thing is that from this common ground each

author moves outward to a different sort of argument. Martin du Gard develops an extended theoretical excursus on the nature of sexuality, and Duvert expands into a definition of an entire relationship (Jonathan and Serge) as biological: they have a symbiotic relationship like that of plants which, by absorbing products which they need from the soil, purify it and make it a viable place for other species of plants to develop. Peyrefitte, like Gide, introduces the theme of nature as a subject for art, and Montherlant, making the implicitly Baudelairean connection between flowers and evil, both inserts his adolescents into a specific literary tradition and raises the issue of the need to temper nature with the art of the mentor. The natural beauty which they all depict is inherently androgynous, a paradox emphasized by Martin du Gard in his description of the arch-masturbator Raoul de Luzac: 'I'd say he was like a girl if he hadn't been so very much the opposite of effeminate.' Only in Montherlant is this androgyny itself an ambiguous quality, tied to a very transient period of desirability (thirteen to sixteen years), and necessarily offset by a countervailing myth of the heroic in order to keep the emphasis of the text on masculine values.

But it is the last of the motifs, the use of literature as a reference point, which is the most important, not least because it often subsumes motifs of the natural, the beautiful and even the moral within itself, but more particularly because it constitutes a basic tool in the difficult process of winning over the reader's sympathies. The idea of male beauty as the natural subject of High Art to which Gide devotes some space in *Corydon*, and the allied presentation of the adolescent as art object (e.g. Nino in *L'Exilé de Capri*) are part of a system of references to the arts in which literature predominates. There are a number of levels of literary reference. The first, to be found in theoretical works, involves bouncing a text off the value system of a pre-existing text. It is striking, for example, that all the four sections of *Corydon* are written 'against' other books: the first dialogue uses a contemporary French translation of Walt Whitman's *Leaves of Grass*, which heterosexualizes the whole of it, as the basis for an attack on current social hypocrisy and the pressures on homosexuals which it creates; the second dialogue responds to and develops Lester Ward's socio-biological theories in *Pure Sociology*; the third dialogue starts from a refutation of Rémy de Gourmont's *Physique de l'amour*; the fourth dialogue is a rebuttal of Léon Blum's *Du mariage*. The first of Duvert's essays, *Le Bon Sexe illustré*, works on the same principle, using the 1973 five-volume Hachette *Encyclopédie de la vie sexuelle* as its enemy text. In this way the writers install their polemic inside a wider framework of heterosexual debate, offsetting to some degree the dangers of marginalization.

In creative works, reference to other literature plays two kinds of role. The first is implicit: the insertion of a text into a specific tradition on a thematic or formal basis. This can be a general relationship created via an aspect of the text, for example the love = death motif which I identified above in *Maumort* and *Les Amitiés particulières*. But the most striking presence of reference to other literature is at the explicit level of references to specific texts. Some of the references have a significant but superficial effect on the reader's response to the form or tone of the text. In *La Ville dont le prince est un enfant* Montherlant underlines the tragic nature of the play with references to Racine, particularly to *Andromaque*, which, play within a play, the boys are currently rehearsing; in *Les Garçons* he presents an episode in which the older boys hymn the charms of one of the younger boys, as a formal poetic exchange between a Greek chorus leader and his chorus, the form thus intensifying the Greekness of the values expressed. But the use of literary reference is much more fundamental and far-reaching than these relatively ornamental examples suggest. Here again we can divide the phenomenon into three aspects: the appeal to a classical model, the appeal to existing French heterosexual traditions and the invitation to an intertextual reading with another pederastic text.

The function of an appeal to a classical model is fairly obvious. For a writer defending Greek love to attempt to assimilate what he writes to a Greek tradition or its reflection in Roman imitators is a logical extension of the appeal to classical authority for the validation of the mentor–pupil relationship in pederastic theory. *L'Exilé de Capri*, by its very setting, is shot through with classical references, many of them with specific pederastic associations: the emperor Tiberius on Capri; the beauty of the young god Mithras; the relationships of Apollo and Hyacinthus, Plato and

Lysis, Virgil and Alexis. References can be as slight as the use of a name to evoke a context of values: Gide, by calling his free spirit in *Les Nourritures terrestres* and *L'Immoraliste* Ménalque, attaches to him the value system of the Virgilian *Eclogues* (idealized pastoral poems in imitation of a Greek genre, which include relationships between adult and adolescent males, particularly in no. 2).

A reference of this sort can become a recurrent motif, as with those to Homer's *Iliad* in *Les Garçons*. The 'society' established under the nickname 'The Protection', which consists of older boys (of about sixteen years old) and their thirteen-year-old protégés and lovers, is defined in terms of the Homeric heroes (e.g. Achilles and Patroclus) such as to give a stamp of traditional masculinity to the relationships as well as putting them under the authority of a Greek example from the purely literary point of view. Consequently Montherlant can play off the 'masculine' and 'feminine' characteristics of the group in apparent paradoxes: 'The *Iliad* of the Protection was fertile in touching scenes.' The motif is at the same time a way of integrating *different* aspects of the value system at work in the novel, in that Montherlant uses it to join the adult pederasty (priestly) with the inter-adolescent relationships:

> In the *Iliad* (the Homeric one) the Gods protect such and such a warrior: when he is defeated a god intervenes and makes him the winner. In the *Iliad* of the Protection, the mere reference to a god protected you from defeat. The *soutane* was the magic armour which made you invisible.

But there is also a more profound sense in which the motif draws attention to the parallels between the society of the school and the society of Greek epic: women are despised (by the headmaster and the Abbé de Pradts); religion is a pervasive force; codes of honour are central; pederastic relations (sublimated or not) are an organizing principle.

On a comparable pattern, Peyrefitte, in *Les Amitiés particulières*, uses a system of literary and artistic references of different kinds to define the values and feelings of Georges and the nature of his relationship with Alexandre. Some of the texts are modern – poems by Fersen and Rostand – some are heterosexual (e.g. *The*

Song of Songs), but the vast majority are classical, many with overt homosexual implications: a print of a sculptured male figure, his father's collection of coins showing Alexander the Great, Virgil, Apollo and Hyacinthus. The references to Alexander and those to Nysus and Euryalus (the warrior lovers from Virgil's *Aeneid*) serve a similar purpose to the Homeric references in *Les Garçons*: they invoke a heroic context. Peyrefitte even extends this to an almost allegorical reading. One of Georges's father's coins, though worn by time (the effect of society on the relationship) shows the hero's profile with an untouched freshness, defying time and man (the lovers' defiance of social prejudice), while the reverse of the coin shows the figure of Victory, one of her wings apparently supporting the name Alexander (an augury that their love will prevail). Similarly, the reader is intended, as Georges does, to link Antinous,[13] Saint Alexander, Alexander the Great, Virgil's Alexis and Georges's beloved (beauty, religion, power, art, classic pederasty), just as he is to connect hyacinths, Hyacinthus and Saint Hyacinthus (nature, classical pederasty and religion). In this way the entire value system on which the heroes depend, and which society fails to comprehend or honour, is given the seal of classical and religious approval, and moral and aesthetic justification, simultaneously.

As I suggested above, the use of classical references is only one aspect of the invitation to intertextual readings. Given their setting, religious texts are to be expected as points of reference in the school stories, although the appeal made by Père de Trennes to Saint Augustine's *Confessions* and to the belief that children are not naturally innocent is an unexpected choice of source.[14] But Montherlant in particular also suggests the Baudelairean equation of beauty and evil, defining his boys as by nature physically exquisite (including some flower imagery) but morally corrupt (notably Linsbourg's beloved, Denie), and suggesting a possible equation sexuality = evil, which automatically relates the theme of pederasty not just to the whole tradition of the artist-pariah but thereby to the wider tradition of French homosexual writing from Proust to Genet which uses that motif. Parallel with this is the complex intertext created by *Les Amitiés particulières*, *La Ville dont le prince est un enfant* and *Les Garçons* themselves, in which the second Montherlant text involves a reworking of the first with a different emphasis.

The 'joint text' which they thus create, and which specifically uses the phrase *amitiés particulières* (special friendships) to define the relationships described, sets up a commentary on, and redefinition of, the view of pederasty represented in Peyrefitte's novel and on the literary means used to convey that view.

What we are dealing with in all these cases of literary reference is an appeal to *authority*. The author attempts to define the validity of his ideas either by demonstrating their superiority to those of an existing text (*Corydon, Le Bon Sexe illustré*) or their coherence with those of an existing text or texts. In the latter case the authority can be one which 'justifies' in some sense the values of the modern text – Georges and Alexandre are placed under the patronage of Virgil's *Eclogues*, the boys of the Protection are authorized by the *Iliad*. Alternatively, one particular thematic aspect of a work is given weight – love = death, beauty and evil are inseparable – which it derives from a particular post-Romantic tradition already exploited by other forms of homosexual literature. Or, lastly, a debate is established between a pederastic text which has already found favour with the general (heterosexual) public – in this case *Les Amitiés particulières* – and two new texts, such that the ideas of the latter are protected by the status of the former, whilst allowing room for emendation and expansion. All these are examples of tying texts outwards to other writings.

At the same time, literary reference also helps to focus systems of motifs *within* the texts, for example: nature, natural behaviour and pastoral literature (Virgil); the feminine/masculine dichotomy and epic values (Homer); sexuality, sinfulness and Baudelaire. The technique is clearly at one level a persuasive device. If the reader accepts the cultural/intellectual respectability of the book, this will influence his judgement of the sexual/'moral' content, an important factor when not just the sexual and emotional relationships but attitudes on such fundamental social issues as the family might tend to alienate the non-pederastic reader. In this respect literary reference is fundamentally a technique of apologia. Perhaps the ultimate paradox is that a literature designed to overthrow conventional principles of moral authority (e.g. the family) should so often have recourse to the invocation of *cultural* authority (literary tradition) in its attempts to control the responses of the non-pederastic reader. It is no accident that the most independent thinkers (for their respective periods) among the writers we have been considering, Gide and Duvert, should have recourse least often to this particular device.

The more closely we look at it, the more clear it becomes that twentieth-century French pederastic literature is about power: social, sexual and textual control. One branch of it presents the writer's attempt to replace the standard patriarchal power structure with one in which the pederast has power. This substitution can be in the form of a mentor/pupil relationship with a broadly educational purpose and designed to allow for the process of development intrinsic to adolescence; but when the substitution is principally or exclusively aimed at sexual possession, it tends to become exploitative, extending via the use of pornography to the metaphorical possession of the adolescent sex object by the reader. Alternatively, pederastic literature takes the form of a genuine literature of liberation focused on the emotional and physical needs of the adolescent, either as viewed in an all-adolescent context or, as in some of the work of Duvert, in a context where adulthood does not confer privileged status.

There is, of course, often no clear divide between the two approaches to pederasty. The confusion is inherent in Gide's work, and there is an accompanying confusion of image. In his early play *Saul* for example, Saul himself represents the need for adult pederastic desire to be repressed, whereas the sublimated love of the two young men, David and Jonathan, for one another is seen as a positive force. After Gide the self-image of the adult pederast goes through a period where sexual fulfilment is excluded and the emphasis of the texts is on the educational and emotional functions of the mentor (although what we know of the private lives of the authors concerned shows that there is no coherence of writing and life at this point). It is only from the late 1960s onward that an explicitly physical adult pederastic literature emerges, but while this shrugs off the sense of guilt, it frequently exacerbates the problem of possession-versus-liberation.

At the same time the writers face an aesthetic paradox: as with mainstream gay literature, there is evidence of a desire to insert texts into existing literary traditions in order to 'legitimize' pederastic desire. Alongside love = death and the artist-pariah motif it is inevitably the Greco-Roman tradition which is of particular significance. This deference to cultural authority is doubly paradoxical. First, texts which are seeking to overthrow accepted social values, particularly in their attacks on the family, are at the same time seeking cultural acceptance and subordinating themselves to the cultural values of that same society. Secondly, the system of intertextual reference gives great weight to the question of *art*, and a subsidiary system of references to the adolescent-as-art-object is developed to support this, whereas thematically the emphasis is on *nature* and the arguments for the naturalness of adolescent pan-eroticism and pederastic desire. It is understandable that, given these paradoxes, and the relatively tightknit set of themes and conventions to which most of the pederastic texts adhere, Duvert's work, or a text like Guibert's *Fou de Vincent*, should consciously try to overthrow *writing* convention, by adopting the techniques of the *nouveau roman*, with its suppression of standard concepts of identity and psychology, as a prerequisite for the sexual and social revolution which such texts imply.

Notes

1. Quoted by Roger Martin du Gard in his *Notes sur André Gide*. See Martin du Gard, *Oeuvres complètes*, vol. 2 (Paris: Gallimard (Bibliothèque de la Pléiade), 1955), p. 1399.
2. Dominique Fernandez, *L'Etoile rose* (Paris: Grasset, 1978), p. 89.
3. My italics. The statement is from a conversation with Henri Rode, recorded in his book, *Marcel Jouhandeau: son oeuvre et ses personnages* (Paris: Feuilles, 1972), p. 110.
4. However eyebrow-raising this sort of literature may seem to the modern Anglo-Saxon reader, we have to remember that until 1942 the age of consent for any type of sexual activity was thirteen years of age. The activities described were perfectly legal.
5. For a detailed account of the genesis of *Corydon* and a useful summary of its arguments, see Patrick Pollard, *André Gide: Homosexual Moralist* (New Haven and London: Yale University Press, 1991), pp. 3–19.
6. For Alyssa and Juliette, see *La Porte étroite* (1909); for Marceline, see *L'Immoraliste* (1902); for the pastor's wife, see *Symphonie pastorale* (1919); for Mme Sophroniska and Pauline, see *Les Faux-monnayeurs* (1926); for Carola, see *Les Caves du Vatican* (1914).

7.   The play, *La Ville dont le prince est un enfant* (first published in 1951, reworked in 1967) develops a central episode of material later published in novel form in *Les Garçons* (1969). There *are* differences of detail and of treatment, but the values of the two works are essentially the same.

8.   Cf. Ch. 2, pp. 61 and 68 and Ch. 5, pp. 133 and 140. Where reader sympathy with irregular sexual liaisons clashes with received notions of social propriety, the author can satisfy both the romantic propensities and the moral prejudices of the reader by killing off the character principally responsible for the irregularity, provided it is done in a suitably tragic manner.

9.   *Si le grain ne meurt*, pt II, ch. 2 in André Gide, *Journal 1939–49, Souvenirs* (Paris: Gallimard (Bibliothèque de la Pléiade), 1954), p. 595.

10. The snake is both a biblical symbol of evil and a phallic symbol = sex = evil. The image here recalls the use of a snake as a belt, with comparable connotations, in Baudelaire's prose poem 'Les Tentations'.

11. See Charles Adam, 'Armed with a pen: Roger Peyrefitte', *Gay Times*, November 1993, pp. 60–2.

12. The choice of a policeman also panders to the stereotypical view of gay males as lusting after men in uniform, a factor designed to underline the raw carnality of the relationship between Jack and Roy.

13. The city of Alexandria played a key role in the life of Antinous, the adolescent lover of the Roman Emperor Hadrian; hence its place in this list. The fact that Antinous committed suicide while on a state visit to Egypt with Hadrian creates a special connection between him and Alexandre, and therefore gives his name a particular resonance here. Hyacinthus, in the next list, similarly introduces associations of untimely death suffered because of love.

14. The idea fits well with Montherlant's frequent implicit references to Baudelairean values; for Baudelaire's belief that children were close to original sin, see the prose poems, 'Le Pauvre et le joujou' and 'Le Gateau'.

Chapter seven

Lesbian (Re)visions (i)

'Lesbianism is much more than homosexuality. . . . Lesbianism opens onto another dimension of the human.'

● *Monique Wittig*[1]

LESBIANISM as a focal subject for French literature first made a substantial appearance, as I showed in Chapter 1, in the last decades of the nineteenth century, particularly in the work of Decadent authors. At the same period the male voyeuristic tradition, which had its roots in the eighteenth-century libertine novel, found a new and more complex expression in Pierre Louÿs's *Chansons de Bilitis*. Meanwhile, Sappho scholarship, largely under the impetus of the discovery of important papyrus fragments in Egypt in 1897, reopened the question of the lesbian element in Sappho's poetry, and thereby revitalized the issue of Sappho as the model *par excellence* for modern lesbian writing.[2] Together with the relaxation of the sexual code, which permitted discreet sexual experiment, at least among women of the upper classes, these factors created a climate in which overt lesbian *self*-expression in literature seemed possible.

However, other factors militated against such self-expression. In the first place, although lesbianism was a frequent theme in male writing between 1880 and 1910, there were unwritten rules on how it could be handled. It is not true to imply, as Virginie Sanders does,[3] that male authors could present lesbianism in whatever form they liked, with impunity: in 1892, for example, Jean Lorrain was convicted of an 'offence against public decency' and fined 3,000 francs for publishing a story 'Sapphic in atmosphere' entitled 'Autour de ces dames' in *L'Echo de Paris*.[4] His fault was to have written a lesbian story with a *contemporary* setting, to have done so without taking a hostile moral stance to his material and to have published the story in a newspaper. If men were not completely free to handle the theme, it is hardly surprising that it was difficult for women to handle it at all. Male critics (most of whom were also novelists or poets themselves), nervous of growing competition from their female counterparts, were quick to portray any form of female emancipation as a denial of the role of wife and mother on which society saw itself as built, and to associate such antisocial behaviour with lesbianism, which they presented as a sign of moral decadence. Accordingly, publishers were very reluctant to take on overtly lesbian works by women: in 1901 one of the leading courtesans of the day, Liane de Pougy, had difficulty in finding a publisher for *Idylle saphique*,[5] the highly moralistic autobiographical novel in which she portrayed her own affair with Natalie Barney.[6] These contextual factors inevitably influenced how far, and in what form, lesbian writing could develop.

The classic account of modern French lesbian writing, Elaine Marks's essay 'Lesbian intertextuality'[7] posits a division into three periods: the *belle époque*, its essence summed up by Colette, who at the same time acts as a transitional figure to the next phase; the Existentialist period, with Violette Leduc as its focus; and the development of lesbian feminism in the 1970s and 1980s, centring on the texts of Monique Wittig. Bridging this tripartite development is the Sappho model, even if it informs the texts of each period in a different way, dependent on whether the focus is the teacher/pupil relationship (Sappho as educator of mind, emotions and senses) or the poetics of the female body and female desire. The idea of lesbian intertextuality and of continuity within development which Marks expounds is a valuable one, but I want to consider the material from a different angle, partly in order to bring out comparisons with male homosexual literature, and partly to show other significant patterns within lesbian writing which highlight the complexities of its own tradition.

Marks's tripartite division implies a movement from 'feminine' writing to 'feminist' writing, but to look at the texts in this way is, to some extent, a distortion. The nature and significance of this distortion becomes apparent if we take as the basis for discussion a division into 'separatist' writing, that is, texts which present lesbianism as separate from male homosexuality or female heterosexuality and which promote the isolation of lesbians from the rest of society, and writings which present lesbianism as part of a sexual spectrum or 'continuum' and relate it, directly or implicitly, to other forms of male or female sexuality. 'Separatist' and 'continuum' perceptions of lesbianism coexist right across the century, and share many of the same literary themes and motifs. The *belle époque* itself provides a good example of this. The focus of lesbian French writing at that period is the circle around Natalie Barney and Renée Vivien – an expatriate American and an expatriate Anglo-American.[8] Their expatriate status was important: they perceived themselves as 'outsiders' in a profound sense, and their lives and work (Barney in particular considered life and work as inseparable) are based on separatist principles – the centrality of women and women's values; the relative superiority of women; the need to reclaim heroic female figures from patriarchal neglect; the need to define and express a non-traditional relationship between emotion and sexuality. Yet, as we shall see, the writings of other members of their group are not separatist at all. The novelist and poet Lucie Delarue-Mardrus married, and much of her work, while focusing on women's issues, does not concern itself primarily with lesbianism.[9] More importantly, Colette, who belonged to the group for a while and shared some of their values, integrated her perceptions of the nature and value of lesbian emotional and physical relations into a general view of the nature of womanhood and of relations between the sexes which is quite at odds with the tradition represented by Barney and Vivien.

In this chapter, then, I am going to look at the development of lesbian separatism, because it represents the dominant tradition in this century. Its roots lie, as I have said, in the expatriate circles of turn-of-the-century Paris. Natalie Barney in particular systematically rejected patriarchal norms: by living abroad; by expressing her lesbianism openly; by spending money inherited from her father on the private publication of lesbian poetry, on theatrical and other all-female entertainments at her Paris house (20, Rue Jacob) and on the *Académie des femmes* (founded 1927), a place for women writers to try out their unpublished works and an institution for subsidizing the printing of commercially unviable works. This conscious cultivation of difference in her lifestyle was paralleled by the systematic expounding of difference in her writing. From her earliest work onward she argues for the separate and superior nature of female values against any form of male domination or manipulation of women. In *Cinq petits dialogues grecs*[10] she represents heterosexual sex as a violation of a woman's wholeness, and the image of man as despoiler is symbolically expanded in the figure of Demetrios in her play *Autour d'une victoire*.[11] Her poems contain attacks on marriage and procreation. For example in 'A une fiancée':

> Vous voulez enfanter, devenir une mère,
> Donner au monde un homme, une âme à la matière,
> Bétail reproduisant le mal de vos aïeux.
> Vautrée en le passé pour taire vos alarmes,
> N'entendez-vous ces cris qui montent jusqu'aux cieux,
> Demandant le non-être au Créateur des larmes?[12]

> (You want to give birth, become a mother,
> Bring a man into the world, give a soul to matter,
> You're just a domestic animal reproducing your ancestors'
> sin.
> Hunched up over the past to silence your own fears,
> Can't you hear the cries mounting to heaven,
> Begging the Creator of tears for non-existence?)

These positions are confirmed and expanded in the arguments of her post-First World War prose works *Pensées d'une amazone* and *Nouvelles pensées d'une amazone*, and her position remains unchanged right up to the belatedly published *Traits et portraits* (1963). She attacks the primacy of heterosexuality, challenging straights over reproduction and overpopulation, rejecting the value of maternity on social, aesthetic and metaphysical grounds, presenting problems such as war and violence as inextricably linked with male sexuality and traditional concepts of masculinity, but also attacking male homosexuals for the pursuit of sensuality as an end in itself.[13] This rejection of the male in general and of heterosexuality in particular, accompanied by a systematic redefinition of female sexuality and female creativity, constitutes, for the period, a fundamental challenge to society's principles.

Exactly the same points are made in the stories and poems of Renée Vivien. From the first poem of her second collection of poems, *Cendres et poussières*, with its all-embracing first-person plurals, she makes it clear that she is addressing an elite female readership, and that men play a relatively small part even among the characters of her poems, which are peopled mainly with goddesses, heroines and female lovers. The implicit rejection of men becomes explicit in her collection of short stories *La Dame à la louve*.[14] Several stories have male narrators who betray the narrowness of their values by the manner of their narration, and some feature male characters who manifest what society has traditionally labelled 'feminine' weaknesses, for example Jim in 'Le Soif ricane' faints when confronted with the danger of death from a prairie fire and has to be saved by his female companion Polly. In this collection male sexuality is associated with violence, the taking of a woman's virginity is presented as a barbarous act of pillage and massacre, and heroines prefer to die rather than submit to men.

As for hostility to male sexuality and rejection of maternity, both openly expounded in her novel *Une Femme m'apparut* in which heterosexuality is scorned as 'an unnatural aberration' and 'an abnormal passion' and marriage denounced as a purely commercial arrangement, these attitudes are reflected constantly in the details of her poems. In her expansion of a fragment of the work of the classical Greek poetess Telesilla, for example, she emphasizes the value of virginity, the rejection of male desire and the animal brutality of straight sex:

> ... les hommes en rut et les femmes passives luttant et se
> mêlant comme les animaux.

> (... rutting men and passive women

struggling together and mating like animals.)

'Litanie de la haine' (from *La Vénus des aveugles*) is even more specific:

> Nous haïssons la face agressive des mâles. ...
> Nous haïssons le rut qui souille le désir.
> Nous jetons l'anathème à l'immonde soupir
> D'ou naîtront les douleurs des êtres à venir.

> (We hate men's aggressive faces. ...
> We hate the lust which soils desire.
> We curse the filthy sigh
> Which will result in the birth of the pain and sorrow of
> those who are to come.)

This direct language is often replaced by symbols familiar from male decadent poetry. Thus in 'Les Succubes disent ...' (from the same collection) the preference for sterility is introduced in images of the moon and of flowers which die without producing fruit, and in associations with spirits which presage death and still birth. In its turn this sterility is linked to a cancellation of sexual potential itself: in the last stanza, the bodies of the speakers are sexless as they gaze on the sterility of eternity.

The corollary of the rejection of others which we have been discussing lies in images of alienation and of rejection of the self *by* others. Vivien in particular protests against heterosexual hostility towards her brand of affection:

> On m'a montrée du doigt en un geste irrité,
> Parceque mon regard cherchait ton regard tendre ...[15]

> (People pointed at me with irritated gestures,
> Because my gaze was looking for your tender gaze ...)

and even more against heterosexual rejection of her *art*:

> O mes chants! nous n'aurons ni honte ni tristesse

De voir nous mépriser ceux qui nous méprisons ....
Et ce n'est plus à la foule que je m'adresse ...
Je n'ai jamais compris les lois ni les raisons.

Allons-nous-en, mes chants dédaignes et moi-même ...
Que nous importe ceux qui n'ont pas écouté?[16]

(O my songs! we shall not be ashamed or saddened
To see ourselves despised by those whom we despise....
It's no longer the crowd that I am addressing ...
I have never understood laws or reasoning.
Let's go, my disdained songs and I ...
What do those who have not listened matter to us?)

The image of rejection is intensified in two short stories published together in 1907 under the joint title *Le Christ, Aphrodite et M. Pépin* which, prefiguring Kazantzakis's *Christ Recrucified* and Denys Arcand's film *Jésus de Montréal*, propose that if the two divinities were to attempt a 'second coming' in contemporary materialist society, they would be rejected.[17] But at the same time we find, running in parallel, an insistence on exile as choice rather than a condition imposed by others, and a proclamation of independence from the world's opinions:

Nous irons voir le clair d'étoiles sur les monts. ...
Que nous importent, à nous, le jugement des hommes?

(We shall go to see the brightness of stars over the
   mountains. ...
What does it matter to us what others think?)

The positive side of alienation is the impetus that it gives the writer to redefine woman. Both Barney and Vivien place great emphasis on the female body, female power, female unity and female creativity. The common element underlying their treatment of all these is the rejection of opposition and confrontation, which they perceive as a male category of thought, and its replacement by an emphasis on similarity and synthesis (although in practice, as we shall see, Vivien is haunted by dualities, many of them imposed or intensified by the traditional poetic discourse to which she adheres). At the physical and emotional level this sense of identity between women is perfectly embodied in Vivien's 'Union' (*Sillages*), the poem moving from similarity of the heart and body to identity of thought and feeling across space and time. But the two writers go beyond this level of unity. Barney wanted to emulate Sappho by gathering around herself a group of women who would be lovers *and* friends *and* writers – hence her proposal to Vivien that they set up a 'school of poetry' on Lesbos (during their 1904 trip there). The same sense of a unity which is not merely physical and spiritual but also *creative* informs such poems as Vivien's 'Nous irons vers les poètes' (*A l'heure des mains jointes*), which describes the ideal separate existence, as far away as possible from the threat of masculine control, in a world exclusively dedicated to art:

> Nous souvenant qu'il est de plus larges planètes,
> Nous entrerons dans le royaume des poètes,
> Ce merveilleux royaume où chantent les poètes.
>
> (Remembering that there are broader plantes,
> We shall enter the kingdom of the poets,
> That wonderful kingdom where the poets sing.)

This escape into art is not merely an escape; it represents the zenith of separatist ambitions precisely because female lovers who were also artists presented a challenge to the conventional natural, social, divine and aesthetic orders all at once.

It is not surprising, then, that the most important of the thematic and stylistic features which underpin the separatist emphasis of both Barney and Vivien's work derive from the figure of Sappho and *her* work. Both women could read Ancient Greek, and Vivien actually translated the extant fragments for a bilingual edition (the 'translations' consisted of both literal prose version and verse translations which are expansions and interpretations).[18] Sappho's significance to Barney is evident right from the *Cinq petits dialogues grecs*, the first of which is devoted to praise of the poetess, who is portrayed as following her nature, an elemental force, goddess and mortal together, whose loves are fleeting, fierce passions which both destroy and glorify. Both women wrote dramatic pieces about Sappho: Barney's *Equivoques*, published in *Actes et entractes*, and Vivien's two dramatic poems 'La Mort de Psappha' and 'Atthis delaisée', in *Evocations*. From Sappho's work they took ways of expressing sensual and emotional love for women, refined values of love and friendship, the idea of an elite, and a whole paraphernalia of classical reference from which Vivien built a quasi-religious picture of Sappho and her followers as priestess and cult. In Vivien's novel *Une Femme m'apparut* San Giovanni, the author's androgynous *alter ego* presents herself as a reincarnation of a follower of Sappho, and the same spiritual kinship is taken up in the poem 'Psappha revit' (*A l'heure des mains jointes*).[19] The transposition of lesbian experience in time and space to classical Mytilene, its placing under the tutelage of Sappho and the goddess Aphrodite, and its presentation through a vocabulary and imagery drawn in part from classical lyric and pastoral poetry emphasize the distance between the modern reader and the world of the poems, even if, particularly in Vivien's work, Sappho has been reinterpreted through a filter of Baudelaire and Swinburne.[20]

There is, then, no doubt about the seriousness of Barney and Vivien's aspiration to separatism or its importance in their work. In life their financially privileged condition gave them the means to live freely, and their expatriate status put them, in a significant sense, outside the dictates of society: Vivien seems to have achieved a life in which contact with men was minimal, and although Barney was less exclusive in this respect – she quite enjoyed flirting with them, had one or two close male friends (including Pierre Louÿs) and included male writers in the activities of her literary salon and even of the *Académie des femmes* – she admitted men into her life strictly on her own terms. But even in life separatism was not easy to sustain as a positive position; we have seen how the fine line between choosing isolation and feeling rejected is reflected in Vivien's poems. Vivien's desire to reach a wider female reading public than her own circle brought her into abrasive contact with the Parisian critics, who treated her early work (up to 1903) kindly because she kept her identity secret, masculinizing her name to René, and thereby contrived to present it without a recognizable lesbian context. Once her real identity was known, she was exposed to a personalized hostility which led her, after 1906, to withhold her work from the critics altogether.[21]

If separatism was difficult in life, it was impossible in literature. Apart from Sappho, there was no female model for Barney or Vivien to follow. They were more or less obliged, therefore, to adhere to forms of discourse which were male-dominated.[22] Barney's main works, the two collections of *Pensées*, are consciously attached, by form and title, to the seventeenth-century male tradition of moral reflections exemplified by La Rochefoucauld and La Bruyère, and to some extent she does manage to subvert that tradition by challenging its assumptions about the relationship between reason and emotion, frivolity and profundity. Vivien, however, had a much harder task. Much of her poetry is firmly rooted in Baudelaire and the post-Baudelairean Decadent tradition. It is shot through with motifs of *ennui*, the fascination of death, the interrelation of love and death; it inverts traditional values, particularly in its preference for sterility and purity over fertility and carnality; its images play with the same oppositions of light and dark, pleasure and pain, nature and art. Susan Gubar claims that Vivien is subversively suggesting that 'the lesbian is the epitome of the decadent and that decadence is fundamentally a lesbian literary tradition',[23] but in much of the poetry there is no evidence of subversion. The 'otherness' of a lesbianism projected across time and space into images of classical antiquity has the same sanitizing effect as the equivalent technique in Jean Lorrain's 'Bathylle';[24] the connection between love and sickness or death, even when ornamented with the baroque (and essentially phallic) conceit of orgasm-as-death in 'Amazone' (*Etudes et préludes*), activates the conception of same-sex love as destructive; the motif of artist-as-outcast integrates Vivien into a *male tradition* (Hugo, Baudelaire, Corbière), just as the sterility-versus-fertility opposition creates a potential intertext with Laforgue. Where Vivien uses motifs from pre-nineteenth-century male traditions the problems are greater still. Both Barney and Vivien were attracted by the courtly love tradition – there are photographs of them playing at page and lady – and motifs of this kind appear, for example, in Vivien's 'Pour le lys' (*Dans un coin de violettes*) and 'La Douve' (*La Vénus des aveugles*). But this implies postures of dominance and submission which underline a frequent inequality in the roles of lover and beloved in Vivien's poetry, an inequality completely at odds with the motifs of unity and equivalence in 'Union' and 'Paroles à l'amie'. Not only, as Jay rightly points out, are such relationships 'inherently pernicious even when played out between women of equal power – or lack of it – within the context of the dominant culture', but they destabilize the already precarious value system of Vivien's poetry, while at the same time drawing attention to the dominant/submissive position in which that poetry stands to the male tradition on which it relies.

In two respects, however, I think Gubar's claim is justified, precisely because it is plain in both that Vivien has created a specifically female perspecctive. The first is her inversion of the symbolic value of traditional female figures, particularly as an expression of spiritual rebellion which takes the Romantic male motif of Satanic revolt and turns it into a genuine subversion of the Judaeo-Christian tradition of God-the-patriarch. In Vivien's prose works Vashti (praised by San Giovanni in *Une Femme m'apparut*) takes a positive role: her disobedience to Ahasuerus is portrayed as a righteous act in 'Le Voile de Vashti' (*La Dame à la louve*), because the latter, in ordering her to unveil herself in front of his drunken courtiers, was treating her as a possession and violating her female privacy. In the same story Lilith (Eve's predecessor, who was created equal with Adam and refused to obey him) is held up as a representative of the aspirations denied to women, and it is in the same role that she speaks in 'Souveraines' (*Evocations*) and is invoked in 'Treize' and 'Litanie de la haine' (*La Vénus des aveugles*). Other figures used the same way range from Delilah to anonymous groups of unjustly persecuted spiritual rebels such as witches ('Enseignements', in *Sillages*). These rehabilitations of female figures are integrated into the standard apparatus of Romantic revolt – e.g. praise of Ashtaroth, Belial, Belzebuth, Eblis – in such a way as to give this too a new feminist force.

The second example of such a 'rewriting' of the male tradition is Vivien's use of the androgyne. When this classic Decadent motif is used by other women writers of the period, such as Rachilde, it usually merely reflects, as in male writers, the idea of emasculation, the feminization of the male. Vivien's lesbian fairy-tale 'Le Prince charmant' (*La Dame à la louve*), on the contrary, presents androgyny as the transcendence of the conventional limitations of masculinity and femininity through the combination of both elements within a single person, in this case Terka, the 'perfect page' with whom Sarolta falls in love under the impression that she is her brother.[25] The same image is reflected in 'Sonnet' (*Evocations*), where the beloved is both Hamlet and Ophelia:

> Ton être double attire ainsi qu'un double aimant,
> Et ta chair brûle avec l'ardeur froide d'un cierge.
>
> Mon coeur déconcerté se trouble quand je vois
> Ton front pensif de prince et tes yeux bleus de vierge,
> Tantôt l'Un, tantôt l'Autre, et les Deux à la fois.

> (Your double being attracts me like a double magnet,
> And your flesh burns with the cold heat of a candle.
> My disconcerted heart is troubled when I see
> Your princely thoughtful brow and your virgin's blue eyes,
> Sometimes One, sometimes the Other, and yet Both
>   together.)

The most complete expression of this view of the androgyne is in the figure of San Giovanni, who emphasizes the importance of the coexistence of the conventionally masculine and feminine within the creative artist, thus justifying in theory (even if it does not entirely work in practice) the assimilation of the male tradition alongside Sappho within Vivien's work.

The problem for both Barney and Vivien, but particularly for the latter, is that the proportion of their work which emancipates itself from the existing male-fashioned discourse is relatively small. There is therefore a constant tension between their separatist aspirations and the literary continuum into which their writing is locked. They lack a language of their own, literally and metaphorically, and even their Sappho is too closely associated with the male

Decadent use of classical motifs, in particular with the *Chansons de Bilitis*. It is to this question of emancipation from existing literary discourse that their successors will particularly address themselves.

The transitional figure in French lesbian separatist writing is Violette Leduc. It may seem odd to call Leduc a separatist at all, given her own evident, continuing bisexuality and the important part played in her work by, for example, positive portraits of non-lesbian forms of sexual 'transgression', such as adolescent heterosexual incest (*Le Taxi*) and successful adult heterosexual relations between a woman of fifty and a much younger man (*La Chasse à l'amour*). My reason for doing so is that the central problems posed in her work, which revolve around interrelated themes of gender, identity and writing, seem only to resolve themselves satisfactorily in brief periods of lesbian relationships and the writing to which those relationships gives birth.

Her main text, the autobiographical narrative *La Bâtarde* (1964),[26] starts with a series of oppositions: between present written self (her birth certificate) and absent newborn self: between paternal absence (she was illegitimate) and female presence (her mother and grandmother); between present writing self and absent past self – oppositions whose resistance to resolution is a fundamental cause of her sense of fragmentation. This dualism continues to be a key feature of the text. Her relationship to the masculine, for example, is always that of dominated and dominator, even though her dominator figures are often, ironically, gay males. This pattern repeats itself both in literary terms (her relationship to the strategies of narration in Rousseau's *Confessions*), and in lived terms, as she writes to please Maurice Sachs or sets up a cult of adoration to Genet. At most she inverts the terms of the relationship, playing the man (right down to her clothes) for her feminized husband, Gabriel, and turning him into an erotic *object* within the text.

Only in her sexual and emotional relations with her schoolfriend Isabelle and her teacher Hermine does she find a temporary fulfilment, a sense of unity and equality which derives from the *sameness* of her partner. Significantly, this fulfilment and sense of unity ally themselves with a new form of writing, the development of a lyrical exploration of the female body and lesbian eroticism reminiscent of the same freeing of the self through a new writing of the *male* body, a few years earlier, in Genet and in Jouhandeau's *Tirésias*. *La Bâtarde*, *Ravages* – an earlier novel which covers part of the same material – and in particular *Thérèse et Isabelle* (a work intended as part of *Ravages*, censored by the publishers, and only belatedly published in 1966) all confirm the same pattern in this respect. Although the wider context of her work covers the general issues of the female condition and of the constriction of the gender roles imposed on both men and women, Leduc's problems as woman and writer achieve a temporary resolution only in episodes which, while they owe something to the Sappho-as-mentor tradition (particularly as reflected in the early work of Colette), are marked by an identification of all-female sexuality, nature and literary creation,[27] a pattern which will recur in later lesbian separatists.

Leduc, writing in the 1950s and 1960s, demonstrates many of the problems of a lesbian writer's relationship to the existing literary traditions. But it is only in the 1970s and 1980s that lesbian writers, turning to extreme separatist solutions, directly addressed the core problem of the constraints of existing discourse. The most influential theorist and creative writer to embrace radical lesbian separatism is Monique Wittig. For her, changing language itself is an important part of, indeed a prerequisite for, changing society. In her key essays, 'The Straight Mind' and 'One is not born a woman',[28] she argues that male values permeate and shape all society's discourse, from structural anthropology to pornography, from the language of fashion to the language of psychoanalysis. The problem is that all of life has been described in a series of binary oppositions, where the first term is neutral, the norm, and the second is negative, that which departs from the norm: 'Straight society is based on the necessity of the different at every level. It cannot work economically, symbolically, linguistically or politically without this concept. ... But what is the different/other if not the dominated?' The concept of the differences of the sexes, then, is designed to ensure that women are 'other', hence inferior: *man* is the unmarked term, *woman* = minus *man*. For lesbians, Wittig argues, it is essential to grasp that 'man' and 'woman' are political concepts of opposition as much as master/slave or white/black. There is no 'essence of man' which genuinely exists in opposition to 'essence of woman'; the function of such concepts of difference is to mask the conflicts of interest between groups, the maintenance of difference being an act of *power*.

Two things follow from this. First, lesbians and gay men who continue to speak of themselves as women and men are conniving in the continuation of heterocracy. If Wittig focuses on lesbianism, it is because it is an active refusal of the male-created category 'woman' and is therefore 'the only social form in which we can live freely'.[29] Second, since 'marked' concepts cannot be redeemed, you cannot abolish the social reality of oppression which they represent unless you first abolish the concept. It is the task of the lesbian writer, therefore, to change the discourse: to reinvent language and create a new system of signs which will free people from their preconceptions. The notion of a literal, physical lesbian separatism which the first of the above points introduces is explored in Wittig's *Les Guérillères*; the reinvention of language and the sign system is central to *Le Corps lesbien*.

Les Guérillères is a mythic Utopian text exploring the potential nature and development of an exclusively lesbian society. The women begin by ridding their 'space' of masculine traditions, then relearn their own bodies, eventually re-conceiving them as a totality: they cease to regard the female genitalia as the supreme defining feature, since to do so is simply to substitute vulva worship for phallus worship. In coming to terms with their bodies the women thus move beyond the narcissistic fixation with their own sexuality which has been imposed on them by their original sexual inequality. The book then records the battle against men, its successful conduct and the foundation of the first monosexual society – a society where a few converted men (significantly, young men with long hair, which I take to be an indication of prior rebellion against gender stereotyping) attain to the same sex-status as the women. I use the terms 'men' and 'women' hesitantly, because the whole point is that these sex-differentiating terms have become irrelevant. All the citizens of the new state are lesbians, because they have achieved *sameness*; the oppositional values of heterosexual society have been eliminated.

Le Corps lesbien focuses on this use of sameness while at the same time going much further than *Les Guérillères* in the pursuit of changing the *discourse* of gender and sexuality. *Le Corps lesbien* is a series of paragraphs resembling something between a monologue and a sequence of prose poems, expressing the love of two female 'voices'. The writing/speaking subject encounters a complete absence of difference in her love relationship, because the body of the other is indistinguishable from the body of the self. In pursuit of this sense of identity between the two, Wittig experiments with language itself. The experiments can be morphological: the French forms of 'I' and 'me' – *je* and *me* – are represented as 'j/e' and 'm/e', to symbolize the fact that the elements of subject and object are both present in the self. But the innovations are more commonly lexical. For example, Wittig takes an attribute of the goddess Aphrodite – *cyprine* (i.e. of Cyprus) – and creates from it a noun which takes on qualities of many kinds of liquids, from *semen* to the *sea* until 'the rising tide spills out into the sky farewell black continent of misery and sorrow farewell ancient cities we are embarking for the bright and radiant islands for the green Cytheras for the black and gold Lesboses'.

At another level Wittig attempts to release the power of language by reworking the existing sign system, as in the use of Freud's metaphor of female sexuality as an unknowable 'black continent', which, in both the above example and the one which follows, Wittig attaches to a Baudelairean image of leaving for the new freedom of the lesbian islands: 'I float my arms in your arms, the wind untangles our hair, it combs it, brushes it, shines it, farewell black continent you are setting sail for the island of the living.'

A more complex example of how to take a male-created concept and reorder it is the use made of Lévi-Strauss's definition of the 'exchange of women' by men as a basic principle of human social organization. Shaktini has shown how this idea is reworked as female control of exchange in an elaborate passage (in 'poem' 43) in which colour attributes are assigned to a group of women, who then create a new order of meaning by exchanging the colours.[30] By implicit reference to Rimbaud's poem 'Voyelles', in which an arbitrary association of sounds with colours means that the sounds of the vowels cease to be part of a system signifying reality but become something which has a meaning in itself, Wittig turns a universalizing structuralist theoretical concept into a random poetic image, thus emphasizing the randomness of the original concept.

Les Guérillères and *Le Corps lesbien* both contain features which recur in Wittig's later works, notably the importance of nature and the physical, the motif of violence and implicit and explicit reference to existing mythology and legend. The first of these stems from the dual desire to move away from the abstract, universalizing tendencies of traditional discourse and to insist on the *real* presence of the female body as opposed to the metaphorical language of traditional literature, which moves the attention of the reader *away* from the body itself into such 'ghetto' images of femininity as flowers. Violence is a more complex feature. In *Les Guérillères* it is a necessary social weapon and, at the same time, by constantly linking the women of the title to an 'Amazon' tradition, emphasizes the voluntary assumption by women of what is traditionally a male characteristic. In *Le Corps lesbien* this male characteristic becomes part of love-making; this again destroys a stereotype of femininity, but it also suggests the power to turn negative 'male' forces into positive forms. Wittig takes, for example, the traditional Homeric idea of the wrath of Zeus, feminizes the deity (Zeyna), and gradually turns what was an authoritarian weapon of male dominance into part of an amorous game. Underlying both texts is therefore an equation of violence with energy, and it is this equation which is duly articulated in the article 'Violence' in Wittig's *Brouillon pour un dictionnaire des amantes* (1976), a text codifying the Utopian visions of her earlier works, in a definition which begins, 'The ardour, energy, force shown by the amazons of every period'. But in her later vision of the hell of contemporary social reality, *Virgile, non* (1985), violence returns to the ordinary status of a negative force used by men against women. It is, however, the third of the recurrent features which I listed above, the reference to myth and legend, which has the most far-reaching implication.

Proper names in Wittig's texts from *Les Guérillères* to *Virgile, non* are largely drawn from Latin and Greek literature; they are the names of goddesses and legendary heroines, or the feminized names of gods and heroes (Ulyssea, Achillea). But this classical element goes beyond the use of proper names: it permeates the whole discourse of the text. For example, the female warriors of *Les Guérillères* are, as I suggested just now, implicitly amazon-figures, and 'amazon' is a term which comes to dominate *Brouillon pour un dictionnaire*. The specific entry 'Amazones' is worth quoting in full:

> In the beginning, if there ever was a beginning, all the lovers [the form in the French text is in the feminine] were called amazons. And living together, loving each other, extolling each other, playing together – in those days when work was still a game – the lovers in the earthly paradise were called amazons throughout the golden age. Then, with the establishment of the first cities, a very large number of lovers broke the original state of harmony and called themselves mothers. For them the word 'amazon' now had the sense 'girl', eternal child, immature, she-who-does-not-face-up-to-her-destiny. The amazons were banished from the cities of the mothers. It was at this time that they became violent and fought to defend harmony. For them the old name of amazon had not changed its meaning. It now meant something more, those who protect harmony. Since that time there have been amazons at all periods, on all continents, islands, ice floes. We owe it to the amazons of all periods that we have been able to enter the age of glory. Blessed may they be.

Here we have not merely the equation all-female-lover = warrior = protector of the unity and harmony of life, but also the idea that lesbian literature should rewrite history, looking 'through' the patriarchal myths and legends to the female truths they have covered and distorted. The passage also demonstrates Wittig's rejection of both urbanization and maternity as weapons of an implied heterocracy. There is also, even in translation, some sense of the tone of oral history mixed with a deliberately *biblical* lyricism. Clearly, like Wittig's cult of Sappho as patron saint of her own writing, or her assumption of the role of Dante in her trip round the modern Inferno, all this universalizes the perception of lesbian values which the texts project. But this very universalization is itself problematic.

Setting aside for the moment the problem of the dependency of the texts on masculine-formulated traditions (which I want to consider later as a general issue) and the extreme literariness, even if it poses as folk memory, of what is evoked — as the first-person voice in *Le Corps lesbien* says of the women in 'poem' 43: 'I know them all from studying them in the books in the library' — a paradox appears. After denouncing, with good reason, the a-historical universalizing methods of structuralist anthropology and psychoanalysis as examples of manipulatory heterocratic discourse posing as fixed truths, Wittig constructs an a-historical mythology of lesbianism, which makes a number of highly disputable assumptions. For example, she claims that the only alternative to binary oppositions is 'sameness' (thus creating a new binary opposition: duality versus unity), that desire is a matter of choice and that it is possible to equate solidarity and love. In so doing Wittig removes her texts from the reality of everyday experience; they have nothing to say about how to deal with oppression *here and now*, with the specific class, racial and cultural issues of the 1970s and 1980s. As Marie-Jo Dhavernas puts it: 'Radical lesbians are obliged to replace our concrete reality — which doesn't fit into their schemes — by recourse to the imagination, to fit women into the stories of other peoples' oppression rather than bringing our own to light'.[31]

Surprisingly, in view of this last point, the creative response to lesbian separatism and to the example given by Wittig's work has been strongest in French Canada, where conservative attitudes to gender and sexual orientation have been seen as an integral part of a general social and political oppression.[32] The link between political activism, feminism and lesbianism is well illustrated by the case of Nicole Brossard, who helped to found *Parti Pris* in 1963, the journal which quickly came to be regarded as the mouthpiece of Quebec nationalism. She went on to co-found *La Barre du Jour* (1965), a literary journal aiming to overthrow the moral and sexual taboos of Quebec society as part of the process of synthesizing sociopolitical analysis with literary experiment; and in 1976, she helped to launch a radical feminist paper, *Les Têtes de Pioches*, in which she took up an openly lesbian stance.

Canadian lesbians such as Brossard echo many of Wittig's main concerns, particularly with language, violence and eroticism, and are very sensitive to the issue of a female tradition, citing other women's writings plentifully in their own and using intertextuality as a tool in the creation of a sense of group purpose which, as the litany of names in Brossard's *Amantes* shows, cuts across divisions of time, space and language.[33] The echoes of Wittig can take the form of motifs: amazons and the spirit of Lesbos in Brossard's *Le Sens apparent*. In particular, the ideas of *Le Corps lesbien* have been developed in French Canadian poetry, which has emphasized the positive dimensions of female sexuality, looking at the ways in which, in a same-sex relationship, mutual pleasure replaces the exercise of power[34] and exploring the coexistence of sameness and difference. But whereas Wittig has maintained that the kind of verbal crudity which characterizes gay male eroticism is a negative feature, Canadian lesbians have tried to harness its violence. In this passage from Louise Cotnoir's *Plusieures*, for example, the pun on *confusion* = confusion, but also *con* = cunt/*fusion* = blending together, creates a mixture of lyricism with physical immediacy which certainly adds an extra dimension to the experience described:

> Sa longue chevelure dans les doigts et ma bouche dans ses lèvres. Le goût n'est pas le même. Pourtant de la coincidence. Retenir les liquides, les grains, les essences. La confusion des règnes. Le poil blond duveteux.[35]

(Her long hair in my fingers and my mouth in her lips. The taste is not the same. Yet something coincides. To retain the liquids, the particles, the essences. The cun[t-]fusion of domains. The downy blond pubic hair.)

One of the most typical examples of a writer whose work develops the issues which concern Wittig is Jovette Marchessault, who, even before she came out as a lesbian in 1979, had already, in *Comme une enfant de la terre* (1975), produced what Rosenfeld calls 'an amazon's quest for the promised land in which women can live in harmony with each other and with their natural surroundings'.[36] Her first truly lesbian work, *La Mère des herbes* (1980) evokes in poetic, mythical terms, the interrelation of the female forces at work in nature and the system of values which the author inherited from her grandmother and mother, thus approaching the issues of women's history and the metaphysics of femaleness in a less intellectualized way than Wittig does. But it is in *Triptique lesbien* that Marchessault is both at her most reminiscent of Wittig and yet also at her most independent. In the three 'panels' of the work she illustrates, through myth and allegory, the history of patriarchal violence against women, prophesies a bright future and offers an example of rebellion. She takes disturbingly violent images (mother/daughter incest in 'Les Vaches de nuit', abortion in 'Les Faiseuses d'anges') which have traditionally negative associations, and turns them, as Wittig does images of erotic violence, into symbols of positive achievement, conscious assertions of personal freedom.

In the course of creating a web of feminist myths and symbols to suggest the 'female' meanings of the past and present which male institutions have conspired to obliterate, she, like Wittig, attacks head-on the problem of male-moulded discourse. As well as playing with grammatical and stylistic issues (destroying the concept of grammatical gender, insisting on a communal 'we' as a focus of group experience, using puns to associate men with negative forces), she explores, like the poets, the violence of sexual language itself. Unlike the poets, she turns this violence against men, in particular using it to attack the connection between male supremacy and the 'rape' of the female mind and body by the Catholic Church, as in the following blasphemous parody of receiving Holy Communion: 'On your knees, little girls! It's the exquisite moment for the divine fellation. On your knees! Open your mouths! Wide! Wider still! Receive the spurt of sperm from the great eucharistic male.' Linguistic liberation has become a prerequisite for the total liberation of the female self, a liberation represented equally by the vehicle of the message (the sexual language) and the imagery itself (the male 'occupation' of the female mouth).

It is in fact in this area of language, literary tradition and the need for new forms of female expression, that the Canadians have principally established their own originality of both theory and practice, and in so doing, to my mind, have largely avoided the problem of the relationship with 'male' texts which is posed by

Wittig's *Virgile, non* and *Le Voyage sans fin.* Because there was already a close relationship between radical social thought and literary experiment in Quebec in the 1960s, whereas in metropolitan France the *nouveau roman* of the same period insisted on the complete separation of literature and life, in the 1970s and 1980s Canadian feminist writers in general and lesbians in particular found the idea of a need for a complete overhaul of systems of representation quite natural. Writers such as Brossard and Louky Bersianik have emphasized the way in which the binary systems of patriarchal thought which have relegated 'subordinate' groups (women, blacks, gays) to negative categories, have permeated all levels of language.

One of the major effects of this concern with language and the process of representation has been a total breaking-down of traditional generic categories; fiction, poetry, the essay all tend to be represented in the same work, such that the author is concurrently commenting on the world and on the problems of representing the world. Brossard's *L'Amèr ou le chapitre effrité* (1977), *Amantes* (1980) and *Picture Theory* (1982) are cases in point. The very title of the first of these is characterized by its phonetic play on 'la mère' (the mother), 'la mer' (the sea) and 'l'amer' (something bitter) and its orthographical play on the same words designed to suggest the suppression of the mute element (the unsounded final *e*) in woman when she takes on her elemental role. This is an indication of the revitalization of language which is integral to the work's attack on male linguistic theory and practice, which suppresses woman's creativity and reduces her to a 'biological destiny' invented to preserve male power. *Amantes* takes the image of a lesbian continent (which occurs in Wittig and Zeig's earlier *Brouillon pour un dictionnaire des amantes*) and dramatizes the theme of lesbian space physically by its experiments with the 'space' of the book itself – black and grey pages divide it into five parts, it is illustrated with photographs of the New York skyline and there are constant shifts between different typefaces. The book is aggressively non-linear, both linguistically (there is no longer a conventional sentence structure) and narratively (it is 'about' four lesbians making love and learning to articulate their feelings, but it is non-directional). *Picture Theory* takes the same idea – of a group of lesbian lovers who live together and write their experiences concurrently -- but develops much further, on both a theoretical plane and in practice, the concept of a lesbian aesthetic, particularly the idea of the spiral as a structural form (taken from natural objects such as shells) which both represents a lesbian sensibility and challenges patriarchal linear norms.

Although Brossard is the French Canadian lesbian writer best known outside Canada, it is perhaps the work of Louky Bersianik which offers the most interesting example of a writer whose writing encompasses the same concerns as Wittig's but moves from a dialogue with the male tradition to the creation of independent forms which discuss the world and the problems of its representation concurrently in a characteristically Canadian form. Bersianik's first two published works, *L'Eugélionne* (1976) and *Le Pique-nique sur l'Acropole* (1979) are modelled on, but fiercely parodic of, classics of the male intellectual tradition; her third book, *Maternative* (1980), contains a series of short texts which seek to provide a female alternative.[37]

L'Eugélionne attacks the misogyny of Judaeo-Christian culture by deconstructing the Bible and biblical discourse. The basic paradic method is simple inversion: the book offers the Testament of a female Christ-figure, a component of the 'Sainte Trigynie' (this parody of the Holy Trinity means 'Holy Three-woman group'), and is told, gospel-style, in chapter and verse, through parable, description and sermon. But as well as parodying the Bible, from 'Emasculated Conception' to a new death and resurrection, the text attacks the twentieth-century equivalent of the Bible, the psychoanalytical theories of Freud and Jacques Lacan (Saint Freud and Saint Jacques Linquant), who are seen as propounders of an insidious myth of the natural predominance of man which springs directly from the myth of Adam. Bersianik excoriates a system of language which defines woman as *lack* or *absence*, as 'that which does not have a penis'; her primary weapon is ridicule, based again on straight-faced inversion, as in the Adam/Eve creation story, where it becomes Eve who is horrified by *Adam*'s body: 'It's not possible. It's the world upside-down. My father-mother is deformed. In the first place he hasn't any breasts. And then, I think he's losing his vulva and all that follows.'

In *Le Pique-nique sur l'Acropole*, Bersianik takes on Plato's *Symposium* with even greater savagery, also linking it (in the footsteps of the French feminist theorist Luce Irrigaray) to the sacred texts of modern psychoanalysis. In *L'Eugélionne* she had shown up the arbitrariness of the symbolism on which so much intellectual discourse is based, by demonstrating that the worship of the phallus could as easily be replaced by a worship of – and consequently a whole symbolic discourse based upon – the hole.[38] In *Le Pique-nique* she displaces the Oedipus myth as the story at the heart of Western culture and substitutes Agamemnon's murder of his daughter Iphigenia. The text is accordingly less light-hearted. Plato's aristocratic banquet and its elegant dialogue between exquisite rhetoricians pondering on the abstract philosophical implications of love is replaced by a picnic at which the women, headed by Socrates' neglected wife, discuss the physical realities of female sexuality, particularly their sexual suffering (rape, clitoridectomy).

Having thus disposed of the main lines of the existing thought through which women's oppression is designed and justified, in *Maternative* Bersianik explores the alternatives. Drawing on both the previous books, in that it starts with a parody of the Gospel according to St John: 'In the beginning was the Flesh/And the Flesh was made Word', and also incorporates some of the female voices from *Le Pique-nique*, *Maternative* synthesizes the problems of language with those of coming to terms with sexuality, showing that it is only in all-female relationships – of which mother-daughter (as in Marchessault) is the archetype – that physical and linguistic communication can come together completely. At the same time it suggests ways in which existing tradition and mythology (Iphigenia, Demeter) can be reread to reveal models for modern experience (the woman who goes mad because her husband does not understand how to communicate with her body, the African child whose father has subjected her to the mutilation of clitoridectomy).

These are very complex texts in their levels of cultural reference alone, and I have barely scratched the surface. In *Le Pique-nique*, for example, each detail of the supposed Platonic banquet menu, such as 'Vol-au-vent d'hirondelle à la sauce Philomèle' (swallow vol-au-vent with Philomela sauce: a reference to yet another myth in which a woman is persecuted and destroyed because of man's desires), is designed to re-enforce the idea that the Greek element in Western culture helps men to devour/digest the women who are subjugated by its discourse. But the complexity of the texts goes well beyond themes and oppositional intertextual resonances. From physical parody of the manner of presentation of Lacanian psychoanalytic texts to the implications of the musical form used to circumscribe the dialogues of *Le Pique-nique*, Bersianik activates all the formal and linguistic devices of her writing. The undermining of male language at a thematic level is sustained by parody and distortion of the linguistic forms which characterize it: for example, the neologism 'manoeuvre freuduleuse' (a freudulent manoeuvre) neatly exemplifies, and disposes of, the sleight of hand concealed by Lacanian jargon.

The greater difficulty is to create the new female language which will fill the silence imposed by male discourse. In *L'Eugélionne* the women demonstrate against the Academy, waving signs which call for the

> revision of the rules of syntax and an in-depth study of the semantics and current usage of the language, which is based on a sexual discrimination according to which animals and inanimate objects are given more importance than women when it comes to grammatical agreements.[39]

But it is very difficult in practice to change the grammatical and syntactic basics of language without rendering comprehension impossible. So, Bersianik puts more weight on elements in the *ordering of discourse* than on grammatical issues as such. Just as Wittig puts great stress on the structural principles of O (the endlessness of the perfect circle) as a female symbol, and Brossard does the same for the spiral, she is looking for a non-linear structure which she can identify as representing an essentially female quality of thought. Already in *Maternative* the litany-like reiterations of *L'Eugélionne* have become the basis for a structuring where repetitions generate other patterns related in sense or sound. In her later text *Axes et eau* (1984), which is built around the same images of the female body, nature and female artistic creativity which came to dominate

Maternative, this structuring becomes what Bersianik herself calls a weaving technique:

> To avoid becoming too enmeshed in the symbols which are so well coded by our culture and which give it its full patriarchal meaning, I have tried to develop a reticular writing which may appear somewhat disconcerting in that it is personal and, therefore, totally peculiar to me. The interest of such writing lies in the fact that it succeeds in decentring the text and producing a new sense out of the extra-sense, i.e., outside of the pre-existing range of symbol, in a travestied, divested language. It is writing which 'pense a cote' and which practises the technique of weaving and the transformations weaving produces.[40]

There is no doubt that Bersianik, like Brossard, has gone further in freeing herself from the constraints of conventional 'male' discourse and cultural tradition than the separatists of the start of the century could have dreamt of. But I wonder whether there is not a paradox in the result. Brossard and Bersianik profess to be writing for women as a totality; their language is shot through with the plural 'we' and the terminology of the type and the group; they deal in myths, legends and the reconstitution of the female past. Yet in practice there is an implicit elitism in what they write which matches the self-conscious sense of the superiority of the artist which permeates the writings of Barney and Vivien. Enormous burdens are imposed upon the reader of texts in which so complex an intellectual substructure supports a revolutionary linguistic superstructure. Returning to the criticisms which Marie-Jo Dhavernas aimed at Wittig, I feel that they apply still more to the Canadians. Intellectually stimulating though their writing undoubtedly is, it not only does not address itself *in any practical sense* to the physical realities of the vast majority of women, it does not even address itself to the vast majority of *lesbians*, who will simply be unable to *read* it, in the most literal sense. For the prophets of communication, this has to be a serious problem.

Notes

1. 'Paradigm', in George Stambolian and Elaine Marks (eds.), *Homosexualities and French Literature: Cultural Contexts/Critical Texts* (Ithaca and London: Cornell University Press, 1979), p. 117.

2. For a history of Sappho scholarship and its influence on creative literature at the period, see Joan DeJean, *Fictions of Sappho 1546–1937* (Chicago and London: Chicago University Press, 1989).

3. Virginie Sanders, *La Poésie de Renée Vivien* (Amsterdam-Atlanta: Rodopi, 1991), p. 122.

4. See Christian Gury, *L'Homosexuel et la loi* (Lausanne: L'Aire, 1981), p. 244.

5. De Pougy herself says so in *Mes cahiers bleus*; see Sanders, *La Poésie de Renée Vivien*, p. 124.

6. Barney actually helped de Pougy to write parts of the novel. For a critical account of it, see Sanders, *La Poésie de Renée Vivien*, pp. 126–30 and Jennifer Waelti-Walters, *Female Novelists of the Belle Epoque* (Bloomington and Indianapolis: Indiana University Press, 1990).

7. In Stambolian and Marks (eds.), *Homosexualities*, pp. 353–77.

8. After decades of critical neglect there is a growing corpus on both writers. The basic accounts are to be found in Shari Benstock, *Women of the Left Bank: Paris, 1900–1940* (London: Virago, 1987); Karla Jay, *The Amazon and the Page: Natalie Clifford Barney and Renée Vivien* (Bloomington and Indianapolis, Indiana University Press, 1988); and Sanders, *La Poésie de Renée Vivien*.

9. The exception is her autobiographical novel, *L'Ange et les pervers* (1930), which evokes her relationship with Barney. Her lesbian poems were only published posthumously.

10. Natalie Barney, *Cinq petits dialogues grecs* (Paris: Editions de la Plume, 1902).

11. Published in *Actes et entractes* (Paris: Sansot, 1910).

12. In Natalie Barney, *Quelques portraits-sonnets de femmes* (Paris: Ollendorff, 1900), p. 47. For similar sentiments in Vivien's work, see 'Je pleure sur toi . . .' in *A l'heure des mains jointes* (*Oeuvre poétique complète*, ed. Jean-Paul Goujon (Paris: Regine Deforges, 1986), p. 276).

13. The point is already made in the *Nouvelles pensées* but is particularly developed in 'Gide et les autres' in *Traits et portraits*.

14. Renée Vivien, *La Dame à la louve* (Paris: Lemerre, 1904).

15. 'Paroles à l'amie', *A l'heure des mains jointes*, in Goujon, *Oeuvre poétique*, p. 258.

16. 'Sans fleurs à votre front', *A l'heure des mains jointes*, in Goujon, *Oeuvre poétique*, p. 274.

17. Christ is perhaps the only male figure with whom Vivien ever presents any empathy. The female figure in 'Le Pilori' (*A l'heure des mains jointes*), for example, suggests Christ suffering ridicule on the cross.

18. *Sapho, traduction nouvelle avec le texte grec* (Paris: Lemerre, 1903). For an account of the translation and its importance see DeJean, *Fictions of Sappho*, pp. 249–51.

19. For an acknowledgement of Sappho's importance as a literary model see the last stanza of 'Invocation' (*Cendres et poussières*).

20. For the modernity of Vivien's Sappho, see the preface to Jean Goujon's edition, p. 12. It should also be observed that the diction of her poems owes something to the contemporary classical revival among *male* poets such as Henri de Regnier.

21. For an account of the critical reception of Vivien's work, see Sanders, *La Poésie de Renée Vivien*, pp. 111–70.

22. Apart from the *roman personnel* and the gothic novel, nineteenth-century French women writers had not managed to find any distinctive forms in which to express themselves. In the last two decades of the century in particular they were largely content to work within those male literary movements, Decadence and Symbolism, which seemed most at odds with the values of contemporary society.

23. Susan Gubar, 'Sapphistries', *Signs*, 10 (1984), pp. 43–62.

24. See above, ch. 1, p. 14.

25. Compare Barney's unpublished play, *Salle des pas perdus*, which portrays characters who find their platonic other half after death and can then move to another phase of existence. An account of the play is given in Jay, *The Amazon and the Page*.

26. Generic labels cannot be very precise, in Leduc's case, because she 'fictionalizes' so much of her autobiography in both themes and techniques, but its three volumes, *La Bâtarde*, *La Folie en tête* and *La Chasse à l'amour*, are clearly documentary in intention in a way that the other writings, even when based on the same material, are not.

27. It is important to note, as Isabelle de Courtivron does in *Violette Leduc* (Boston: Twayne, 1985), p. 112 that Leduc is capable of using *male* sexual imagery to convey her sensations when confronted with the natural beauty of a landscape, e.g. (from *Trésors à prendre*): 'My prick nicks the hymen, knocks against it, but is unable to deflower it between the branches, after lunch my prick fights a dual with the silver of the poplars'. This seems to prefigure Christiane Rochefort's claim that the act of writing is itself sexually stimulating, but the choice of male imagery is unexpected. Perhaps the gender-masquerade is less surprising, however, if we bear in

mind the implicit identification of pen and penis in *La Bâtarde*, and Leduc's struggle to achieve the 'masculine' status of writer without destroying her reality as a woman.

28. Monique Wittig, *The Straight Mind and Other Essays* (New York and London: Harvester, 1992). Originally 'La Pensée straight' was published in *Questions féministes* no. 7, 1980 and 'On ne naît pas femme' in *Questions féministes* no. 8, 1980. References will be to the English version.

29. 'One is not born a woman', *The Straight Mind*, p. 20.

30. Namascar Shaktini, 'A revolutionary signifier: *The Lesbian Body*', in Karla Jay and Joanne Glasgow, *Lesbian Texts and Contexts; Radical Revisions* (New York and London: New York University Press, 1990), pp. 291–303.

31. Marie-Jo Dhavernas, 'Hating masculinity not men', in Claire Duchen, *French Connections: Voices from the women's movement in France* (London and Melbourne: Hutchinson, 1987), pp.101–10. The point Dhavernas makes is similar to that made by Toril Moi in criticizing the Utopian writings of Wittig's *bête noire*, Helene Cixous: 'Stirring and seductive though such a vision is, it can say nothing of the actual inequities, deprivations and violations that women, as social beings rather than as mythological archetypes, must constantly suffer'. (See *Sexual/Textual Politics: Feminist Literary Theory* (London and New York: Routledge, 1988), p. 123.)

32. In writing this section I have found the following essays of particular interest:
Dupré, Louise. 'From experimentation to experience: Quebecois modernity in the feminine', in Shirley Neuman and Smaro Kamboureli (eds.), *A Mazing Space: Writing Canadian Women Writing* (Edmonton: Longspoon/NeWest, 1986), pp. 355–60.
Forsyth, Louise H. 'Beyond the myths and fictions of traditionalism and nationalism: the political in the work of Nicole Brossard', in Paul Gilbert Lewis (ed.), *Traditionalism, Nationalism and Feminism* (Westport, CT and London: Greenwood, 1985), pp. 157–72.
Hajdukowski-Ahmed, Maroussia. 'Louky Bersianik: feminist dialogisms', in Gilbert Lewis, *Traditionalism*, pp. 205–25.
Neuman, Shirley. 'Importing difference', in Neuman and Kamboureli, *A Mazing Space*, pp. 392–405.
Parker, Alice, 'Nicole Brossard: A differential equation of lesbian love', in Jay and Glasgow, *Lesbian Texts*, pp. 304–29.
Rosenfeld, Marthe. 'The development of a lesbian sensibility in the work of Jovette Marchessault and Nicole Brossard', in Gilbert Lewis, *Traditionalism*, pp. 227–40.
Rosenfeld, Marthe. 'Modernity and lesbian identity in the later

works of Nicole Brossard', in Susan J. Wolfe and Julia Penelope, *Sexual Practice, Textual Theory: Lesbian Cultural Criticism* (Cambridge MA and Oxford: Blackwell, 1993), pp. 199–207.

Waelti-Walters, Jennifer. 'When caryatids move: Bersianik's view of culture', in Neuman and Kamboureli, *A Mazing Space*, pp. 298–306.

33. Nicole Brossard, *Amantes* (Montreal: Quinze, 1980), p. 180: 'my multiple continent of those women who have signed: Djuna Barnes, Jane Bowles, Gertrude Stein, Natalie Barney, Michèle Causse, Marie-Clair Blais, Jouvette Marchessault, Adrienne Rich, Mary Daly, Colette and Virginia, the other drowned women, Cristina Perri Rossi, Louky Bersianik, Pol Pelletier, the so-attentive Maryvonne, Monique Wittig, Sande Zeig, Anna d'Argentine, Kate Millett, Jeanne d'Arc Jutral, Marie Lafleur, Jane Rule, Renée Vivien, Romaine Brooks …'

34. For example, Germaine Beaulieu, *Archives distraites* (Trois Rivières: Ecrits des Forges, 1984).

35. Louise Cotnoir, *Plusieures* (Trois Rivières: Ecrits des Forges, 1984).

36. See Marthe Rosenfeld, 'The development of a lesbian sensibility in the work of Jovette Marchessault and Nicole Brossard', in Gilbert Lewis, *Traditionalism*, pp. 227–40.

37. Three of the nine sections of *Maternative* were written much earlier than *L'Eugélionne* or *Le Pique-nique* (see Maroussia Hajdukowski-Ahmed 'Louky Bersianik: feminist dialogisms', in Gilbert Lewis, *Traditionalism*, p. 205). So we should regard the progression between the three works as a deliberate arrangement, rather than an accident of intellectual development.

38. The comic climax of her argument is her impeccable demonstration that, since the physical and functional focus of the penis is the seminal canal, the symbolic centre of the phallus itself is a hole.

39. This is a reference to the grammatical rule which says that in groups involving both grammatical genders, the masculine form always predominates. As grammatical gender is arbitrary, this means that, for example, a plural pronoun to describe 'a girl and her dog' or 'the woman and her book' would have to be masculine.

40. See Louky Bersianik, 'Aristotle's lantern: an essay on criticism' (trans. A. J. Holden Verburg) in Neuman and Kamboureli, *A Mazing Space*, pp. 38–48.

Chapter eight

Lesbian (Re)visions (ii)

'I've loved people, and sometimes it's been women,
sometimes men, that's all there is to it.'
● *Christiane Rochefort*[1]

PARALLEL with the separatist tradition which develops
from Barney and Vivien, through Leduc (the only French forerunner acknowledged by Wittig) to Wittig, Nicole Brossard and the
other Quebec radicals, there is, as I said at the start of the previous
chapter, a quite different pattern of writing about lesbianism,
which places or maintains all-female sexuality as a point on a
continuum and looks at problems of integration as much as at
separation. Such writers tend to take the view articulated by Bonnie
Zimmerman that 'lesbian identity and perspective are fluid, overlapping with heterosexual female or gay male perspectives'.[2] Inevitably, the two traditions are not as distinct as I have made them
sound. It is difficult, for example, to read Leduc's account of
schoolgirl lesbianism without linking it back to Colette's *Claudine
à l'école*, and there are other respects too – the male as erotic object,
the poeticization of female sensuality – in which there is a clear
connection between Leduc and Colette. Equally, Colette, although
she is the first twentieth-century proponent of the 'continuum'
approach to lesbianism, belonged for a while to the Barney/Vivien
circle (principally at a period after the relationship between the
latter two had finally broken up). But despite the links between
different sorts of lesbian writing, it is necessary, I think, to look at

non-separatist lesbian writing as a tradition in its own right, because it represents a fundamentally different approach to sexual identity. To do this I intend to focus on the work of Colette, Christiane Rochefort and (rather more contentiously) Marguerite Yourcenar.

Whilst Barney's circle may have given an impetus to Colette's willingness to explore her own physical and emotional potential for lesbian relations, its values were very different from her own. Her writing on the subject mirrors her life in its pattern of development. It is very important to remember that Colette had a rural childhood and was married very young; she had no experience or comprehension of Parisian *décadence* or the literary and intellectual lesbianism of the period 1880–1900. She had therefore no preconceptions, no intellectual programme behind her experiments with same-sex relationships. For her, lesbianism was a way of escaping from the restrictions imposed on her by male domination, a chance to plunge herself into unfettered femaleness and, in so doing, to discover her 'real' identity. Her husband Henri Gauthier-Villars (better known by his only-too-revealing pen-name, Willy) was a much older man, who encouraged her in lesbian experimentation for his own titillation while demanding from her a heterosexual fidelity which he himself did not observe. As a result she gave herself up to a brief period of exclusive lesbianism, in the form of a relationship with a much older woman. From this she emerged into a primarily heterosexual lifestyle which did not, however, exclude further lesbian relationships, and which was also marked by two relationships with much younger *men*, thus inverting the mentor–pupil pattern of her own early experiences.

Her writing was similarly initiated by a period of male domination, during which she wrote the 'Claudine' books in collaboration with her husband. This period shades into a transitional phase of gradual emancipation, which starts as early as the third of the Claudine books, *Claudine en ménage* (1902), the novel which draws on Colette's own affair with another married woman, and encompasses *La Retraite sentimentale* (1907), in which she focuses on the conflicting claims of desire and emotion, promiscuity and monogamous attachment. The final phase of the development of her ideas on sexuality is the long period from *Chéri* (1920) to *Le*

Pur et l'impur (1932, originally entitled *Ces Plaisirs*), the text in which she reflects most fully on different kinds of sexuality and their relationship to the desire/emotion dichotomy. In emancipating herself from male control, she also freed herself from the constraints of existing literary traditions (the male voyeur version of the Sappho-as-mentor-and-sexual-initiator motif and the contemporary pederastic male school-story). She was not in any sense a 'separatist', and came to reject the lesbian ghetto society, in which she once moved, as a pale shadow of the heterosexual society from which it purported to offer an escape. It is nonetheless significant that the period of lesbian experiment which gave her the opportunity not just to discover herself as a woman but to come to terms with the 'masculine' side of her nature too, also helped to stimulate in her an independent *female* creativity.

It is easy to write off the lesbian motifs of the early Claudine novels as the contribution of Willy. Colette herself, in her autobiographical sketch *Mes apprentissages*, claims that he was responsible for 'hotting up' the erotic elements in the books. But by the time she wrote *Mes apprentissages* Colette had tired of the notoriety of her early image, and was happy to distance herself from her first writings. The fact is that even *Claudine à l'école* is much more than a 'formula' book. Its basis is highly autobiographical, and the motif of a lesbian headmistress and lesbian fascination among the girls is not merely a parody of the Sappho-as-instructress motif. It is significant that a female writer and critic such as Rachilde should not only have praised the book when it appeared under Willy's name but should have voiced the suspicion that it must really have been written by a woman.

Claudine à Paris begins the process of portraying the physical and sentimental dimensions of relationships between girls more seriously (in the flashbacks on Luce and her unfulfilled attachment to Claudine), but it also introduces reflections on male homosexuality which indicate the direction that Colette's later preoccupations with sexuality will take. Colette's understanding of male homosexuality at this period is confused, resulting in the superimposition of two clichés which are a little difficult to reconcile: the adolescent pederast with a taste for younger boys and the transvestite. However, although the element of the feminine within the male is to some extent ridiculed (in the portrayal of Marcel and in the photograph of Jules dressed as a girl), an attitude which Colette herself will later regret in *Le Pur et l'impur*, it does introduce the idea of the natural coexistence of conventionally gender-divided elements within individuals of one sex. At the same time there is a certain envy expressed of Marcel and Charlie's togetherness which, for all its ironic touches, poeticizes the notion of the couple:

> Those two handsome boys, they'll be looking for a cool place under the trees, somewhere in the suburbs. The greenery will be making them feel romantic, bringing colour to their cheeks, giving a sea-blue tint to Marcel's eyes and brightening the dark eyes of his dear friend. . . . They'll come back by the evening train, melancholy, arm-in-arm, and split up with an expressive look in their eyes. . . . And I'll be all on my own, just like I am now.

Complementarily to this envy of togetherness, all suggestion of sexual promiscuity (Charlie's past escapades, for example) is heavily criticized. Both of these are attitudes which will be taken up in the context of various forms of sexuality in later texts.

Claudine en ménage, however, is definitely the key text of the four Claudine novels. As I said earlier, it initiates a transitional phase; it rehearses the schoolgirl-lesbian motif, so dear to Willy, in the form of the visit by Claudine and her husband Renaud to Claudine's home town and old school. This in turn introduces two important new ideas: the concept of a cause-and-effect relationship between different kinds of sexual desire, and (implicitly) the notion of male *licence* for female sexual experiment. Having described how her husband has taught her the secret of physical passion and awareness of the power and possibilities of her own body (described, incidentally, in very boyish terms), Claudine goes on to observe that this new 'power' which she uses half-instinctively on her husband, she was very tempted to try out on Hélène, a fifteen-year-old schoolgirl whom she had impulsively kissed in the school. This is the first acknowledgement of lesbian desire on the part of *Claudine* (in the earlier books she acts as an observer, or as the object of the desire of others), and it serves to introduce and justify the real theme of the book: the affair with another married woman, Rézi, which forms the focus of the text, an affair facilitated and encouraged by Renaud, and which comes to an end only because Claudine discovers that *he* is also sharing Rézi's favours.

This account of the text may appear to suggest that it is every bit as well integrated into the 'male fantasy' tradition as the earlier books. Renaud at one point actually makes a reference to that tradition by addressing Rézi as 'O Bilitis', as he installs the two women in the apartment which he has arranged for their – and his – love-making. The patronizing terms in which he speaks of certain women's need for other women in order to preserve their taste in *men* could certainly be seen as underlining the sense of a purely male perspective:

'You women, you can do anything you like. It's charming and it's of no significance ...'
'No significance? ... I don't agree with you.'
'Oh, yes, I'm right! Between you pretty little animals it's, how can I put it? ... a consolation, a diversion which gives you a little rest from us ...'
'Oh?'
' ... or at any rate, which offers you some compensation, the logical pursuit of a more perfect partner, of a beauty closer to your own, in which your sensitivity and weaknesses can find themselves reflected. ... If I dared (which I don't) I'd say that certain women need a relationship with another woman to preserve their taste for men.'

However, assertion of male control, via explanation and implicit permission, is undermined *even in its context*. Interestingly, Colette uses the motif of male homosexuality to achieve her effect. Prior to the passage quoted, Renaud has been fulminating against his son Marcel's passion for adolescent boys, and Claudine, puzzled, has queried the difference between that passion and her own schoolgirl adventures or her current relationship with Rézi. Immediately *after* the passage quoted Claudine herself simply reinserts Renaud's attitude to lesbians into the male soft-porn tradition: 'I can only make sense of what my husband has just said as a flattering paradox which disguises his somewhat voyeuristic libertine tendencies'.

The paradoxes are beginning to flow thick and fast here. Renaud's explanation is, ultimately, the one which seems to apply to Colette's life and work, where lesbianism does indeed offer Colette/Claudine the chance to rest and reappraise her sexual potential as a basically heterosexual woman. But it is only a meaningful explanation, seen not as the product of gracious patriarchal permission but as a process of genuine, independent experiment and liberation, such that the return to heterosexuality becomes a matter of choice. Moreover, there is a fundamental challenging of Renaud/Willy's view of lesbianism in the novel, a challenge which is implicit in the particular nature of the Claudine/Rézi relationship and the manner of its portrayal.[3] There is nothing salacious about the terms in which Colette transfers her autobiographical material into fiction. From the first confidences of the two women, to their first kisses, the preparation of sexual acts, the undressing and then the ellipse of the acts themselves, the emphasis is on the intensity of physical and emotional communication, and not on *pleasure* at all. An excellent example of this is the exploration of feminine physicality in the scene in which Claudine is brushing Rézi's hair. Furthermore, there is a subtle complexity in the presentation of sexual identity within the Claudine/Rézi couple. Claudine is initially the tomboy, taken for a lesbian in society because of her short hair and boyish frame; Rézi is the personification of turn-of-the-century femininity, all curves and spirals, lace and frills. Yet Rézi is the seductress, Claudine the seduced. On the other hand, whilst, in seducing Claudine, Rézi *feminizes* her, Claudine remains the psychologically dominant partner within the relationship. As Nicole Ward-Jouve puts it: 'It is almost as if Claudine learnt to love her own muffled or suppressed femininity by loving Rézi'.[4]

Although five years elapsed, and other texts were written between the publication of the relevant works, the release of feminine potential via lesbianism in *Claudine en ménage* was the final new element which Colette had to explore before she was ready for the extended meditation on the relative importance of sensuality and emotion which constitutes *La Retraite sentimentale*. This novel should be 'read against' two short texts from *Les Vrilles de la vigne*

(1908), 'Le Miroir' and 'Nuits blanches', as well as against the reflections on male homosexual promiscuity and togetherness in *Claudine à Paris*. Both Annie and Marcel in *La Retraite* represent the dangerous attraction of physical pleasure, particularly the obsession with 'fresh young flesh'; Claudine's voice, in contrast, upholds monogamy and censoriously rejects promiscuity. But it would be simplistic to make a simple identification between Claudine's voice and Colette's. The former is, as 'Le Miroir' reminds us, a faithful projection of certain images of Colette, but lacks her human complexity. What Colette seems to value is not the monogamous heterosexuality preached by Claudine in *La Retraite*, a novel from which the heterosexual male, in the form of Renaud, is uncomfortably absent (he is indeed eventually 'abolished' by death), and in which his influence is accordingly very theoretical. What she *does* seem to value is the *generalized*, primarily non-genital sensuality described in 'Nuits blanches', one of the few texts directly reflecting her relationship with Missy.[5] 'Nuits blanches', poetically evoking the experience of sleepless nights beside a loved one, recreates the intensity of physical togetherness, as opposed to the erotic consumerism of Marcel or Annie. Sexual pleasure, when it finally occurs, becomes an expression of maternal tenderness rather than of ordinary desire.

Rather than a simple opposition of heterosexuality and homosexuality, or of marriage and promiscuity, this group of texts between them constructs a critique of relationships which involve domination, manipulation or mere consumption of another human being. Renaud's marriage to Claudine is ultimately seen as diminishing her by the constraints it puts upon her, just as much as Marcel and Annie's frenetic obsession with physical pleasure diminishes them or as Claudine's manipulatory attempts to involve Marcel in a sexual encounter with Annie damage him. It is the physical images of Colette and Missy asleep together which suggest, on the contrary, how a mentor–pupil relationship can achieve a genuine balance of communication and pleasure.

It makes no sense, from this point on in Colette's writing, to treat the topic of women's sexual/emotional relationships with other women separately from two other key motifs, the mother/daughter bond and the older woman/younger man relationship.

Elaine Marks, having quoted an extended image of embracing and cradling the beloved from *Les Vrilles de la vigne*, sums the point up aptly:

> All of Colette's empathetic attitudes towards women loving women are contained within this image and will be repeated in non-lesbian situations: in the relationships between 'Colette' and 'Sido', between Chéri and Léa, between all those who love passionately and exclusively. What is involved is someone younger needing protection, someone older offering a refuge and caring.[6]

Hence, Colette's 'feminized' male heroes in *Chéri*, *La Fin de Chéri* and *Le Blé en herbe* do not represent, as the genuinely feminized men in the novels of Rachilde do, a sort of woman's revenge, an inversion of patriarchal values where women become the victors. Chéri is not defeated by Léa, but by the obligation which time imposes upon him, to go out alone into the world of the conventional heterosexual male. He and Phil are younger partners in relationships for which an idealized lesbianism seems to have provided the model. Their androgyny is the androgyny of the child, the refusal of traditional adult macho values. At the same time Colette cannot fully escape the *temptations* of power, and the sexual control linked with it, temptations revealed in the masculine imagery of penetration in which she talks about her relationship to the young: 'Moreover this has left me with a facility for piercing and frustrating the artifice which childhood and adolescence deploy. Accordingly, I enjoy, more than many adults, the forbidden pleasure of penetrating the young.'[7] Accordingly, like the Claudine novels, the value scales of novels such as *Chéri* come to take on their fullest sense when read as part of a long movement towards the complex 'sexual manifesto' constituted by *Le Pur et l'impur*.

   Le Pur et l'impur is undoubtedly the most important French text on lesbianism and on women's sexuality in general in the first half of the century. It has been variously represented as the equivalent of Gide's *Corydon* and as a repudiation of the portrait of lesbianism in Proust. But it is a difficult text to evaluate; or rather, perhaps I should say that it is a difficult text to evaluate if you try to reduce it to a statement about lesbianism in the sense that *Corydon* is a text about pederasty, or to a redefinition of the social and psychological mechanisms of lesbianism in the sense which you might look for such a definition in *A la recherche du temps perdu*. There are in fact at least three overlapping subject centres in *Le Pur et l'impur*: the constrictions of 'normality', the distinctive natures of male and female sexuality and the desire/emotion dichotomy. It is true that it offers a series of sketches of people whose lives depend on pleasures and attachments outside the norm – opium addiction, donjuanism, transvestism, lesbianism, male homosexuality, relationships between younger men and older men or women. In this respect it can be seen as part of Colette's growing protest against the exploitative and limiting world created by normative patriarchal values. It is also true that most of it concerns sexual issues, and that much of it *is* about lesbians, notably the essays on Renée Vivien and on the famous 'Ladies of Llangollen', Lady Eleanor Butler and Miss Sarah Ponsonby. In this respect it is certainly the most extended set of reflections on lesbianism to be published in France before the 1960s. However, the importance of the work does not lie in either of these individual aspects, but in the synthesis of male and female sexuality, straight and gay, into a single set of problems, to which social pressures and gender differences (which Colette sees as in part biologically determined) prevent there being a single set of answers.

I say 'problems', because, with one exception, all the types of relationship which Colette explores present apparently insurmountable difficulties. Heterosexual relationships are represented as destabilized by the inequality of sensual pleasure between the sexes – as Damien, one of the dissatisfied Don Juan figures, puts it: 'The fact that I'm their master in pleasure but never their equal, that's what I'll never be able to forgive them'. Such relationships are equally threatened by the inability of the adult male to accept any feminine dimension in himself, and by what Colette claims is the male tendency to pursue a masculine element even in the female body: 'Men go to what can reassure them, to what they can recognise, in the hollows of the female body, whose characteristics are the complete inverse of their own.' Lesbianism has the advantage of offering a woman the opportunity to develop both the feminine and masculine aspects of her character, and to respond to both aspects in another woman; Colette speaks with approval of natural androgyny, whilst castigating any attempt at 'playing' at being a man. But although a lesbian relationship brings a woman to a fuller awareness of her own female identity and its potential, it seems rarely, in Colette's eyes, to achieve more than a transitional value, unless, like the 'Ladies of Llangollen', the couple isolate themselves from the world.

Much has been made of the 'Ladies of Llangollen' section, but I think it is easy to overstress both its significance and its coherence. Earlier in the text Colette has scathingly rejected lesbian separatism in a (rather ungrateful) portrait of Missy as 'La Chevalière', doyenne of a society of grotesques and misfits which pathetically apes the 'real' society on which it purports to turn its back. Equally scathingly she rejects any form of pursuit of lesbian sensuality for its own sake, in her portrait of Renée Vivien, in whom she decries 'an immodest overvaluing of *the senses* and the technique of pleasure'. But although she appears to find, in the relationship of Lady Eleanor and Miss Sarah, all the psychological benefits of lesbianism, and to admire the couple's courage in braving a hostile world, she also reveals an impatience with a replication of heterosexual power structures which she implies is inevitable within long-term lesbian relationships: 'Robust Lady Eleanor, responsible for all the decisions about daily life, so sincerely "lost" in your beloved, didn't you realise that two women can never create an entirely female couple? You were the wise gaoler, the male.' The implication is that a lesbian relationship can never offer a permanent solution to a woman's needs, because it will always result in one of the women becoming a substitute man.

What Lady Eleanor and her friend do have in their favour is the constancy of the emotional dimension of their relationship and the degree of communication which it reveals. It is communication which matters most to Colette, through whatever form of bond it is achieved. Hence her hostility to all forms of sexual consumerism, which she regards as both a negation of communication and a danger to the self. This is surely the *real* centre of the work. Consistently, within the relationships studied, Colette separates out addiction – the distortion or limitation of the self which comes from excessive devotion to physical pleasure – from what she sees as the true ends of love, defined as 'the burning, pure space which holds together more tightly than any bond of the flesh'. Unexpectedly, it is only certain *male* homosexual relationships which seem to fulfil her definition. She speaks with affectionate respect of the relationship formed by an older man (a poet) and his proud young peasant lover, a relationship in which all the positive elements of masculinity are preserved, and she approves the natural transposition of their friendship into sexual terms: 'Friendship, masculine friendship, unfathomable emotion. Why should the physical pleasure associated with love be the only sob of exaltation forbidden you?...'[8] In the light of this example, it seems to me that the concepts of 'purity' and 'impurity' in the title of the book refer not to a simplistic opposition of emotion and desire, but to the *balance or imbalance* of emotion and desire within individuals and relationships. In this sense, this relationship alone, in the whole of *Le Pur et l'impur*, represents purity, a quality which, consequently, the reader must infer to be only possible in sexual terms (as opposed to in the mother/child relationship) in a mentor–pupil relationship between two *men*.

This last example makes me doubt whether it is a sufficient explanation to say, as Elaine Marks does, that for Colette 'Lesbianism is a *pis-aller*. It is a copy of either mother–daughter or male–female love or both'.[9] What Colette approves of is an older/younger partnership, based on friendship, and for whom sexual expression of their feelings is a natural extension of the range of means of communication, rather than an independent expression of desire. Certain gay male relationships fulfil that pattern; in her novels older woman/younger man partnerships fulfil it for a time; mother/daughter relationships fulfil it without the sexual dimension. As a result of social indoctrination other forms of heterosexual relationship rarely seem to achieve the same degree of communication. But on lesbian relationships her position is not really clear or entirely coherent. The picture of her relationship in 'Nuits blanches' fits the approved pattern, but for some unexplained reason she does not seem to think that such a relationship is sustainable in the way that the male equivalent apparently is. Given the rest of her argument about the nature of love between two women, it ought to constitute the most perfect form of communication, and yet it is rejected as insufficient (there is a disturbingly Freudian air about the images of emptiness in which she couches this insufficiency). Whatever the reason for this rejection – which must lie in the nature of Colette's own sexual make-up – this gap between the logic of female sexuality and its reality for her is surely the source of the sadness under whose sign the book is placed from the beginning – 'this book which will speak sadly of pleasure' – a sadness which is associated with such otherwise positive qualities as androgyny, and whose counterpart is the mood of compromise on which the book closes.

Colette does, nonetheless, communicate a positive message about lesbianism in *Le Pur et l'impur*: it has a natural place in the spectrum of human sexuality and a woman should be free to move in and out of it without having to conform to socially created images of the lesbian (e.g. transvestism, promiscuity) which, in life and in literature alike, can obscure the reality and importance of woman-to-woman relationships. This is coherent with the fact that, from the 1920s onwards, in her own writing she favours a technique of indirection, of concentrating on the communication of a female sensibility that will leave lesbian desire as one possible ingredient, which the reader can 'read between the lines'. Only the emphasis on the female body and on the mentor/pupil pattern remain as reminders of the literary tradition (the Sappho model) in which her writings initially took root.

By *Le Pur et l'impur*, then, Colette has more or less integrated lesbianism into the spectrum of human sexuality, looking through it onto the problem of the relationship between desire and emotion and between the masculine and the feminine. In all of this her primary concern is the individual as a physical and emotional entity; in so far as she deals with society, it is to look at its effects on the individual. In this respect her work shares a feature with that of her separatist sisters of the same period; Barney and Vivien, too, consider sexuality in terms of the individual woman and the constraints put on her by society. The furthest any of the three writers goes beyond this is in extending their consideration to the relationship between sexuality and artistic creation. It is entirely understandable that a *belle époque* writer should focus on individual psychology in this way; it was a preoccupation of much literature of the period, and in any case the first problem for women in general, and lesbians in particular, was to come to terms with their own identity and the problems of self-fulfilment in a masculine-dominated world.

The next significant lesbian writer to share Colette's 'continuum' view of sexuality, Christiane Rochefort, was in a very different position. Although born in 1917, her first novel, *Le Repos du guerrier*, was not published until 1958, and the works with which we shall be concerned appeared across the period 1963–82. She was therefore writing not only in an increasingly more enlightened climate, from a sexual point of view, but also in a context where other dimensions of social oppression had become targets for literature, and where, therefore, connections were being drawn between problems of gender, sexual orientation and class. Accordingly, as we shall see, Rochefort places lesbianism not only in a sexual continuum, but three-dimensionally within the broader issues of the need for concurrent personal, social and intellectual liberation.

Although Rochefort's stance on issues important to her, such as militant feminism, evolves across the period from *Le Repos du guerrier* to *Quand tu vas chez les femmes* (1982), there are two ideas underlying her writing which remain more or less stable: the importance of 'absolute love' and the inherent dangers of language itself – both ideas deriving from a mistrust of reason and the conscious mind, and a belief in the positive powers of emotion, instinct and the subconscious mind. For Rochefort lesbianism and male homosexuality cannot be in any sense 'a problem', because she does not believe in the validity of the terms themselves. Like colour terms, they are arbitrary divisions of a spectrum, used for purposes of differentiation. As such they are a prime example of the way in which language functions as a policing system, structuring and ordering. The 'bourgeois'[10] world has divided and labelled the whole of life in order to create hierarchical structures which facilitate social control. It is because sexuality is a basic form of energy that conventional societies are always particularly anxious to channel it into controllable forms, defined in terms of acceptable and unacceptable behaviour and relationships. To escape from the bourgeois concept of love, you have first to refuse its component labels. Rochefort records that in her first draft of *Printemps au parking* the two boys around whose relationship the novel is built were just friends. When, on rewriting, she realized instinctively that they should become lovers, she initially rejected the idea, only to become aware that this rejection stemmed from a desire that they should not be labelled as gay. This 'bourgeois' reaction and her own surmounting of it are transposed, in the novel, into Christophe's sense of shock at his own love for Thomas and his response to that shock; his first thought is that his love makes him a 'queer', then he realizes that 'queer' is just an arbitrary division. As he puts it to his best friend Nicolas:

> It's the morality of the barrier-raisers.... . Once you've got across to the other side, you turn round and there *aren't* any barriers any longer, they were imaginary, you put them there yourself, stupid sod that you were, like a well-trained dog. ... I'm not shocked at all any more, I feel absolutely fine about it all. That's freedom, mate.[11]

Once you remove the terminology of sexual orientation and patriarchal sexual values (and with it even such apparently progressive concepts as 'sexual liberation'), you are left with what Rochefort calls 'absolute love'. This concept is articulated in her work as early as *Les Stances à Sophie*. Céline mockingly begins a Dictionary of Neo-Bourgeois Semantics, in which, under the entry 'love', she writes: 'A: for a woman; total self-dedication to domestic life, including night duties. B: for a man; being happy like that.' Her rebellious young sister-in-law Stéphanie offers the positive conceptual counterpart, an Absolute Dictionary, in which the definition is: 'Love: acceptance and contemplation of someone/something other than one's self, taken just as it is, without expecting anything in return.' It is a love which acknowledges no subdivisions, no categories of the licit and illicit, and which, more importantly still, makes no distinction between sexual love and any other forms of love for people, places or things. It imposes no choices; it leaves the individual open to all aspects of life, giving him or her the ability to appreciate the unity of the world.

Rochefort's ideal world is, accordingly, a paradise of direct communication, sincerity and solidarity, of the type portrayed in her Utopian novel *Archaos*, where natural polysexuality is given free reign as the basis – and the prime symbol – of communication and unity. Not for nothing is government business in Archaos transacted in a brothel; the political, sexual and linguistic message of the whole book can be summed up in a key piece of wordplay:

Comme dit le proverbe: bordel n'est pas mortel.
Tandis que l'ordre, l'est.

(As the proverb puts it, disorder won't kill you.
Whereas order will.)

Here the slang word used for disorder – *bordel* – which literally means 'brothel', links sexual disorder to 'disordered' lifestyle, the refusal of hierarchy, of repression and the Protestant work ethic which characterize Archaote society. Archaos is, of course, only a vision of the desirable, but Rochefort is anxious to stress the importance of such visions. The lesson of a realistic novel such as *Printemps au parking* is that you must always hope; never resign yourself to the universe you have, look towards the one you want to create. In so doing, your sexual freedom, as Christophe and Thomas discover, is the first weapon against the constrictions which prevent you from realizing your ideals.

Given the radical nature of this concept of love, and its implications for all aspects of life concurrently, it is not surprising that Rochefort's works tend to consider personal, social and intellectual issues side by side. Initially she was drawn towards a militant feminist position in *Les Stances à Sophie*, in which there is an *almost* total identification of 'bourgeois' (in the Rochefortian sense) domination with masculine values – I say 'almost' because the novel specifically suggests that the closer men are to nature, the more acceptable they are, and that there *are* individual men even in an urban society (Céline's friend Thomas, for example) who transcend the standard limitations of their sex. Nonetheless, the central subject is the oppression of women by men, especially within marriage. From the outset Philippe, the classical hypocritical dominator, moulds Céline to his own values, and her status as his possession after marriage is marked by the loss of her own name – henceforth her 'label' is Mme Philippe Aignan. It is only through a sexual relationship with another married woman, Julia (who is experiencing the same sense of oppression in her own marriage), that Céline begins to find her own identity again. Note how Céline resists *labelling* their relationship:

> 'When it comes to it,' said Julia, 'it must be marriage that makes you into a lesbian. I wasn't one before.'
>
> 'What makes you think you're one now? Just because we're having something on the side, we don't have to *catalogue* ourselves.'[12]

Sexual categorization is just a sub-branch of the general social oppression which women have been trained to accept. Céline's sexual emancipation is therefore, like Claudine's in *Claudine en ménage*, part of the process of freeing herself from the world of marriage, but it doesn't commit her to a new limitation (represented by the term 'lesbian'). It leaves her open to a wider range of possibilities of experience.

By *Printemps au parking* and *Archaos* Rochefort has distanced herself from too simplistic an identification of 'male' with 'oppressor'. The former focuses sympathetically on two male characters, who, as men, belong to the oppressing class, but, by refusing the constrictions of 'normal' sexuality, potentially join the oppressed, especially given that (1) Christophe is under age for gay sex according to the laws in force at the period; (2) he is also a victim of the oppression of the family; and (3) his relationship with Thomas defies social norms twice over by being not only homosexual but also conducted across *class* boundaries. In *Archaos*, which envisages the liberation of both sexes from the bourgeois code, the attitude to men relaxes still further. But it is not until *Quand tu vas chez les femmes* that she sets aside conventional gender boundaries to take an across-gender look at the dominator/dominated issue and its relationship to the problem of militancy itself.

This novel has been interpreted as everything from a feminist revenge novel to an attempt to out-Sade Sade, but it is nothing of the kind. In it Rochefort returns to the issue of the dangers of labelling, in order to show the oversimplification inherent in any form of rebellion which simply seeks to invert existing values. Bertrand's masochism makes him a parody of woman's traditional acceptance of the role of the dominated; at the same time his public acceptance of his sexual 'perversity' makes him a rebel against patriarchal norms. He thus demonstrates the problems and dangers of *re*labelling, and in the process offers a parallel to the problems posed by various representatives of social, sexual and intellectual militancy who, in attempting to assume a dominant role in society, begin to reproduce the distorting patterns of bourgeois values against which they are rebelling. Bertrand's ex-wife Malaure (the militant feminist), his daughter Simone (the militant lesbian) and Gilles-Henri (the militant theorist who writes incomprehensible articles for 'fringe' and pornographic newspapers), all have impeccable, politically correct ideas, rooted in concepts of love, solidarity and freedom, but in trying to impose them on others as the single acceptable form of the truth, they are dealing in prejudice, division and domination. The equivalent group manifestation of the problem is the 'progressive' movement 'Jeunes au service de la civilisation', which becomes a negative force used as a vehicle for hatred and destruction. All these people are trying to impose different forms of arbitrary structure, a fact neatly satirized in Gilles-Henri's plans for a demonstration celebrating sexual perversity, plans which instantly come down to redefinitions of hierarchy:

'Since we're on the subject, where will the women go?'

'The women. ... That's a point, there's the women as well. That makes quite a crowd. And they have the right to be represented, after all, they suffer too. The gay women, at any rate.'

'So we put the gay female masochists at the front of the parade?'

'Oh no, a female masochist is less abnormal than a bloke. Even a gay female masochist.'

'Obviously. So that gives us ... have you got a bit of paper? ... gay male masochists, then gay female masochists – or should it be straight male masochists next? Which attracts more oppression – masochism or homosexuality? We need a computer.'[13]

The novel in fact embodies an element of self-critique in that it exemplifies the dangers of the polarizations (emotion versus reason, rebellion versus acceptance) which are fundamental to Rochefort's own writings. Even her own thought, she seems to be saying, must not be allowed to rigidify into a system. This takes us back to the fundamental notions of absolute love and the dangers of all forms of hierarchy. Rochefort has taken the idea of the sexual continuum, which I identified as at least embryonic in Colette's work, and has extended it into a general libertarian principle. In the process she abolishes the limitations placed on lesbianism by Colette, together with any sense of an inherent difference between men and women. Rochefort's difficulties are not with sexuality or gender, but with how to prevent revolutionary attitudes from becoming new orthodoxies.

For lesbian separatists the synonymy of sexual and cultural separation from any form of male tradition is axiomatic. Logically a comparable integralist equation, at least as regards heterosexual female or gay male literature, ought to exist too. But it is one thing for lesbian or bisexual women to see themselves as part of a sexual spectrum, another to place themselves on an equivalent *cultural* spectrum. A contributory problem is the lack of sensitivity to the sexual identity of their opposite-sex counterparts among female and male homosexual writers. Whilst links between women writers' views of female emotions and sensuality are plentiful, whether they are separatist lesbians or heterosexual feminists, there are relatively few comparable links with male writing. It is true that the concept of the sexual continuum implicit in Christiane Rochefort's work can equally be found in Duvert, whose arguments about the social imposition of gender roles in *Le Bon Sexe illustré* are designed to show binary divisions of the male/female, adult/minor type as reflections of the basic unit of social control possessor/possessed. But although reference to adolescent female sexuality does occur occasionally in his fiction (e.g. in *Le Voyageur*), there is a distinctly misogynist strain in his writing too, which is not confined to the portraits of mothers, but surfaces in, for example, the sexism of the article 'Garçons' in *Abécédaire malveillant*. A rare example of the translation of the continuum into male fiction, Jean Demelier's *Le Rêve de Job*,[14] insists on the pleasure of all types of sexuality, including both heterosexual and homosexual incest, at both the physical and the emotional level, but the novel itself focuses almost exclusively on male sexuality. Even a bisexual writer like Cyril Collard is very *hetero*sexist in his treatment of women characters.[15] The fact is that gay male writers have paid very little attention to female sexuality at all, and when they have done so it is nearly always in terms of their own sexual values and preoccupations.

In particular, perception and presentation of lesbians in male literature has not been very sensitive to their realities. Oddly enough, the heterosexual Sartre, who trivializes male homosexual desire in an obtuse and patronizing fashion in both *La Nausée* (the caricature of Gidean pederasty in the person of 'l'Autodidacte') and *Les Chemins de la liberté* (the predatory and neurotic Daniel), makes Ines, his stereotypical butch lesbian in *Huis clos*, at least more sympathetic than her heterosexual counterparts in the play. Gay male writers have a less creditable record. Proust's portrait of Mlle Vinteuil degrading her father's picture while making love with her friend, or his use of images of illness, insanity, even treason, to define lesbian tendencies, place it in the same condemned category as male homosexuality. And the narrator's fascination with the possible lesbianism of Albertine, while it offers opportunities for an in-depth study of the alienating effect that a sense of complete sexual otherness can have, tells us nothing about the *girl*, whose sexuality remains a perfect example of Freud's 'dark continent' as far as Marcel (and presumably Proust himself) is concerned. *A la recherche du temps perdu* does, it is true, suggest that people may move between different sexual personae, and hints at how conventional sexual labels merely mask the complexities of desire, in the episodes of the letter from the lesbian actress Léa to Morel, in which she implies that he has a 'gay' taste in women, and of Rachel's suggestion to a very feminine young male dancer that she would enjoy a threesome with him and a female friend. However, Proust does not develop his ideas on the subject with any real consistency.

Like Proust (and with less excuse) more recent gay male writers have also seen lesbianism in terms of their own preoccupations. Renaud Camus, for example, resolutely insists on assuming that female desire ought to function like male desire, which he sees, equally tendentiously, as only completely freed from social constraint when completely promiscuous. Consequently, aside from such occasional outrageous remarks as: 'Women deplore being treated as objects of desire. Perhaps they're wrong about that, since it isn't unpleasant, in so far as I've had the opportunity to judge', he returns constantly to the idea that lesbian insistence that for women there is a necessary link between sexual fulfilment and emotion must merely indicate that women have been unable to escape from the patriarchal preconceptions by which they have been moulded.[16] Only Michel Tremblay portrays the positive side of the integration of gay males and lesbians into a mutually supportive social grouping, in *Le Coeur découvert*. No Francophone male writer gives lesbianism the kind of broad empathetic study that it gets from Armistead Maupin in the *Tales of the City* cycle.[17]

This degree of incomprehension, or at least of mutual mistrust, is all the more striking given the overlap of concerns between lesbian and gay writers. The importance of the theme of textuality, and the identification of text and body, occurs in such writers as Genet and Yves Navarre just as much as in Leduc, Rochefort, Wittig and the Canadians, even if there is a difference of focus between, say, Navarre or Hocquenghem's preoccupations with fathering/giving birth to the text and the lesbian stress on the relationship between physical and linguistic communication. This ties in with a shared eagerness to explore the poetics of homosexual eroticism – Genet and Leduc, for example, initiate this type of writing at a comparable period. Equally there are shared currents of ideas, particularly in radical writers. Wittig's arguments in 'Paradigm' on the 'sexual economy' imposed by the dominant heterocracy are essentially the same as those of Tony Duvert in his essays, and their position is mirrored in the implicit critique of 'real' society in Rochefort's Utopian *Archaos*. Collard, in the texts preserved in *L'Ange sauvage*, makes observations about gay male exploitation of third-world boys as financially dependent sex objects which would confirm the views of some radical lesbians that some gays are more patriarchal in their values than they would care to admit; he also criticizes contemporary psychology as part of the normative power base in a way coherent with the positions of Wittig and Bersianik.[18] But these points of overlap are not part of any systematic network of intellectual contact. They cannot disguise the fact that lesbians' identity as a doubly oppressed group – as women and as homosexuals – makes their relationship to the existing 'male' literary tradition even more problematic than it is for gay male writers.

In the early part of the century, in particular, the influence of male traditions was very strong. As we saw in the last chapter, the motifs of Baudelaire and the Decadents permeate the poetry of Vivien, a fact which – given that binary oppositions within style, within content, and between style and content are the lifeblood of Baudelairean poetry – inserts her separatist visions into precisely the set of values from which she is trying to escape. Even the Decadent praise of sterility and its attendant images, which attracts Barney and Vivien as a vehicle for rejecting the conventional identification of women with motherhood, is a trap, in that it brings with it resonances of a highly misogynistic tradition, from Baudelaire to Laforgue, in which woman is represented as inferior, purely animal – nature's prime weapon in its war against the male. At the same time lesbian writers had difficulty disentangling Sappho, the symbol of lesbian creativity, from the male-voyeur approach to lesbianism into which Louÿs's *Chansons de Bilitis* had entangled her.

The most effective forms of escape from existing literary discourse were generic. First, Vivien's short stories launched a new type of 'Lesbian fairy-tale' which, although it was connected with aspects of Decadent writing, also had roots in female gothic, and leads into the utopian fantasy tradition (Rochefort's *Archaos*, Wittig's *Les Guérillères*) of later in the century. Second, Colette and Leduc dismantled the barriers between fiction and non-fiction, posing themselves as first-person narrators in texts which cannot be pigeon-holed as autobiography or novel, such as *La Naissance du jour* and *La Bâtarde*. Marks, discussing the use of characters who refer to a world outside the text, suggests that 'because lesbianism is considered unusual, it requires the kind of validation that only real names can confer'.[19] But what Colette and Leduc are doing is to consciously break free from the dual limitations of realism (which reflects the constrictions of reality) and fiction (a merely theoretical projection of the possible) in order to explore the nature of the female self/female sexuality. This might sound like Gide, but neither woman is interested in the system of intellectual oppositions which Gidean irony imposes on the same enterprise. By insisting on the equivalent value of 'biography' and 'fiction' in self-representation, they step outside conventional processes of categorization, so as to integrate, for example, intellect and emotion, documentary and psychological truth. To the same end they also initiate the rejection of linearity, preparing the way for the experiments in non-linear literary exposition of Wittig, Brossard and Bersianik. Such breaks with traditional methods of representation have been invaluable to women writers.[20] But since the reader is obliged to read them 'against' the literary strategies with which s/he is familiar, even the most determined separatists have found it impossible to free themselves from male forms and male language entirely.

What is slightly less expected is the degree to which separatist writing tries to *harness* the male tradition. Obviously, a critical, parodic dialogue with the dominant value system of the type conducted in *L'Eugélionne* and *Le Pique-nique sur l'Acropole* is a natural part of lesbian self-definition. But to write *non-parodically* within a pattern determined by a previous male text, as Wittig does in *Virgile, non* (Dante's *Inferno*) and *Le Voyage sans fin* (Cervantes' *Don Quixote*) risks confining the imagination to a predetermined pattern of male-defined issues. Is there such a gap between Leduc's obsession, in *La Bâtarde*, with finding a male authority to put a seal of approval on what she writes, and the capitulation to the authority of a male tradition exemplified by the way in which Wittig's rebellion in these texts is totally defined for her by the things she is rebelling against? It reminds me of Rimbaud's discussion, in *Une Saison en enfer*, of the way in which his involuntary infant baptism into the Catholic Church controlled the terms in which he could react to religion. Only pagans can *ignore* hell; lapsed Catholics have to *deny* it. By using Dante and Cervantes as models, Wittig is obliged to create a 'world upside-down' which demonstrates the very system of binary oppositions she is seeking to discredit.

I do not mean to suggest that a female author can never be positively influenced by a male author. It is because the colour imagery of Rimbaud's 'Voyelles', a poem which itself is refusing to be bound by the traditional limits of language, is non-referential, and therefore has no gender-based associations, that Wittig can borrow it and mobilize its resonances of linguistic rebellion to attack Lévi-Strauss's doctrine of 'exchange of women' in *Le Corps lesbien*. For Wittig to relate her concept of freedom to images from Baudelaire's 'Femmes damnées' and 'Voyage à Cithère' is a different matter, given that *no* Baudelairean reference can be divorced from the context of the viciously contemptuous misogyny which disfigures *Les Fleurs du mal* from one end to the other. I cannot reconcile the separatist aspirations of *Brouillon pour un dictionnaire des amantes* with the uncritical respect for the authority of the patriarchal literary canon which Wittig's remarks on literature and her creative response to it reveal.

Wittig is not by any means the most problematic of all lesbian writers when it comes to the issue of the relationship – sexual, thematic and stylistic – to the male tradition. That distinction goes to Marguerite Yourcenar. In the first place, any sexual label attached to her has to be hypothetical. She always tightly limited the biographical information available about her private life, restricting herself to such discouraging statements as, 'Because I lived with a woman for forty years, people assume I'm a lesbian'.[21] In assuming her homosexuality, I can only plead that most critics do, and that the thematic weight of her work seems to justify this. As we shall see, she writes about Sappho in terms of the inter-war international lesbian community in a way which shows familiarity with it, to say the least. But the key feature of the handling of sexuality in Yourcenar's work is that, while Wittig suppresses gender as an issue by eliminating the male, Yourcenar does it by suppressing the female. All Yourcenar's work features alternative sexuality – brother/sister incest in *Anna, soror*, for example. But virtually all the alternative sexuality in question is *male* homosexuality. Eric Bentley produces a provocative explanation for this in commenting on her choice of the life of a Roman emperor as the subject of her best-known work, *Les Mémoires d'Hadrien*.[22] Coupling her with Mary Renault, whose novels (e.g. her trilogy about

Alexander the Great) also revel in portraying male homosexuality
in classical settings, he observed that

> They are both ... on a power trip. Madly identifying them-
> selves with male power. If it is remarkable, in this day and
> age, to make much of Antinous and Bagoas, it is even more
> remarkable that a woman should make much of Alexander
> or Hadrian.

And when asked whether he thought that these were instances of
women's liberation or the opposite, he added: 'A bit of both, I
suspect.' Without completely discounting Bentley's point, I want to
suggest that Yourcenar is an extreme example of integrationism,
the mirror image of the extreme separatism of Wittig, and that
consequently, since extremes always meet, she and Wittig have
significant traits in common.[23]

If Bentley were right in supposing that Yourcenar is identifying herself with male power, it could be argued that this was a
logical model for lesbian writing, especially in someone of her
generation (she was born in 1903). By this I mean that the adoption
of some degree of masculine identity, often symbolized by cross-
dressing, was frequent among female 'modernists' in the 1900–30
period, as a means of escaping the constrictions of society-defined
femininity by adopting a form of dress which was seen as an emblem of freedom. It would be possible to argue that Yourcenar is
attempting the intellectual equivalent, on the hypothesis that a
woman could arrogate to herself some of the freedom of the 'ruling
class' by transposing her values into male images. For a homosexual woman to do so would (given the exclusion of male homosexuals from power in contemporary society) require her to find a
period when male power and male homosexuality were compatible,
which, like the Decadents, projects us safely back into classical
antiquity. This would account for the choice of the Emperor Hadrian as subject matter. But *Les Mémoires d'Hadrien* has to be seen
as the last in a *line* of texts, starting with *Alexis*, which feature
homosexuals in different walks of life at different periods of
history, not to mention Yourcenar's translations from, and essay
on, the modern Greek homosexual poet Constantine Cavafy. We

can hardly talk about 'male power' in respect to most of these texts too. Like Wittig, Yourcenar does not believe in gender difference as an essence; unlike Wittig, it is precisely with masculine values that she identifies, not in a patriarchal sense but in a 'feminized' form which she associates with male homosexuality. It is also because she sees lesbianism as a culturally 'marked' form – i.e. as arousing certain sorts of preconception which she wishes to avoid – that she prefers to work through male images, which she feels have a generalizing capacity denied to their female equivalents.

Alexis ou le traité du vain combat (1929) explores in a Gidean form (the short first-person narrative) various Gidean themes: homosexuality as the product of a puritan upbringing dominated by women; the separation of love from sexual satisfaction; the impossibility for a married homosexual to be 'authentic' until he leaves his marriage. Here, what Yourcenar seems to be doing is to focus on the philosophical issues of identity and personal liberty, laying claim to equal status with male writers by inserting herself into a *male* homosexual writing tradition (Gidean) and by taking on what would traditionally be defined as a 'male' (i.e. abstract) approach.

Alexis, interesting though it is, is a beginner's piece. *Feux*, a volume of expressionist prose poems, is a quite different kettle of fish. The question of sex and gender runs right through the work, which declines from the outset to define the gender of the person to whom these love poems/fragments of lyric prose are addressed. This is not a question of 'discretion'; the writer and the beloved are clearly deliberately rendered as ungendered, so that the issues handled become depersonalized, generalized. Within this framework several of the 'stories' have clear sex/gender thematic focuses. In particular 'Achille ou le mensonge', based on the legend of the unsuccessful concealment of Achilles on the island of Lemnos by his mother, the goddess Thetis, to prevent his taking part in the Trojan War, deals with the issue of gender as a social construct. To do this it features a male hero, who, in his disguise as a woman, has become what is conventionally regarded as feminine at one level but not at another, a conventional 'feminine' character (Déidamie), and Misandre (the name means 'man-hating'), a girl more conventionally masculine than Achilles, more apt for war but ultimately disbarred by social assumptions about gender roles. Added into the equation is the relationship between gender, love and friendship; Achilles' beloved, Patroclus, rejects him in his female manifestation.

Gender/gender roles and their relationship to desire and emotion are thus seen as kaleidoscopically interchangeable in reality, but 'fixed' by the prejudices of a heterocratic society which asserts control through categorization. Note that Yourcenar suggests that these attitudes are not confined to heterosexuals; Patroclus is gay, as are Harmodios and Aristogiton in 'Lena ou le secret', where the male power structure can absorb a cross-class relationship (Yourcenar changes the myth by making Aristogiton a boxer, rather than an upper-class youth like his lover) but excludes women from real communication with men.

The most important poem/story from our point of view, however, is the last, the culmination of the collection, 'Sappho ou le suicide'. Here Yourcenar ceases to embroider, to offer simple re-readings of classical legend and opts instead for a metaphorical application. Her Sappho is a comment on the 'type' of the lesbian artist-figure, a wholly contemporary reference: as she puts it in the preface, 'this "Sappho the acrobat" belongs to the inter-war world of international pleasure'. She downgrades the creative artist into the technician of performance – although the choice of music-hall acrobat also smacks of a reference to Colette, Missy and the world described in Colette's *L'Envers du music-hall*, *Mitsou* and *La Vagabonde*. The focus of the text is again the complex relationship between gender, sexual identity and desire. In what is an exceptionally physical text (exceptionally for Yourcenar, that is) the lesbian element is presented as a paradox. Female nature is endowed with a fundamental narcissism of a kind more readily acknowledged in gay male writing: 'All women love a woman: they are madly in love with themselves, their own body usually being the only form in which they consent to detect any beauty.' But Sappho, who loves in young girls the softness which her own lean, gymnastic body lacks, is condemned to pursue not what she is but what she desires to be. In an inversion of the Proustian man-woman, it is Sappho who, in Yourcenar's terms, has the body of a man but the soul of a woman. Hence, she comes to realize that what she desires in Phaon is not his maleness, but the inferior copy of femaleness which he represents, a truth only revealed to her when he cross-dresses. Sappho attempts, and fails, suicide; she cannot escape from her fate, the eternal pursuit of the image she wishes that her mirror could reflect.

The 'poems' of *Feux* have philosophical and political levels of reference which I have not touched upon here, though the co-existence of these levels with the kaleidoscope of sexual/gender ambiguities on which I have focused is an important part of Your-cenar's presentation of the relationship between personal and general, concrete and abstract, in her writing. What I want to stress is the way in which, just as *Alexis* inserts itself into a Gidean view of homosexuality, so *Feux* comments on, and inserts itself into, the literary worlds of Barney and Colette, but at the same time into those of Gide and Proust. If we add to this Yourcenar's translations from Cavafy, in whose Decadent-cum-modernist poetry homoero-ticism is inseparable from the theme of transcending time through art, we can see Yourcenar developing a practice of writing which allows her to retain categories of conventional male thought and values, and to distance herself from aspects of patriarchal normati-veness, while at the same time resisting assimilation to any sort of 'female' writing.

Is this selling out to the patriarchal model – going for power – as Eric Bentley suggests? We have to remember that the gay male is usually considered as excluded from the power structure by his sexuality. (Christiane Rochefort takes this view.) Hadrian may be an exception, but Yourcenar's other male heroes – Alexis, Eric in *Le Coup de grâce*, Zenon in *L'Oeuvre au noir* – are not. Some French feminists, however, believe that the masculinity of male homosexuals places them in the patriarchal camp whether they like it or not. (Helene Cixous takes this view.) Which view does Yource-nar take? If there is an answer to this question, it has to be provided by the central text in the Yourcenar corpus, *Les Mémoires d'Had-rien* (1951). As middle-aged ruler and philosophical thinker, Had-rian is the epitome of male supremacy; as aesthete, sensualist and lover of an eighteen-year-old boy, he is a classic example of the Gidean pederastic mentor, and, as first-person narrator, is sub-jected to a process of Gidean irony in his self-revelations too. But Yourcenar applies to the themes of love and sensuality a more instinctive, Colette-like physicality. The theory of the fluidity of gender-identity which emerges from *Feux* in particular is fully applicable to Hadrian, as to all Yourcenar's gay heroes (Sappho included). Man/woman is just as much a socially constructed opposition for her as it is for Wittig. But whereas for Wittig the natural resolution of that opposition is provided by the amazon, a female figure who absorbs and naturalizes certain 'masculine' qualities, for Yourcenar the resolution is to be found in a form of male-based androgyny, for which the gay male provides the obvious symbol. By projecting herself into her gay male heroes, she can examine the nature and limits of masculinity – physical, social and intellectual – as freed from the deformations of heterosexuality, without losing sight of essential aspects of the female.

At the same time, as I suggested earlier, this strategy allows her to explore such issues as the separation of love and physical desire, and the pederastic tradition (mentor and younger follower) raised by Barney's circle, and by Colette, without in any way committing herself to their values. In other words it allows her to insert herself into a man's world – and in non-fictional texts she makes it plain that she sees the world pragmatically as a man's world – without espousing its central prejudices. The result is necessarily ambiguous, interpretable as both a sell-out to the male tradition or as a covert take-over of it.

As we have seen, French lesbian writing has its own patterns of development in the twentieth century which, whilst they overlap with gay male writing in some respects, are very different in others. Lesbian separatism developed long before gay male writers started to express any sense of corporate identity, and lesbian writers formulated much sooner than their male counterparts the problems of relating to the dominant language/discourse. A relative emancipation (apart from Vivien and to a certain extent Leduc) from the images of sickness and death, criminality, sin and the artist-as-pariah which permeate gay male writing, at least in the first half of the century, was facilitated by the existence of a positive model, the Sappho tradition, and later by the development of distinctive female patterns of writing. The fact that the gap between the values and aspirations of the separatists and those who see sexuality as a continuum has not led to a simple division into different types of writing can be put down to the complexities lesbian writers experience in concurrently relating to (or reacting against) not only the patriarchal tradition but also the growing traditions of gay male, heterosexual female and lesbian writing. The situation is further complicated by the fundamental split within French feminist theory between those who think that the difference between 'masculine' and 'feminine' is purely a social construct and those who think that there is an *essential* difference between the two, even if it is not biologically determined or even gender-related. The consequence of the need to situate itself in relation to so many different literary and intellectual traditions, combined with the desire to face up to the issue of gender-bias in language itself, is that there is an intense intellectuality about much contemporary lesbian literature, especially in Quebec, which is both a strength (its power to stimulate further debate) and a weakness (its extreme elitism).

Notes

1. 'The privilege of consciousness', in George Stambolian and Elaine Marks, *Homosexualities and French Literature: Cultural Contexts/Critical Texts* (Ithaca and London: Cornell University Press, 1979), p. 105.
2. Bonnie Zimmerman, 'Perverse reading: the lesbian appropriation of literature', in Susan J. Wolfe and Julia Penelope, *Sexual Practice, Textual Theory: Lesbian Cultural Criticism* (Cambridge, MA and Oxford: Blackwell, 1993), p. 136.
3. It is probably significant that the novel reproduces very clearly autobiographical material, especially as, in her autobiographical works proper, Colette was to remain silent on this particular affair. Rézi was an American, Mme Georgie Raoul-Duval; Colette had what appears to have been her first post-school lesbian experiences with her; and it seems fairly certain that the affair came to an end when she found herself sharing Georgie's favours with Willy.
4. Nicole Ward-Jouve, *Colette* (Brighton: Harvester Press, 1987), p. 92.
5. See ch. 1, p. 23.
6. Elaine Marks, 'Lesbian intertextuality' in Stambolian and Marks, *Homosexualities*, p. 364.
7. *Le Pur et l'impur*, in Colette, *Oeuvres*, vol. iii (Paris: Gallimard (Bibliothèque de la Pléiade), 1991), p. 642.
8. Ibid., p. 638.
9. Marks, 'Lesbian intertextuality', p. 369.

10. The term 'bourgeois', in Rochefort's work, does not merely mean 'middle class'; it defines an attitude to the world which is (1) fundamentally hypocritical and (2) primarily interested in possession and domination.

11. Christiane Rochefort, *Printemps au parking* (Paris: Grasset, 1969), p. 262.

12. Christiane Rochefort, *Les Stances à Sophie* (Paris: Grasset, 1963), p. 138.

13. Christiane Rochefort, *Quand tu vas chez les femmes* (Paris: Grasset, 1982), p. 137.

14. Jean Demelier, *Le Rêve de Job* (Paris: Gallimard, 1971).

15. His sense of incomprehension is precisely recorded in his comment on the way he portrays women in his films: 'Woman-child, sweet and inaccessible'. See Cyril Collard, *L'Ange sauvage:* Carnets (Paris: Flammarion, 1993), p. 175.

16. See Renaud Camus, *Notes achriennes* (Paris: POL, 1982), pp. 101–4, and *Chroniques achriennes* (Paris: POL, 1984), pp. 48–50, 146–50.

17. It is interesting, in this respect, to compare Tremblay's critique of lesbian separatism in *Le Coeur découvert* with Maupin's more detailed anatomy of it in *Significant Others*.

18. See, for example, Collard, *L'Ange sauvage*, pp. 189, 194.

19. Marks, 'Lesbian intertextuality', p. 359.

20. For a discussion of the difference between the effect of such techniques in the work of male and female post-modernist writers, see Martha Noel Evans, *Masks of Tradition: Women and the Politics of Writing in Twentieth-Century France* (Ithaca and London: Cornell University Press, 1987), pp. 223–8.

21. In a *New York Times* interview quoted by Joan DeJean, *Fictions of Sappho 1546–1937* (Chicago and London: Chicago University Press, 1989), p. 356, n. 103.

22. 'We are in history', in Stambolian and Marks, *Homosexualities*, p. 131.

23. My train of thought on this subject was set off by various points of comparison between the two writers proposed by Adele King in *French Women Novelists: Defining a Female Style* (London: Macmillan, 1989).

Chapter nine

The Body in the Text

'There is something disconcerting about a man's naked
body being presented as a sexual object.'
● *Gene Thornton*[1]

THE literary representation of the body and of desire, especially the representation of the sexual parts and the sexually
explicit expression of desire, has long been controversial even in a
heterosexual context. But whereas we are accustomed to recognize
the difference in world-view between those who think that all artistic representation of the sex act should be clothed in periphrases
and those who find such an attitude indicative of what Renaud
Camus calls 'a long, painful disease of civilisation', we may be less
alert to the politics of bodily representation itself within a text. Yet
the two are closely connected. In the case of the evocation of
physical presence in fiction, there is a deeply rooted tradition in
patriarchal culture that the male and female body should be portrayed according to different sets of conventions, denoting the
different roles and status of men and women in society. The male,
as the subject of desire, tends to be less physically visible, whereas
the female, as object of desire, is exposed to the view of both the
males within the text and the reader. In consequence, bodily
descriptions of men in conventional fiction tend to connote attributes of character (strength of will, intelligence, determination if he
is a 'real' man, their absence if he is not), whereas women are
primarily defined as a set of decorative surfaces, as potential sexual
possessions.

An author who radically challenges these conventions, particularly if that author is a woman, risks being told that s/he does not know how to portray male characters. The only readily acceptable variation on the tradition is its direct inversion, since this in practice reaffirms the validity of the tradition itself. Thus in Rachilde's *Monsieur Vénus*, a Decadent 'revenge' novel in which a man is subjected to sexual humiliation by a woman, the conventions of physical description are simply reversed. Right from the start Jacques is systematically feminized and animalized; when we first see him, he is garlanded with the artificial flowers he is making, and the details of his body are directed away from areas of potential body strength onto purple lips, milk-white teeth, dimpled chin, smooth child-like skin. In so far as there is anything connotative about the description, it is expressed through dog images which suggest humility, submission, powerlessness. In short, he is not a 'man', in visual terms, as the passage itself concludes: 'quite broad hands, a sulky voice, the way his thick hair grew, were the only things about him which gave away his sex'. In other words, Jacques is immediately defined as an *object* of desire and given a 'female' description to fit his female role.

The first major French writer to challenge the theory and practice of the existing conventions of description was Colette, who substantially dismantled the notions of conventional masculinity and femininity of her period and their relationship to the presentation of both the female and the male body. It is not just that women in her works are assessed in terms of such non-sexual qualities as healthiness, strength, their ability to withstand the ageing process; men are viewed from a completely different angle too. For the first time the distinction between inner and outer man is abolished. Chéri's body *is* his character: his firm shield-like chest establishes his masculinity, but the fact that we first see it as the setting for Léa's pearl necklace concurrently indicates his femininity. Futhermore, as Diana Holmes has pointed out, the reader's physical image of a Colette hero includes a host of details which are not conventionally part of either male or female characterization: 'the shape of his nostrils, knees and neck, the precise shading of skin and hair on different parts of his body, his characteristic smell and whether or not he is eating well'.[2] These details form part of an evaluation of the character's sensuality and erotic potential; they place him firmly as the *object* of desire. But this is not presented as a form of subjection, as it is in Rachilde; on the contrary, it is a question of equalization. The fact that the relationship between May and Jean in *L'Entrave*, for example, is emphatically freed from the customary dominated/dominator structure is not only spelt out by the narrator, who expresses her amazement at 'this couple where the woman is only treated as a woman in bed', but is represented in the physical portraits of Jean. One of these is particularly interesting because, like the portrait of Jacques in *Monsieur Vénus* to which I just referred, it uses the mouth as a point of sensual focus:

> I had never noticed how much a mouth, set in a clean-shaven face, with full sulky lips but finely delineated at the corners, gives away about the weaknesses and charms of a man's character, or that his chin was obstinate and yet feminine at the same time, or that his low collar revealed a neck which was strong but smoothly rounded such that the muscles did not show.[3]

The reason why the effect is quite different from that obtained by Rachilde is that Colette removes the 'feminine' references from a simple contrastive power structure. In *Monsieur Vénus* Jacques' femininity is contrasted with the 'masculinity' of Raoule. In *L'Entrave*, Jean's femininity has nothing to do with power, except in so far as a man's sexual attractiveness is made dependent on his blending of masculine and feminine characteristics. The same is true even in those texts where the presentation of a young male in particular is part of a contrastive system which places him against one or more women, older or younger, with sometimes a second male figure who represents conventional masculinity. In these cases it is the failure of gender to coincide with the conventionally masculine and feminine which is important. The opening of Colette's *Le Blé en herbe*, for example, deliberately presents two androgynous figures side by side. Vinca, with her short hair and flat chest, a sunburnt tomboy striding down towards the rocks, is described as tucking up her clothes prior to wading into the sea 'as calmly as a boy'. Phil, her male counterpart, has 'slim, sixteen-year-old arms and legs which had a fullness which still disguised their muscularity – limbs of which a young girl would be no less proud than a young man'. His status as an object of female desire emerges as he blushes, bare-chested, under the smiling gaze of the unknown woman-in-white. And his later sexual initiation at her hands, whilst it turns him into a 'man', precisely accentuates the feminine in his appearance. As he hurries to look in the mirror, he sees:

> in a face hollow with weariness, languishing eyes made larger by the dark rings around them, lips which, from touching a made-up mouth, had retained a little of its red colour, black hair tumbling over his forehead – doleful features, less like those of a man than those of a bruised girl.[4]

Phil's physical ambiguity is a source of his desirability, but to be an object of desire is not a question of submission. His androgyny depends upon, and brings to the surface, an equivalent androgyny in both Vinca and Mme Dalleray. It is therefore a prerequisite not only for their power over him but also for his power over them.

What Colette does in her descriptions, then, is to abolish the old system of physical representation as a prerequisite for rethinking the experience of being a woman. Finding a new discourse in which to explore the female body has been a critically recognized, naturally developing trend in women's literature in general – and in lesbian literature in particular – from Colette onwards. To a certain extent the complementary re-identification of the male body from a female perspective also develops, at least in heterosexual and bisexual women's writing – Leduc's portrait of Gabriel in *La Bâtarde*, for example, follows a similar pattern to those of Colette's heroes. What as yet no one seems to have asked is how far, and in what ways, a similar revision of the male and male desirability has taken place in gay male literature. By definition a gay male reader's perception of, and relation to, the male characters in what he reads is quite different from that of a male heterosexual reader, and though it may share perspectives with that of a heterosexual female reader, it is influenced by different criteria of desire. If this is the case, then the perceptions of the gay male *writer* must affect the presentation of his male characters in the same way. In fact, in the course of this book, we have already seen a number of competing views of the male body or contrastive ways of presenting it – androgyny and the macho, natural images and parallels with art or literature, explicit and indirect presentation of sexual acts – most of which cut across the division between pederastic and adult homosexual writings. The question is, do these contrastive approaches fit into any coherent typology?

At first glance it would seem easy to show a difference in body presentation between texts which promote anonymous sexual fulfilment and those which contain a more conventional association of sex with emotion. In the latter, perception is a two-way process: by emphasizing not just the eyes but also the *glance* of the desired one, the author stresses that the desirer is as much object as subject. Thus, when Jean-Marc sees Mathieu across the disco floor in *Le Coeur découvert*, he passes from the role of perceiver to perceived:

> It was while I was watching the movements of an inspired dancer who was astonishingly unaware of what was happening around him that I first noticed the dark eyes which were staring at me from the other side of the dance-floor with almost comic seriousness.

Similarly, when Julien Green first sees Mark, he defines him as 'the young student with the dark eyes', and it is these eyes which define the terms of their relationship: 'The purity of Mark's gaze made me pure too'.

If, on the other hand, we look at description in Renaud Camus, this reciprocity seems to be absent. Parallel with his personification of desire itself (the individual being merely the vehicle of desire) Camus, in *Notes achriennes*, presents sight as a one-way process. The eyes of his partners are merely mentioned as coloured surfaces. This matches the rest of his descriptive technique. The males he encounters are seen in terms of a few superficial details, noted in the telegraphese of the small ad – hair and eye colour, facial and body hair, build – and even reduced to the purely formulaic: 'le beau brun de l'avant-veille' (the good-looking dark boy from the night before last); 'le brun du Crisco' (the dark boy from the Crisco club), with the adjective *beau* often left to stand alone, as though it were self-explicit. In specifically sexual contexts this stylization is intensified by the concentration of the focus of the text on the sexual parts in close-up. In an encounter in the Crisco 'back room', for example, the reader first experiences Camus's partner as 'his already hard cock, long and quite thick, but not too thick, heavy and pleasant-smelling, very beautiful',[5] the camera only gradually panning up – thighs, stomach, chest – to show that he is blond and mustached, and eventually to suggest an imagined background for him: perhaps he is a young married man out for a secret fling. This choice of perspective, foregrounding the erect penis, emphasizes that the sole role of the sexual partner is as an agent of pleasure; when Camus's eyes reach his face, the man is, significantly, looking away.

What we must observe, however, is that the difference between Tremblay and Green on the one hand and Camus on the other is not a simple case of an opposition between a mutual envisioning, which makes the surface of the body relatively unimportant, and a one-way perception which presents the body detachedly as an object of desire. Of course, examples of genuine, selective one-way perception are plentiful in gay writing, but as detached appreciations of beauty rather than in contexts of desire. Collard's description of an Italian boy seen across the harbour is a good example:

> There are probably few things more beautiful than the shoulder and arm of a bronzed, muscular Italian boy as they project from his tank top. He crosses the bar at the tiller of a fishing boat, body leaning forward, cock at rest in his red shorts.[6]

The boy is evoked in the terms of someone admiring a picture; he has been entirely aestheticized, rendered as desirable rather than as desired. But, with the other examples which we have discussed, it is really a case of two different views as to where the experience of the body is centred, and how that can be translated into language. Tremblay and Green privilege sight over the other senses, something to which Camus explicitly objects: 'Language and the eyes are not the sole vehicles of knowledge, and we should not neglect those rare places which give back their powers of exploration to hands and lips.'[7]

In contexts of actual desire, the tactile is indeed frequently privileged over the visual in 'promiscuous' texts. The extreme example is Guy Hocquenghem's *L'Amour en relief*, where the central character, blinded in a motor-scooter accident, is freed from the tyranny of sight to experience physical love on a quite different sensory plane. In ordinary 'sighted' texts, a relatively abrupt way of listing visual aspects of the body in sexual encounters is often balanced by an insistence on, for example, verbs of touch. Thus the first physical encounter between the bisexual Sylvain and his girl-friend Carol in Collard's *Condamné amour* is characterized by the way her fingers brush over his body and stroke him through his underpants, the mutuality lying in the return of the caresses as he fondles her breasts. Camus's anonymous partners similarly communicate by fingers and mouth, in masturbation and oral sex. This counter-privileging of touch over sight is even made explicit in a scene in *L'Ange sauvage* where, as Collard is willingly gang-banged by the group of Mexican boys who have been feeling him up, he notes that, lying on his stomach, he can no longer see 'the reflections of the adolescent orgy in the mirrors facing the bed'. Both sets of texts, therefore, deal in mutuality, but one does it via the body as object seen, the other via the body as object felt.

Another possible distinction is between the insistence on parts of the body as a reality in themselves, and the use of them to suggest something deeper. In women's writing, there is a fundamental division, in physical description, between the literal and the metaphorical. Some feminists regard all use of metaphorical language for the female body with mistrust as distracting from the tangible physical reality, a way of 'covering' the female body in a cloak of language. The problem is neatly encapsulated in the caption to a cartoon in a radical lesbian pamphlet which mocks 'metaphor as evasion':

> I will now sing a short song comparing my lover's clitoris to a pearl, her labia to a persimmon fruit and her vagina to a vanilla pod, because quite frankly that's the only way I can cope with it all.[8]

Others argue that, precisely because patriarchal metaphors are 'dead', metaphorical language can and should be re-energized to specifically female ends.

For women writers, then, the question is, when is directness a failure of imagination, when is metaphor a failure of nerve? In gay male texts the dichotomy between literal and metaphorical presentation does not generate the same dilemma. Again, the division is in fact rather misleading. In the first place focus on individual parts of the body very easily gives way to synecdoche,[9] with an automatically symbolic effect, as when Genet represents Harcamone as a giant penis, stressing the equation between sexual power and 'moral' authority.[10] In the second place, metaphorical application of a description is not solely dependent on the use of metaphorical language as a vehicle of the description. Although a writer like Green to some extent builds in the metaphorical associations of his physical references through his choice of detail, he also uses structural devices to point up his meaning. In the long-delayed description of Mark, for example, with his lightly tanned skin and coal-black eyes, neat nose and fleshy lips, the final paradox of the co-existence of an impression of sensuality with one of chastity and virginity is achieved by juxtaposing pairs of features with different potential connotations. This is not essentially different from the structural device used by Renaud Camus in describing yet another sexual encounter in the Crisco club. The bald references to 'my hands on his thighs, his buttocks or his pecs, his hands in my hair' seem to limit us to the physical act, but the way in which the two partners keep changing place, one kneeling, one standing, until they end up in an embrace on the same plane, crouching half-overbalanced, represents the mutuality of pleasure, the absence of any attempt to play master and mastered. In both texts the choice of direct or indirect language has less influence on the metaphorical power of the description as a whole than the patterning devices which accompany that language.

There is in fact very little bodily description in gay male writers which is not harnessed to some level of meaning beyond itself. At its most direct, the further level can merely be a sense of potential psychological elements created by the use of abstractions, as when Collard, in describing a young Canadian as a strange mixture of beauty and ugliness, refers to 'the heaviness of his forehead, the emptiness of his washed-out eyes, the narrowness of his mouth'. Usually, however, one of three techniques is used: comparison with nature, comparison with art and definition by association or context. As we saw in Chapter 6, comparisons with nature are particularly frequent in representations of the adolescent male body in pederastic writing, where they perform the dual task of activating 'feminine' associations (particularly through images of flowers) and of naturalizing pederastic desire itself. The description, for example, of Diego's crutch in Duvert's *Journal d'un innocent*, plays on details of nature vocabulary, 'the neat pouch of his scrotum with its fine parallel furrows, the little plump half-moons which close around the hole', then draws these together by defining the ensemble, objectified by Diego's perception of it in a fragment of mirror glass, as 'the simplicity and radiance of this young landscape with the rounded hillocks of its sleepy cheeks'. A wide range of writers from Proust and Genet to Bory and Yves Navarre apply nature images to the adult male too, but for a more disparate range of effects. It is rare for the primary purpose of such images to be to make the visual experience of the body more immediate. Sometimes the writer is referring to a convention of writing rather than to a reality. Renaud Camus, for example, uses conventional images of strength – tiger, mane, lion – to suggest that a blond Italian friend misleadingly fits a heterosexual stereotype.[11] More often we are dealing with a metaphorical system. Collard, for example, introduces a beach scene with the image of 'an avalanche of muscular, sun-tanned bodies' in order to integrate himself, sunbathing, into the natural order, an integration which is a prerequisite for presenting himself as the vehicle of a natural force, desire.[12] In Jouhandeau's *Tirésias* and Navarre's *Le petit galopin de nos corps* this use of natural images is expanded to provide a running commentary on the sexual and emotional experiences at the centre of the texts – respectively, release of male 'femininity' through anal sex, and expression of the natural force of passion. There is an inherent stylization at work in the way gay writers use these images. They are drawn from a narrow range of elements – fruit, flowers, animals, landscape features. When applied to the adolescent body they usually suggest freshness, fragility and grace; applied to an adult male they either indicate macho qualities such as strength or they are markers of androgyny; applied to males of any age they are also used to symbolize the force and naturalness of homosexual desire.

Stylization is even more evident in definitions of the body in terms of art or literature. If comparisons with flowers and landscapes naturalize desire for the male body, comparisons with classical sculpture make it intellectually respectable. They also lock the body into a one-way objectifying perspective, keeping a safe distance between beholder and beheld. Very rarely is sculpture presented as something tactile; I can only think of one example, the narrator's response, in Eekhoud's *Voyous de velours*, to the half-naked body of the young gymnast Bugutte: 'I felt a desire to run my hands over that admirable statue of flesh and to mould it, passionately'. A more typical use is that made by Julien Green, who harps on the visual aspect of statuary in *Terre lointaine*, evoking the desire aroused in him by the reproductions of Greek sculptures in the University of Virginia and the particular erotic effect of the androgynous bronze Narcissus, a copy of which he obtains from a Naples museum, then comparing and contrasting these desires with his response to the bodies of the young men he sees around him. By transforming the latter into art metaphors, he objectifies and possesses them whilst keeping them at a safe distance. The process applies as much to casual encounters – the sailor in summer uniform 'who seemed like a silver statue, for his impeccable uniform was exactly moulded to his body to the point of becoming a new form of nudity'[13] – as to Mark, whose naked photograph becomes the repository of his desires and thus allows him the illusion that his feelings for Mark himself are 'pure'.

The mirror image of the process, interestingly, occurs in *Journal d'un innocent*. The narrator finds the attractions of Diego pall precisely because he is readily assimilable to a picture, and therefore too readily objectifiable, as though he were no more than an image in a pornographic magazine: 'Diego is nothing more than a perfect, banal picture; I can only draw up a boring list of his physical perfection. ... Even his erections have the fixity of a photograph.'[14] Green uses art to fix bodies at a distance, in an effort to neutralize their erotic power over him; Duvert becomes indifferent to a body which has a self-distancing quality, because he *wants* erotic involvement.

Comparisons with nature and art, then, tend to use the body to project other values or ideas. Inversely, we also find contextual associations used to project qualities *onto* bodies, by implication. The most obvious example of this is the 'masculinization' of a figure by references to stereotypically male objects – uniforms, guns, cars. This can be ironic; Tremblay, in a very funny scene in *Le Coeur découvert*, makes the boyishly attractive Mathieu fail dismally to achieve the right macho image in an audition for a beer advert, as much because of as despite the accoutrements of foaming tankard and hunting rifle. (The point is underscored at the end of the novel when Mathieu's adolescent charm wins him a profitable contract as the flashing smile in a campaign to promote *milk*.) But more often the stereotyping is straight-faced. In Cocteau or Genet a sailor's uniform is just as much a guarantee of a muscular physique as it is in Tom of Finland. Similarly, the macho power of Jack's body in Peyrefitte's *Roy* is prepared for by the police badge and pistol which he sets down before undressing. And in Bory's *La Peau des zèbres*, the sexual charge of Paul's body, and François-Charles's growing desire for it, is suggested only half-ironically by Paul's car and the way he handles it: 'Paul was driving a very low-slung red convertible with mortar shells for wings, a mortar shell where the bonnet should have been and the two of us squeezed together inside another shell hollowed out into an aircraft cockpit.'[15] However unwillingly, both François-Charles and the reader begin to identify Paul with the classic heterosexual visual symbolism of the car-as-weapon, endowing him with a sexual fascination which the text has previously denied him.

What redeems this last example from being a mere cliché, in fact, is that it is part of a wider system of contextual association.[16] The attraction which will arise between François-Charles and Paul is governed by the terms of the presentation of the context in which they meet. It is a beach scene in which all the human element is instantly transferred to the landscape. Human attributes pass to the sun, which 'kills' colour, to the sand 'brushed, combed titivated (perhaps even perfumed at the *Carlton* end)', to the naked, watery-blue sky (the adjective *lavé*, meaning watery *and* washed, cleverly combines inanimate and human associations). People, when they appear, are merely a part of the landscape: 'as if the immobility of it all – sun sky sea people – were false', the whiteness of Hubert's body matching the washed-out quality of the sun-bleached *plage*. At best people are reduced to animals: 'The cattle which are currently splashing, blowing and mooing in the water will come back dripping and collapse onto the meadow of powdered flint'. Paul, when he eventually appears, is described in terms which have hints (shellfish, flowers) of the same register: 'being a blond, his pale skin had turned lobster-red, clashing horribly with bathing trunks the same shade of geranium as mine'. At the same time, he begins to break free from the constraints of the white, still landscape because of his colour and his action (he is seen running, flicking glittering water from his heels). For such time as François-Charles is unaware of, or fighting against, his attraction for Paul, the young man is evoked in the same narrow set of references, which define him as tied to an environment (connoting his relationship with Hubert) from which he is struggling to emancipate himself. It is only during the subsequent car ride, therefore, that Paul escapes from his image as the big, blue-eyed, sunburnt blond, and that François-Charles starts to perceive him as an individual physical presence rather than a type, a process characterized by a quite different sort of physical reference: 'Paul has misbuttoned his silk shirt; as his arm moves with the steering wheel, through the gap in his shirt above the plaited leather belt holding up his trousers, I can catch glimpses of his stomach.'[17] The desire, which was absent when presented with his nearly nude body before, is now activated by a mere hint of bare flesh.

In the Bory example which we have just discussed, the text still does not quite escape from a certain masculine stereotyping. The most interesting examples of the connotational and metaphorical approaches to the presentation of the male body use the technique to face up to the special nature of gay male desire more openly. Genet in particular uses the compression of masculine and feminine elements into the same metaphor to highlight the potential abolition of gender roles implicit in gay desire. Trying to come to terms with the idea that boys who play a 'male' role in a relationship with one boy can play a 'female' role in a relationship with another, the narrator of *Miracle de la rose* creates an image which partakes of both qualities:

> I was still overwhelmed by the idea that each male had his own wonderful male partner, that the world of virile beauty and strength forged a chain of love-links in this way, forming a garland of muscular and contorted, or stiff and prickly, flowers.[18]

Although implicitly dealing in hierarchy, Genet avoids the obvious pyramid metaphor, replacing it with a double image, the chain and the garland, which emphasizes equality. At the same time, with their oxymoronic connotations of weight and constriction, lightness and celebration, and the further paradox of the identification between feminine (flowers) and masculine (muscularity, stiffness, prickles), the images insist on the coexistence of traditionally opposed qualities within and between the partners in a homosexual relationship. '

What interests me in this image is less its suggestion of androgyny than its emphasis on balance, the chain or garland as a series of interlinked elements equivalent in kind and status. I am not trying to play down the importance of suppressing the patriarchal masculine/feminine dichotomy. Indeed, I have some sympathy with Dominique Fernandez' subjective assertion that art only captures male beauty perfectly when it projects it as bisexual.[19] Once writers escape from the Proustian view of the male homosexual as a woman trapped in a man's body, they cease to present androgyny, Decadent style, as a dilution of the male and begin to depict a genuine male 'femininity' – in other words all those qualities which involve softness, gentleness, languor, receptiveness – in the same way that women writers do, as a normal part of man's experience which the heterosexual code requires him to suppress. The representation of the body necessarily plays an integral part in this process. To a certain extent the feminization is achieved by borrowing the techniques of women writers, such as the choice of 'nonstandard' parts of the body for focus. Yves Navarre, in *Ce sont amis que vent emporte*, for example, defines Roch's desire for David in terms of knees, leg hair, chest hair, pubic hair in one description, and David's desire for Roch in terms of mouth, armpits and the nape of his neck in another, using reference to smell and taste (as opposed to sight) to enhance the sense of intimate exploration.[20] Other writers emphasize posture. Collard's evocation of a portrait of Saint Vincent, for example, establishes masculinity by the contours of the penis, visible through his loincloth, but balances this assertion of the male by the femininity of his stance: 'His body is offered, lightly curling around itself. When it comes to it, what is there to distinguish him from a gigolo in any city of the world, leaning against a wall.'[21] This duality Collard specifically interprets as expressing the coexistence of violence and tenderness, tracing the fine line between the two. In another passage he evokes two ostensibly clashing images of the same boy – a young tough filled with coiled energy, and a fragile, wet-eyed figure sucking his thumb – and laconically joins them: 'Half-warrior of the night, half seeker after love: that's the way I like you',[22] equating masculinity with one set of body language, femininity with another, but showing both as necessary to the creation of his desire.

This brings me back to my initial point. It is surely the case that in this sort of writing, just as in the Genet metaphor, it is *balance* that is the central issue. Androgyny in itself is less important than harmony, the refusal to privilege one set of values over another. The same point is made inversely by Yves Navarre in *Killer*. The absurdity of the *im*balance which results from artificially suppressing the feminine – the suppression excoriated by Fernandez in his assessment of fascist sculpture – is satirically rendered in an incident in which Killer picks up a muscle-man at Parsons Pleasure, the nude bathing place in Oxford. Everything about the man is a cliché of gay macho, from the size of his genitals to his leather gear and motorcycle. But the resulting sexual encounter consists of a series of *tableaux vivants*. Killer is obliged to 'act out' a series of photographs (objectification of the body) showing couples in poses which suggest the physical victory of one over the other. The muscle-man, although sexually excited, is afraid of real sexual contact, because that obliges him, in experiencing an orgasm triggered by another man, to acknowledge his feminine dimension. In fact he only comes when Killer forces him into a situation where he has to submit to masturbation. What Navarre suggests is that by denying his femininity, he paradoxically emasculates himself. If the release of the suppressed feminine is an important part of male beauty and consequently of homosexual desire, it is because it represents a refusal to accept a power imbalance.

This, I think, is the real key to a specifically gay male representation of the male body and of desire. Whether interested primarily in sex as an end in itself or as a part of emotional communication, whether giving primacy to sight, touch or some other sense, whether privileging literal or metaphorical language as the best medium for communicating the physical, gay writers who are at ease with their sexuality find techniques to suggest equality of perception (via whatever sense or senses) and balance of desire. If a character, like the narrator of *Terre lointaine,* is not at ease with his sexuality, imbalance is inevitable; the young Julien's objectification of other men's bodies is a technique for escaping from the dangers of desire by reducing the desired to a controllable state. Objectification of this kind can equally be a way of forcing the desired to accept a role he would otherwise reject. The extreme and most disturbing example of such an imbalance of desire which I have found in a gay text is the portrait of group necrophilia in Navarre's *Les Loukoums,* where the body of a beautiful youth murdered expressly for the purpose is sullied by the sperm of his desirers as it lies on display in the Chapel of Rest. This is a good indicator that we should be careful not to make a simple equation between the role of desiring subject = good and the role of desired object = bad. It is true that women writers have struggled to impose themselves as desiring subjects, but that is precisely because the existing heterosexual discourse denied them that role. Gay male writers, on the contrary, have had to reclaim the role of *object,* for the inverse reason. Even in *Terre lointaine,* power often resides in the object of sight; when Green sees the beautiful Nicolls, he is wracked with desire: 'When I ceased to see Nicolls, I almost ceased to think about him, but to see him set me on fire, I was like a mad man, motionless or dumb, given up to the flames'. His problem is that he has no more power over Nicolls than the dead boy in *Les Loukoums* has over the necrophiliacs. Hence the importance of mutuality of experience, in whatever form it is represented. In pursuit of that mutuality, binary oppositions such as masculine and feminine, active and passive, seeing and seen, subject and object, have to be deprived of any value significance by the literary systems into which they are integrated.

What these systems are and how they work has, inevitably, a lot to do with the particular concept of beauty and forms of desire which an author is seeking to express. My analysis so far has concentrated on the abstract implications of individual patterns in texts. Naturally, the use of a given set of concrete elements in the context of radically different codes of sexual and emotional behaviour will lead to very different surface effects. Let us look at some examples of how different literary systems work, to establish to what extent, and in what ways, equivalence of desire and mutuality of pleasure play a part in them.

I shall start with the power of the experience of anonymous desire, because this automatically eliminates the problem of competing individual desires, focusing instead on the relationship of individual to group. In, for example, William Cliff's *Conrad Detrez*, a poetic elegy for the Belgian writer, the problem is tackled by the gradual creation of a context in which generalized physical details are interwoven with other levels of reference, particularly to nature, to establish parallels between human sexuality and other natural forces. The reader is acclimatized from the first canto to sharp shifts between biographical narrative, evocations of nature and personal reflections; these shifts encompass both literal recording of the body and a personification of desire which reduces the individual to a vehicle for the anonymous forces of his appetites:

> ... car nos désirs
> dans les détails pour trouver leur pitance
> étaient forcés de souvent s'avilir
> parking pissoirs bar parcs ...[23]

(... for our desires
when it came down to detail were often forced, in order to find
basic sustenance, to debase themselves,
parking lots lavatories bars parks ...)

In the opening stanzas of the third canto, personifications of desire, corporeal synecdoches designed to concentrate the essence of the body into sexual functions, nature imagery and a certain social realism alternate in such a way as to make each a reinforcement of the other, the totality of which is intended to 'place' Detrez' sexuality into a broader philosophy of existence. The canto plunges us into the intensity of physical experience which characterizes Rio de Janeiro, equating the energy and freshness of the natural environment, of sun and sea, with the vibrancy and unsuppressible appetites of the flesh. Starting as an accumulation of the general – 'sensual bodies' – of the sexual particular – 'great greedy mouths' – and of the abstract – 'fleshly desires for constant coupling' – man as a species is finally identified, by synecdoche, with his cock:

> oh! ces queues brunes, ces queues parcourues
> du brûlant vouloir d'aller s'enforner
> au milieu des muqueuses déchirées

(Oh, those brown cocks, those cocks thrilling in their whole length
with the burning desire to thrust themselves
in among torn mucuous membranes.)

The images continue in this fashion: man as long spurts of cum, as genitals with an irrepressible desire to touch each other, such that the male, his sexual organs and his desire become completely interchangeable entities. This vision of man as co-extential with his sexuality, reminiscent of Genet's presentation of Harcamone as a giant erection in *Miracle de la rose*, in turn links him back to nature – the beach as the brothel where the sexual gold of semen is expended – and then contrastively links him to social themes through images of sexual exploitation and prostitution. This elaborate system is then used to represent both generalized anonymous sexuality and its personalized version in the character of Detrez: he exemplifies it, it symbolizes him. The powerful explosions of the volcanoes of Central America, the crash of the sea rollers against deserted beaches and the intensity of his orgasms with chance young pick-ups on the road mirror each other as the release of uncontrollable natural forces; his experience of, and taste for, anonymous sex becomes part of the natural system reflected in the instinctive carnality of young Brazilians.

Even if some of the same elements play an important part, the question of mutuality has to be handled through a completely different pattern of presentation in a text with a personalized focus. In Navarre's *Le petit galopin de nos corps*, for example, the three 'portraits'[24] – Joseph's description of Roland, Roland's answering picture of Joseph and the subsequent lyrical prose poem in which Joseph shifts to a still more intimate evocation of his beloved – also interrelate the human and the natural, and are also at points sexually specific, but the focus is different. Apart from the obvious widening of the physical basis of the description to include more parts of the body, it is noticeable that Joseph's portrait of Roland insists on the body as a process rather than a state, and seeks to define what is individual about that process even when relating it back to more general or abstract forces. The body as process is represented by the way the eyes shift between green and blue (there are associations of sky and water, changeable elements), the way the skin can be soft and yielding or tense and hard, the way the hair moves between winter brown and summer gold. This mobility is itself a subsidiary term inside the paradox 'change within continuity', the latter also translated into bodily terms. The hands, for example, characterized as 'broad, long, solid', become symbols of protection and strength, then stand as an image of stability by taking on the representative status of peasant hands across the centuries. Even a sexual reference, to the dark colour of Roland's penis, is used to reinforce the point about historical continuity: it suggests Arab blood from earlier invaders, the exotic, the powerful. And sexuality itself is used simply as a symbol of unity: 'The one thing that really brings us together is the simultaneity of our orgasms, at the moment when our bodies can no longer withstand the effects of our mutual embrace.'

Roland's portrait of Joseph is even more orientated towards metaphor. In taking the idea of breath, and its organ the nose, and drawing the portrait out of the consequent associations, Navarre uses some of the same techniques as William Cliff, notably synecdoche and personification: 'His nostrils make a real choice, they detect and literally filch the best of the air around them'. But the function of these rhetorical figures in context is the opposite of Cliff's. It is not that the literal physicality of Joseph is centred on his nose in the way that Cliff's Brazilians are embodiments of the penis, but that Navarre wants to build up a system of values around a single focus point; the quest for purity of air, for example, is linked to Joseph's rejection of both the unknown and the overfamiliar in life. Breathing brings with it a language of automatic metaphor (e.g. breathing freely, choking) which is easily extendable into more abstract character analysis. At the same time it connects with the theme of nature (recurrently used throughout the novel to connote the naturalness of the sexuality portrayed) in two ways: through the biology of the body, the oxygenization of the blood and the idea of life-rhythms, and through images of the wind.

In the third descriptive section, with the refrain, 'You have the body of the days and the seasons', the metaphorical patterns of the earlier descriptions are repeated in more detailed forms. It is interesting to see that, however precise the physical images – Joseph touching the indentation on Roland's skin left by an overtight belt, or stroking the point on the arch of the foot where the bones converge – the movement of the text is always toward a meaning *beyond* physical immediacy. Consequently, the value of the synecdoche *penis = man* is entirely different from what it was in Cliff's text. Rather than concentrating man into carnality, it prepares us for the way in which the subsequent extended description of oral sex followed by anal penetration evolves into a set of symbols of the union of difference in sameness. Where direct description of the body occurs, it is surrounded by passages of openly metaphorical writing which link the presentation of the human back into images of the natural cycle, to stress the idea of continuity within change – a trace of shit on Joseph's cock reminds him of river mud, murky wells, of looking at the snot in your handkerchief when you blow your nose. At the same time a vocabulary of natural function – breathing, eating – occurs side by side with that of sexual intercourse, placing the latter in a natural continuum in ordinary human terms.

What a man learns from exploring another man in this way is, of course, to appreciate the male body fully, but this physical dimension is still only a preparation for a more abstract form of learning. As Joseph himself articulates it: 'The body is not the only thing; but everything is connected through the body, the pages of the spirit'. Yet at the same time this preference for the metaphorical over the purely visual is different in kind from the comparable approach to the presentation of the male body in heterosexual writing, not only because there is a conscious 'feminization' through images of softness, instability, sexual receptiveness which are each part of a set of polarities within the description, but also because *both* men see each other in these terms. There is no question of privileging one partner over the other, one gender over the other, by a contrast between the metaphorical and the literal. Equally, although there is diversity, which expresses itself in complementarity of temperament, of body, even of desire, it is a diversity held in check by a unity of style.

My last text, Jouhandeau's *Tirésias*, offers the greatest ostensible challenge to a theory that mutuality and balance are the key elements in a genuinely gay representation of desire. On the one hand, as the title suggests, it is about the coexistence of the masculine and the feminine within an individual's sexual experience.[25] The question of harmony within the individual is therefore central to it. On the other hand, it recounts four sets of relationships with rent-boys; it is their bodies which are the objects of desire, their sex acts which are poeticized. Since commercial sex is usually viewed as a one-way transaction as far as *desire* is concerned, this would seem to exclude mutuality. Hot sex with male hustlers is the stuff of hardcore pornography, where the stereotypes are in fact merely translations of heterosexual dominator/dominated patterns into a homosexual mode. The objectification of the impossibly beautiful, improbably overendowed, eternally randy stud in the text allows the one-handed reader the illusion of possessing him repeatedly (and for free) whenever he wants to. At one point in *Tirésias* Jouhandeau touches specifically on the issue of reciprocity and prostitution, but only in commercial terms: he pays well for good value. However, as we shall see, his literary technique is designed to counter the associations of inequality inherent in his theme by creating parallels and alternations which underline motifs of mutuality of desire and unity in pleasure.

The way in which motifs are structured is the key issue. The text is a sexual *Bildungsroman*, describing Marcel's initiation into the mysteries of passive sodomy. Richard is his first mentor; Philippe shows him that this pleasure is something he can derive from more than one beautiful man; a brief experience with a dwarf suggests that it may be the act itself which counts; then Pierre completes the process of his physical and psychological 'formation'. Within this linear progression, there are a number of constants, both thematic – e.g. Marcel's sense of sexual duality – and metaphoric – e.g. images drawn from nature and mythology. But these constants themselves fluctuate in their application. Marcel asserts his sense of being both male and female, but he also at one point specifically sees himself as woman to Pierre's man. The boys are natural forces – lion, bull, pedigree dogs – conventional images of masculine strength and pride which, at one level, suggest superiority over Marcel. But nature images are also used to feminize them: Richard stripping is compared to a snake sloughing its skin; Pierre's body hair is metaphorized as sweet smelling undergrowth; and Philippe has wide periwinkle-blue eyes and a mouth which twists and contracts like an oyster at the moment of his orgasm. In this respect they are put on a par with Marcel, who is also a natural force, a stretch of fallow land now ploughed and ready to bear fruit, and whose sphincter becomes a sea urchin, half-animal, half-plant. Similarly the boys, whilst sometimes their animality could be interpreted as placing them on a plane below Marcel, are frequently gods, on a plane above him; but through the image of the centaur (the mythological creature half-man, half-horse) which is applied to the joined bodies of Marcel and Philippe, and which itself picks up the riding images used of all three boys as they have sex with Marcel, the domains of the mythological and the animal are joined in the human.

We have then a narrative, progressing in a linear fashion at one level, but repeating and embroidering itself at another, interwoven with a network of references which create a balance of similarity and contrast. At the centre of this network are set pieces of sexual description which hold the key to the physical value system of the work. In the first, which opens the book, Richard is defined initially as an object of gaze and desire: 'my gaze focused on the axis of his body', but as subject (initiator and dominator) of the sexual act: 'he threw himself on me, biting my shoulder'. The terms in which he is introduced concentrate on physical surfaces – handsome, dark colossus, pale grey eyes – with a slightly surreal colouring to the sexual focus in the phrase, 'au bassin nacré opulent' (literally, 'with ample, pearly pelvis'). His status as animal is connoted by the red lion and yellow leopard on the blue pullover which Marcel encourages him to leave on for a moment, symbolically between their naked bodies, an animality promptly echoed in the rosettes of black hair on his tanned thighs, 'like the spots on a panther's coat'. The metaphorical basis then expands to include a reference to Malatesta, a Renaissance tyrant, and the first of a series of weapon metaphors for the penis which will continue throughout the book. Gradually the motif of power is being passed from subject of desire to object.

All the description I have looked at so far is designed to convey conventional qualities of 'manliness'. But at the same time, Richard's mouth is rendered as a half-open pomegranate, an image customarily applied to the female genitalia, and whose androgynizing element will be picked up in a later description of a drop of milk forming on his nipple at the moment of his orgasm (i.e. what is ostensibly the supreme 'male' moment). This is the first of a series of textual dualities, both thematic and formal (the two levels being completely interlinked), which reflect and develop the duality of the subject/object role – Marcel the viewing eye but sexual possessed, Richard the object of gaze but sexual possessor. As the series unfolds, anal sex is defined as delight and pain (using the words *douceur* and *douleur* to make the two concepts almost homophonous), the oxymoron then being repeated in a set of variations: 'It was all the same to me whether I lived or died, and I told him so, so much did the torture and the pleasure intensify one another'. Richard's murmurs about the narrowness of the passage are antiphonally matched by Marcel's cries as to how imperious its traverser is, until the paradox of equality of experience in dominator and dominated comes to a verbal and thematic peak in a phrase which is, in form, a piece of pure baroque imagery but in content a piece of direct physical realism, Richard's 'Déchiré par ton anneau que je déchire ne me demande pas plus merci que moi à toi' (literally, 'torn (as I am) by your ring which I am tearing, you should no more ask me for mercy than I you'). This in turn prepares us for the image of their physical inseparability as 'a strange knot of intertwined roots', followed by simultaneous orgasm, the form of the phrase again underlining the mutuality of the experience: 'his sweetness spread through me, my sweetness flooded his hands'. The passage thus offers a movement from a (rapidly destabilized) master/mastered duality to a state of equality in pleasure, a movement confirmed antithetically, as Jouhandeau follows the harmony of the joint climax with an account of his one previous experience of passive anal sex, many years before, in which he had been to all intents and purposes raped, and where the pleasure was not reciprocal.

The beginning of the section on Pierre, a little over halfway through the text, repeats the basic structure of the Richard episode which we have just been discussing, but with extension and variation. Pierre, too, is introduced as an object of gaze, but an 'object' self-metamorphosed into a subject by its insistence on provoking desire in the perceiver:

> While I undress, slowly as usual, I am secretly watching
> him. Pierre, who, quick as a flash, has shed his trousers, his
> pullover and his sandals, watches me as, already naked, he
> lies stretched out on the bed, his hands clasped behind his
> neck, with the secret intention of displaying his charms to
> excite me.[26]

Accordingly, whereas Richard's body was primarily translated into metaphors representing Marcel's perceptions, Pierre's is visible primarily in his own realist terms:

> the tufts of hair in his armpits and groin create a triangular
> definition to the full roundedness of his ample figure, which
> is 'tied off', as it were, by his knotted biceps, his swelling
> pectorals, his pear-shaped calves.

The only metaphor, comparing his resting penis in its context to an enormous dark package of coiled rope hanging over the side of a ship, is a much more down-to-earth image than most of those applied to Richard, carrying with it traditional associations of potential for adventure and sailor's machismo.

Just as the 'body' section is a variant in the Richard episode,
so is the description of the sex act itself. This is similarly based on a
series of oppositions – victim/dominator, verbal sweetness and flat-
tery/vulgarity, insult and threat – which also extend to include
Marcel: 'his caress excites me and calms me'. But these oppositions
are concerned less with the anal experience itself than with a duality
of behaviour, 'masculine' and 'feminine' in conventional terms, on
Pierre's part. This latter aspect (as with Richard) is underlined by
feminizing physical detail – here, the sensitivity of his nipples – just
as the former is confirmed by types of image also shared with the
Richard episode: the phallus as piercing instrument, Pierre as rider,
the use of mythological reference. This passage too reaches its
zenith in mutual pleasure, but whereas before Jouhandeau stressed
the importance of equality of pleasure by directly juxtaposing the
account of it with an incident from which it had been absent, this
time he continues into a set of extended reflections on the balance
of pleasure between the two men, to the point at which Pierre
himself defines them as the right and left hands of a single body,
and it is Pierre who is frustrated on an occasion when their orgasms
do not coincide. The unity of Richard and Marcel is, like that of
Joseph and Roland in *Le petit galopin*, a balance achieved through
complementarity; the unity of Pierre and Marcel, although built on
exactly the same sort of complementarity, is *represented* as deriving
far more from shared dualities. Accordingly the balance between
theme and form which was created in the Richard passage through
a series of antitheses is here achieved by variations on a single
theme, the 'perfecting of sexual harmony', in increasingly physically precise terms.

Taken as a whole, what *Tirésias* is doing at the level of its
physical themes[27] is to establish reciprocity of desire and fulfilment
as coherent with a series of apparently irreconcilable differences
(age, beauty, intellect, the rent-boy contract) and as themselves
overriding other patterns of behaviour between the partners – mas-
culine/feminine, dominator/dominated – which would normally
create physical and psychological inequality. To do this, the text
uses an elaborate network of repetition, alternation, contrast and
balance, reinterpreting apparent opposites, such as male/female,
pleasure/pain, subject/object, as ambiguous sliding scales of experi-

ence, and clothing the whole in a language which is both (indigestibly?) metaphorical and sexually precise. The result is that the young men are both physically very real, very visible within the text, and yet as important to Marcel and the reader for the symbolic role they play; they are both individual presences and the anonymous agents of complete sexual fulfilment. In consequence, Marcel can simultaneously experience his own duality and his unity with another, and can experience that 'other' as both an individual and a representative force.

The three texts which I have examined 'embody' three quite different approaches to sex itself: anonymous pleasure, sex within an emotional relationship, and sex within a purely physical relationship. Yet they have in common a rejection of most of the binary oppositions which delineate the separate roles of sexual subject and sexual object in a heterosexual text; or, to be more accurate, they find ways of neutralizing the hierarchical implications which heterosexual texts attribute to these oppositions. I am not, of course, suggesting that this is how *all* gay male writing presents the male body and male desire. For one thing, to do so would be a-historical; most of the material I have looked at in detail is post-1960. For another, it would be an obvious overgeneralization, contradicted by plentiful examples even within the text of this book. What I *do* want to suggest is that, where they exist in texts by male homosexual writers, such phenomena as the suppression of male visibility; the presentation of men only in terms of an approved 'masculine' discourse of the body; the insistence on a traditional dichotomy between desiring subject (real men) and desired object (sexual subordinates); in short any retention of a power imbalance, thematic or formal, constitute departures from a gay male writing 'norm'.[28] In an unequivocally gay male text, the surface of the body, the physical experience of desire and the metaphorical associations of both are projected through literary systems which, disregarding the conventional categories of 'masculine' and 'feminine' representation, play with different kinds of stylistic balance and reciprocity.

The importance given to a 'gay' representation of the body and desire in many of the texts at which we have been looking connects logically with the insistence on the body *as* text which I noted as important in certain AIDS writings. I think there is a very real sense in which gay readers refuse the significance of the argument that literature, as merely a system of signs, cannot represent life. Regarding this as a truism, they happily collude with the texts they read in the 'experience' of gay desire, deciphering the literary systems as a translation of lived or liveable experience. The bodies which 'unfold and stretch between the sheets' of the pages we read take on the immediacy of bodies we have met, or want to meet, between the sheets of real life, but this immediacy is experienced aesthetically, as a set of responses to a particular literary discourse. The text takes on the function of the mirror, reflecting what is 'other' but recognizably part of ourselves. In this way the specifically gay male representation of the male body and male homosexual desire in literary texts becomes, at the very least, the guarantee, for both writer and reader, of the legitimacy of their sexuality, or, looking at it more positively, the celebration of the validity of that sexuality.

Notes

1. Art critic of the *New York Times*, quoted by George Stambolian in his foreword to Allen Ellenzweig, *The Homoerotic Photograph* (New York: Columbia University Press, 1992), p. xvi.
2. Diana Holmes, *Colette* (London: Macmillan, 1991), p. 78.
3. Colette, *Oeuvres*, vol. ii (Paris: Gallimard (Bibliothèque de la Pléiade), 1986), p. 338.
4. Ibid., p. 1225.
5. Renaud Camus, *Notes achriennes* (Paris: POL, 1982), p. 216.
6. Cyril Collard, *L'Ange sauvage* (Paris: Flammarion, 1993), p. 71.
7. Camus, *Notes achriennes*, p. 239.
8. Quoted by Helena Michie, *The Flesh Made Word: Female Figures and Women's Bodies* (New York and Oxford: Oxford University Press, 1989), p. 147.
9. Synecdoche is the figure of speech in which the term for part of something is used to denote its totality. We use a 'dead' version of this rhetorical device every time we call someone an arsehole or a dickhead.
10. Jean Genet, *Miracle de la rose* (Paris: Gallimard (Folio), 1988), p. 198.
11. Camus, *Notes achriennes*, p. 174.
12. Collard, *L'Ange sauvage*, p. 47.

13. Julien Green, *Terre lointaine* (Paris: Grasset, 1966), p. 125.
14. Tony Duvert, *Journal d'un innocent* (Paris: Editions de Minuit, 1976), pp. 151–2.
15. Jean-Louis Bory, *La Peau des zèbres* (Paris: Gallimard, 1981), pp. 299–300.
16. Ibid., pp. 229ff.
17. Ibid., p. 303.
18. Genet, *Miracle*, p. 288.
19. Dominique Fernandez, *Le Rapt de Ganymède* (Paris: Grasset, 1989), pp. 177–84.
20. Yves Navarre, *Ce sont amis que vent emporte* (Paris: Flammarion, 1991), pp. 28, 50.
21. Collard, *L'Ange sauvage*, pp. 98–9.
22. Ibid., p. 71.
23. William Cliff, *Conrad Detrez*, can. I, st. 7 (Paris: Le Dilettante, 1990), p. 16. Detrez died of AIDS in 1985. His best-known works are *L'Herbe a brûler*, a novel evoking his experiences in a Brazilian seminary, which won the Prix Renaudot in 1978, his posthumously published political novel, *La Ceinture de feu* (1985) and a volume of essays, *La Mélancolie du voyeur* (1986). The sex and nature parallels which Cliff uses are in part references to a comparable set of parallels in *La Ceinture de feu*.
24. Yves Navarre, *Le petit galopin de nos corps* (Paris: R. Lafont, 1977), pp. 46–66, 155–63.
25. In Greek mythology, Tiresias accidentally acquired the power to change sex. He was punished with blindness by the goddess Hera for revealing before Zeus that women experience greater pleasure in sex than men do, but recompensed by Zeus with the gift of foretelling the future.
26. *Tirésias: écrits secrets*, iii (Paris: Arlea, 1988), p. 59.
27. I am ignoring, as not relevant to the topic under discussion, the elements in the language of the text which, by raising the Baudelairean angel/devil dichotomy, put the whole narration into a perspective of moral debate typical of Jouhandeau's work up to the end of the 1960s. In practice, the *end* of the text is directed to precisely these issues.
28. In other words, gay writers who choose to write about the male body and inter-male desire in any form *not* based on balance and mutuality are using a non-gay form of discourse. The manner of writing becomes the definer of gayness, not the matter.

Further Reading

This bibliography gives a selection of important *non-fictional* texts by French creative writers (sections 1 and 2), and critical works of a general kind which I have found useful in writing this book (section 3). I have listed the editions which I have used; in some cases there will be several editions easily available. For novels, plays and poems, consult the text itself; for specialist criticism on individual authors, see the notes at the end of each chapter. Most of the works in section 3 contain substantial bibliographies for further reading.

(1) Essays on aspects of sexual orientation

Bory, Jean-Louis and Guy Hocquenghem. *Comment nous appelez-vous déjà?*, Paris, Calmann-Levy, 1977
Colette. *Le Pur et l'impur* in *Oeuvres*, vol. iii, Paris, Gallimard (Bibliothèque de la Pléiade), 1991
Duvert, Tony. *Le Bon Sexe illustré*, Paris, Editions de Minuit, 1974
Duvert, Tony. *L'Enfant au masculin*, Paris, Editions de Minuit, 1980
Fernandez, Dominique. *Le Rapt de Ganymède*, Paris, Grasset, 1989
Genet, Jean. *Fragments ... et autres textes*, Paris, Gallimard, 1990
Gide, André. *Corydon*, Paris, Gallimard (Folio), 1991
Hocquenghem, Guy. *Le Désir homosexuel*, Paris, Editions universitaires, 1972
Jouhandeau, Marcel. *Tirésias: écrits secrets*, iii, Paris, Arlea, 1988
Wittig, Monique. *The Straight Mind and Other Essays*, New York and London, Harvester, 1992

(2) Autobiographies, self-portraits and memoirs by homosexual or bisexual writers

Bory, Jean-Louis. *Ma Moitié d'orange*, Paris, Julliard, 1973

Camus, Renaud. *Journal d'un voyage en France*, Paris, POL, 1981

Camus, Renaud. *Notes achriennes*, Paris, POL, 1982

Camus, Renaud. *Tricks*, Paris, Persona, 1982

Colette. *Mes apprentissages*, in *Oeuvres*, vol. iii, Paris, Gallimard (Bibliothèque de la Pléiade), 1991

Gide, André. *Si le grain ne meur* in *Journal 1939–49, Souvenirs*, Paris, Gallimard (Bibliothèque de la Pléiade), 1954

Green, Julien. *Partir avant le jour*, Paris, Livre de Poche, 1972

Green, Julien. *Mille chemins ouverts*, Paris, Livre de Poche, 1973

Green, Julien. *Terre lointaine*, Paris, Grasset, 1966

Green, Julien. *Jeunesse*, Paris, Plon, 1974

Guérin, Daniel. *Autobiographie de jeunesse: d'une dissidence sexuelle au socialisme*, Paris, Pierre Belfond, 1971

Guérin, Daniel. *Son testament*, Paris, Encre, 1979

Jouhandeau, Marcel. *Ces messieurs*, Paris, Lilac ed., 1951

Leduc, Violette. *La Bâtarde*, Paris, Gallimard (Folio), 1964

Peyrefitte, Roger. *Propos secrets*, Paris, Albin Michel, 1977

Peyrefitte, Roger. *L'Innominato: nouveaux propos secrets*, Paris, Albin Michel, 1989

Rochefort, Christiane. *Ma vie revue et corrigée par l'auteur*, Paris, Stock, 1975

Sachs, Maurice. *Le Sabbat*, Paris, Gallimard (Imaginaire), 1960

(3) General secondary criticism

Benstock, Shari. *Women of the Left Bank: Paris, 1900–1940*, London, Virago, 1987

Courouve, Claude. *Vocabulaire de l'homosexualité masculine*, Paris, Payot, 1985

DeJean, Joan. *Fictions of Sappho 1546–1937*, Chicago and London, Chicago University Press, 1989

Dollimore, Jonathan. *Sexual Dissidence: Augustine to Wilde, Freud to Foucault*, Oxford, Clarendon Press, 1991

Duchen, Claire (ed. and trans.). *French Connections: Voices from the Women's Movement in France*, London and Melbourne, Hutchinson, 1987

Evans, Martha Noel. *Masks of Tradition: Women and the Politics of Writing in Twentieth-Century France*, Ithaca and London, Cornell University Press, 1987

Gay, Peter. *The Bourgeois Experience: Victoria to Freud*, vol. II, *The Tender Passion*, New York and Oxford, Oxford University Press, 1986

Gury, Christian. *L'Homosexuel et la loi*, Lausanne, L'Aire, 1981

Jay, Karla and Glasgow, Joanne (eds.). *Lesbian Texts and Contexts: Radical Revisions*, New York and London, New York University Press, 1990

Lilly, Mark. *Gay Men's Literature in the Twentieth Century*, London, Macmillan, 1993

Mossuz-Lavau, Janine. *Les Lois de l'amour: les politiques de la sexualité en France (1950–1990)*, Paris, Payot, 1991

Murphy, Timothy F. and Poirier, Suzanne (eds.). *Writing AIDS: Gay Literature, Language and Analysis*, New York, Columbia University Press, 1993

Neuman, Shirley and Kamboureli, Smaro (eds.). *A Mazing Space: Writing Canadian Women Writing*, Edmonton, Longspoon/NeWest, 1986

Showalter, Elaine. *Sexual Anarchy: Gender and Culture at the Fin-de-siècle*, London, Bloomsbury, 1991

Silverman, Kaja. *Male Subjectivity at the Margins*, New York and London, Routledge, 1992

Stambolian, George and Marks, Elaine (eds.). *Homosexualities and French Literature: Cultural Contexts/Critical Texts*, Ithaca and London, Cornell University Press, 1979

Weeks, Jeffrey. *Against Nature: Essays on History, Sexuality and Identity*, London, Rivers Oram, 1991

Wolfe, Susan J. and Penelope, Julia. *Sexual Practice, Textual Theory: Lesbian Cultural Criticism*, Cambridge MA and Oxford, Blackwell, 1993

Yaguello, Marina. *Les Mots et les femmes*, Paris, Payot, 1978

Index